ALSO BY MICHAEL SCHUMACHER

Published by the University of Minnesota Press

DHARMA LION: A BIOGRAPHY
OF ALLEN GINSBERG

FIRST THOUGHT: CONVERSATIONS
WITH ALLEN GINSBERG

IRON CURTAIN JOURNALS

UNIVERSITY OF
MINNESOTA PRESS

MINNEAPOLIS

Allen Ginsberg

IRON CURTAIN JOURNALS

JANUARY-MAY 1965

EDITED BY

MICHAEL SCHUMACHER

Photographs on pages 326, 345, and 347 courtesy of
the Estate of John Hopkins. All other photographs
courtesy of the Estate of Allen Ginsberg.

Published by the University of Minnesota Press
111 Third Avenue South, Suite 290
Minneapolis, MN 55401-2520
http://www.upress.umn.edu

Printed in the United States of America on acid-free paper

The University of Minnesota is an equal-opportunity educator and employer.

24 23 22 21 20 19 18   10 9 8 7 6 5 4 3 2 1

*

Library of Congress Cataloging-in-Publication Data
Ginsberg, Allen, 1926–1997, author. | Schumacher, Michael, editor.
Iron Curtain journals : January–May 1965 /
Allen Ginsberg ; edited by Michael Schumacher.
Minneapolis : University of Minnesota Press, [2018] |
Includes bibliographical references. | LCCN 2018016684 (print) |
ISBN 978-0-8166-9959-9 (hc) | ISBN 978-0-8166-9960-5 (pb)
Subjects: LCSH: Ginsberg, Allen, 1926–1997—Diaries. | Ginsberg,
Allen, 1926–1997—Notebooks, sketchbooks, etc. | Ginsberg, Allen,
1926–1997—Travel—Communist countries. | Poets, American—
20th century—Diaries. | Communist countries—Description and travel.
Classification: LCC PS3513.I74 Z46 2018 (print) | DDC 811/.54 [B] —dc23
LC record available at https://lccn.loc.gov/2018016684

CONTENTS

Allen Ginsberg with Russian poet
Andrei Voznesensky in Moscow, 1965

EDITOR'S INTRODUCTION

When Allen Ginsberg wrote "Howl," his breakthrough work and masterpiece, he had no intention of offering it for publication. He considered it too private. It had been an exercise. He'd sat down at a typewriter during a time of personal loneliness and depression, and in one lengthy writing session poured out his sympathies for "the best minds of my generation, destroyed by madness." Freed from concerns about how his work would look to potential publishers, he let his mind take flight. Words rushed out of him, his raw, uncensored, unedited thoughts rising up, one after another, until, like Icarus, he risked flying too close to the sun. But unlike the Greek mythological legend, he survived, strong and clear-voiced. Ginsberg's survival from a troubled past surprised his mentor, William Carlos Williams, who gladly introduced *Howl and Other Poems*, the first of Ginsberg's many collections of poems to be published by City Lights Books.

"He avoids nothing but experiences it to the hilt," Williams wrote in his Introduction. "He contains it. Claims it as his own—and, we believe, laughs at it and has the time and effrontery to love a fellow of his choice and record that love in a well-made poem."

I mention this because Ginsberg treated his journals in similar fashion. Like most writers' journals, Ginsberg's journals were intended to be a private record of raw materials, flights of fancy, and inspiration that might be worked into something useful. When he was on the road, separated from family, friends, and country—which was often—he would fill notebook after notebook (there were five from Cuba alone) with whatever he felt like writing, whether that be detailed descriptions of his surroundings, scraps of conversations, accounts of daily events, new poems, random observations, dream notations, or even graphic records of his sexual activities. He had no need for secrets or editing, spelling or proper punctuation.

These raw materials, predictably, were certain, authoritative, wistful, silly. His entries stood as light beams probing body and soul. Ginsberg believed that one should "notice what you notice," and his journal entries offered insight into what he noticed enough to notate. The process could be imprecise, which is why he argued, sometimes irritably, that his poems and journals were not autobiography, at least not in the strictest sense. He'd pass over important events, neglect to report his first impressions of seminal figures in his life. In this way, he was no different from anyone else.

The issues of content and privacy changed when he decided to publish his *Indian Journals* in 1970. Ginsberg's long sojourn to India and the Far East brought about significant self-discovery and spiritual growth. His journals depicted the paths he'd taken in all parts of the subcontinent, his many meetings with Indian holy men, his thoughts on life and suffering and death (spurred on, in part, by his musings at the burning ghats near the banks of the Ganges); he wrote new poetry reflective of his experiences. Publishing the entirety of his journals would have been impractical. Instead, he gathered the best selections into a book that was manageable for both publisher and reader, and he would continue this approach in the published journals that followed.

Ginsberg was aware of how things appeared on the naked page.

Editor's Introduction

Thoughts recorded decades ago could appear to be awkward, fatuous, or embarrassing; they were *honest* at the time of the writing, and they were no less honest many years later. Ginsberg's youthful journals, begun when he was a teenager and running through his college years at Columbia University, illustrate the dilemma. Ginsberg was embarrassed by the egotism of his youth, some of his early efforts to write traditional rhymed poetry, and his naïveté about worldly issues, and while he was certain that the journals would be published one day, he made a point of, first, assigning the editing to people he trusted implicitly, and, second, making certain that it was understood that these journals would not be published until after his death. And so it was. Juanita Lieberman-Plimpton, and later Bill Morgan, worked on the editing, and the volume *The Book of Martyrdom and Artifice* (a title that the young Allen Ginsberg actually used in one of his journals) was published after his death in 1997.

This was of much less concern with later journals, as Ginsberg matured into the person he became in his advancing years. His dedication to Buddhism and meditation guided him and his self-awareness. Of more concern, in terms of privacy, was the privacy of others mentioned in his journals. Carl Solomon never quite escaped being at the center of "Howl," and Lucien Carr, one of the central figures in the early Beat Generation group, wanted no mention in the writings of his famous contemporaries. At one point, near the beginning of my research for *Dharma Lion*, Ginsberg pulled me aside and addressed the privacy issue. "You've been reading my journals," he said, "and you need to keep in mind that there are many living sensibilities in these journals." I assured him that I had no intention of making headlines by invading anyone's privacy and that was the last time it was ever discussed.

Ironically, Ginsberg's privacy concerns bothered him more at the time of the journals' composition than later, when they were being con-

Editor's Introduction

sidered for publication. He used initials once in a while, but he used actual names throughout most of the journals. When his Czechoslovakian journal(s) disappeared, reappeared in police custody, and were never returned, Ginsberg worried about the welfare of those appearing on the pages of his journals, especially the young people. He'd been expelled from Cuba and Czechoslovakia for being a bad influence on the countries' youths, and here it was, concise evidence for one and all to see. He was relieved when nothing came of it.

My introduction to these journals occurred in the mid-1980s, when I was researching my Ginsberg biography. I saw the original journals, as well as transcripts. I was impressed by the depth and range of his writing, and I felt strongly that the journals would be useful to those following Ginsberg's life and career, as well as to poets curious about how the twentieth century's answer to Walt Whitman worked as an artist. The journals contained the first drafts of two Ginsberg classics ("Kral Majales," "Who Be Kind To"), five other strong offerings ("Café in Warsaw," "The Moments Return," "Guru," "Drowse Murmurs," "Studying the Signs"), and a hefty selection of poems unpublished until now. Two poems ("Message II," "Big Beat") were lost in journals confiscated by the police, but Ginsberg had the presence of mind to make copies of them as a kind of insurance against just this type of misadventure. Aside from the accounts of his day-to-day life in Cuba and the Iron Curtain countries, Ginsberg included a detailed list of all of his travels to date and, perhaps most important, a powerful account of his mother's family in Russia and the family's move to the United States. Ginsberg, Jack Kerouac, and others had been logging their dreams in their journals to explore their interests on the workings of the mind in this level of consciousness, and Ginsberg jotted down a strong sampling of his dreams in his journals. The journals also contained accounts of Ginsberg's meetings and conversations with such notable poets as Yevgeny Yevtushenko, Andrei Voznesensky, and Alexander Yessenin-Volpin.

A subtle but ultimately important shift was taking place in Ginsberg's life at this point: he was moving from being an American poet to becoming an international presence. He had traveled extensively prior to his departure for Cuba in January 1965, and his work had been translated into many languages, but he was still, in essence, an American poet writing as an American—more a case of an American expat living in other countries for extended periods of time, not all that different from William Burroughs, Gregory Corso, Gary Snyder, and others, who, tired of the cult of celebrity suffocating the Beat Generation, were living and studying outside the United States. Ginsberg's boundless curiosity about other countries' histories, Eastern religion, international poetry, and even music drove him toward a strange sense of assimilation into wherever he chose to light down. He was still an American, seeing the world through the filter of his own experience, but he was no Ugly American. This comes across in the journal entries, and, more to the point, in his interactions with the youths in other countries.

Ginsberg's disagreements with the authorities on freedom of speech, homosexuality, and drugs might have led to his expulsions from Cuba and Czechoslovakia—and these journals report some of the disagreements and disappointments—but the international reportage of the expulsions led to further discussion of the issues. I recall discussing this with him after the publication of *Dharma Lion*. He felt that I should have been a little more empathetic with some of his travails; I countered that I had no difficulty whatsoever with his message but that he shouldn't have expected to speak freely in a nation run by a dictator with

Editor's Introduction

opposing views. He, of course, disagreed. His messages here are *human*, not political, and leaders tangling with these issues were, sadly, making these issues political. These points were made in these journals and I must confess, all these years later, that he was correct.

Ginsberg advised putative poets to be "hometown heroes"—to make your place in your own city or region. He had only to look at William Carlos Williams, who lived in New Jersey and (at least initially) earned his reputation there, writing some of his poems on prescription pads while working as a pediatrician. Ginsberg's ambitions ran higher, and as these journals illustrate, his global wanderings not only promoted his work on an international level but also promoted a core value that the world would not break down by boundaries and ideological conflicts. What better message could one offer, then and now, when differences bring about terrorism and conflict rather than tenderness between strangers?

ACKNOWLEDGMENTS

First and foremost, my thanks to the late Allen Ginsberg, who supplied the richness of material that made this book a challenge and a pleasure to edit. I had read these journals when I was working on *Dharma Lion*, my biography of Allen published in 1992, and I remember how impressed I was with the sheer volume of his writing while he was on the road and preoccupied, and how I felt that the journals afforded a reader a valuable glimpse into the thinking of one of American poetry's most creative and influential voices.

I owe a huge debt of gratitude to Gordon Ball, editor of two previous volumes of Ginsberg journals (*Journals Early Fifties, Early Sixties* and *Journals Mid-Fifties*). At one time, he was going to edit this volume, but

Editor's Introduction

eventually decided against it. Gordon was exceptionally generous with his time, his materials from his earlier efforts, his advice, and, most important, his friendship. Thanks also to Kathy Ball, who put up with all my phone calls.

Peter Hale, who has overseen the Ginsberg estate since 1997, was also extremely helpful, whether he was supplying me with information or photographs, offering advice, or simply helping me move things along when I hit a speed bump in the road. His friendship was always a beacon.

Thanks to Bob Rosenthal, Ginsberg's longtime office manager and friend, for all the help and encouragement he has given me over the years.

Jeff Pasternak at Andrew Wylie Associates, a longtime overseer of Ginsberg's publishing interests, assisted with the details of seeing this book into print.

Special thanks to editors (and friends) Erik Anderson and Kristian Tvedten, as well as the production staff, at the University of Minnesota Press. Their enthusiasm made this project much easier than it might have been.

Editor's Introduction

A NOTE ON EDITING
ALLEN GINSBERG

A few words about the process of editing this volume ...

One does not edit Allen Ginsberg—or any other writer, for that mat-
ter—without making a lot of decisions. Writers are very protective
about the words they publish (or they ought to be), and there are obli-
gations one faces when publishing words that weren't originally in-
tended for publication. Fortunately, I had occasion to observe Ginsberg
working with editor Gordon Ball on his *Journals Mid-Fifties*. Ball, a col-
lege professor, is fastidious with every word and detail; he is, quite lit-
erally, a literary caretaker. This was fortunate, because Ginsberg could
be very exacting during the editing process. He and Gordon would go
over a manuscript, word by word, line by line, matching text with the
original handwritten journals, making vital decisions about how the
material was to be presented. Misspellings were silently corrected; a
punctuation mark, here and there, quietly inserted. First and foremost,
the journals had to be readable.

I did not have occasion to work with Ginsberg on these journals,
though I did confer with him, though only to a minor extent, when I
was editing *Family Business,* the book of selected correspondence be-
tween Allen and his father, Louis. Gordon Ball was very generous with
his help and advice on editing Ginsberg. All final decisions, of course,

were mine, and I can only hope that Allen would have been pleased with how this volume turned out had he lived to see it.

The reader should keep the following in mind:

1. Ginsberg's spelling could be spotty, especially in the case of proper names; it was not uncommon for him to use two or more spellings of a proper Czech or Russian name. I silently corrected what I knew to be misspellings, knowing that he would have done the same. When in doubt, I maintained Ginsberg's spelling. The same applies to his spellings of Spanish or French words. I left intact obviously intended misspellings ("stept" instead of "stepped," "mexcity" for "Mexico City," for example), just as Allen had in work published during his lifetime: there's a charming playfulness to this.

2. I retained capitalizations exactly as Ginsberg wrote them in his journals. It's possible that he might have corrected some of them, but I doubt it, given the quirky capitalization found in the journals published while he was alive and could supervise the editing.

3. I silently inserted a punctuation mark on a rare occasion, but only if the prose became unreadable without the mark. Ginsberg wrote in bursts of mental energy, his words sprawling out onto the printed page as quickly as he thought, and the unpunctuated passages give the reader an indication of the workings of his emotions and mind.

4. I corrected his misdatings. Quite often, when dating his journals in the early months of the year, or the early days of a month, he used the previous year or month in his dates. I know, from my conversations with him, that he would have made these corrections. However, he was very often wrong when giving the day of the week for an entry: the calendar date did not match the day of the week that he provided. In most cases, this was only a single day. Nevertheless, I had a decision to make, and I opted to use *[sic]* in these instances, and I did not correct the manuscript.

Editing Allen Ginsberg

5. On occasion, the reader will note a question mark within brackets:
   [?]. This indicates a missing word. Ginsberg's handwriting was usu-
   ally legible, but every so often a word would be scribbled in such a
   way that even Ginsberg himself could not determine what he had
   written. Those transcribing the journals years ago had no more an-
   swers than I did, so, rather than cut a line or paragraph containing
   an illegible word, I inserted [?] to indicate a missing word. As a gen-
   eral rule, the loss of the word did not affect the overall meaning of
   the passage.

6. I indicated the excising of a longer passage with bracketed ellipses:
   [...]. In most cases, it was simply a matter of cutting brief passages
   that were repetitious and, I felt, unnecessary. On a rare occasion I
   cut a passage that was so full of missing words that it would have
   been confusing to the reader.

Finally, it should be noted that the photographs in this book were not
part of the journals. They were neither affixed to the pages nor tipped
in afterward. The Ginsberg Estate generously provided them for this
volume as illustrative of his trips.

Editing Allen Ginsberg

IRON CURTA

N JOURNALS

Miguel Grinberg, poet and editor of
Eco Contemporáneo, with Ginsberg
in Havana, January 1965

Cuba

JANUARY—MARCH 1965

By the end of 1964, when he received an invitation from Cuba's minister of culture to participate in a writers' conference in Havana, Allen Ginsberg had devoted a large block of his life to living in and exploring countries outside the United States. He'd lived in Mexico for several months in 1954, spending most of his time examining the Mayan ruins on the Yucatán Peninsula. Then, three years later, following the publication of "Howl" and establishing his reputation as a major young poet, he was off to Europe, where he settled in Paris but visited Spain, Italy, and England, among other countries, over a two-year stretch. In 1960, after participating in a conference in Chile, he spent months wandering all over South America, including an extended stay in Peru, where he explored Machu Picchu and searched the Amazon region for the powerful hallucinogenic drug ayahuasca, a consciousness-altering substance recommended by his friend and former mentor William S. Burroughs. In his most recent extended stay away from the United States, beginning in 1961, he had embarked on an extraordinary journey with an itinerary that included Paris, Tangier, eastern Africa, Israel, and Greece, prior to a fifteen-month stay in India. He concluded the trip with a jaunt to the Far East, including stops in Cambodia, Vietnam, and Japan.

Ginsberg kept detailed journals throughout his travels. He filled hundreds of pages with observations, new poetry, dialogue, sketches, travel descriptions, dream notations, and other musings. He was an endlessly curious traveler, open to any adventure and gregarious with people he met. All of his journals written prior to 1965 would be published, beginning with fragments presented in magazines and, eventually, the first of his book-length journal writings, Indian Journals, in 1970.

The travel arrangements for Cuba might have given Ginsberg an inkling of difficulties ahead. The State Department delayed in issuing the necessary travel papers, relenting only when Ginsberg threatened legal action. Even then, he had to make convoluted travel arrangements to get to Cuba and back. The State Department, adhering to strict Cold War policies, did not permit Americans to travel directly from the United States to Cuba, which meant that he would have to fly first to Mexico City before taking a flight from Mexico to Havana. Returning to the United States would be even more difficult. He was not allowed to fly back to Mexico; instead, he had to travel to an Iron Curtain country (in this case, Czechoslovakia) before heading back to the States. He shrugged it off. He was delighted by the opportunity to visit Czechoslovakia, where his work was popular, and if all went well and he was able to line up a few paying readings, he might be able to travel to other countries in the region.

Recent months had primed Ginsberg for his visits to totalitarian regimes. Censorship, a Ginsberg obsession since the "Howl" obscenity trial in 1957, stood front and center in his activities. He'd decried censorship in statements, essays, and interviews, and in December 1964, just before departing for Cuba, he, along with Norman Mailer and poet John Ciardi, testified in Boston at a hearing designed to determine whether William S. Burroughs's novel Naked Lunch was obscene. Ginsberg defended the book's literary merits—to no avail—and as he prepared to embark on a journey to a country where he was expected to talk about poetry and judge a poetry contest, freedom of speech was very much on his mind. It was something, he decided, that needed to be discussed openly. The same could be said about homosexuality, which was oppressed in Cuba, and capital punishment, which was practiced. Ginsberg surmised (incorrectly, as it turned out) that Cuba would offer him a forum for his ideas.

He flew to Mexico City on Friday, January 15, 1965. He spent the weekend relaxing, wandering around the city, and stopping in some of the museums. He was in his full travel mode, eager for adventure, his senses sharpened as he jotted in his journal, his mood upbeat after a pleasant stay in Mexico. He was prepared for whatever lay ahead.

The journals open with his flight to Mexico City.

Cuba

Kennedy Airport 5:40—Coughing all day, a cold and itch in breast pipes from cigarette smoke—

Goodbye to Gene,[1] with his hand cupped at his ear to hear—me say what? Arthur C. Clarke[2] and planetary sovereignty he sayd.

Out on the inky oil field to the silver giant plane—sudden exultation walking out with strap bag over my shoulder under a bright full moon over the Eastern Airline building—I remember pointing with Gene to the lady sat in dais before red velvet curtains in the Control Room Paging Booth uplifted above the entrance doors surveying the terminal, she like a mannequin sat enthroned—

But on the glare black field in front of the terminal the huge plane I paced toward looked up to the full moon a few silver clouds drifted near and a burst of music in my head the Ride of the Valkyries.

I was at last stepping on the giant bird to fly to the Island of Cuba and premonitions of Marxist Historical Revolutionary Futurity with Wagnerian overtones lifted my heart, an abstract passion seized the Airfield.

In the plane the Muzak with staccatoed symphony cream scratching over my Wagnerian Exile thought—scribbles.

A field of blue lights

Flying is too abstract—going back fast
over old smelly jungle Roads.
"Para descargar mis pensamientos"—
a "thought Song on the plane"

1. Eugene Brooks, Ginsberg's older brother.
2. Science-fiction writer, author of *2001: A Space Odyssey* and *Childhood's End*.

Cuba

"Spine silence"—written on back of matchbook cover.
"I thought you was the Boy"
the gas station attendant said
the old Sociologist, mistaking him for Pretty
     Boy Floyd. Anecdote at NY party weeks ago.

How green the Zocalo! And there is life again! A garden, the iron benches in the grass, large leafed plants upspringing like friendly green dogs—a place to sit quiet at night—

The smell, Mex Tabac and detritus and tropic rank earth perfume—which I smelt as I stept from the plane—Naked Lunch's[3] benches, where the old tragic Garver[4] draped his dying bones & is begone—and now another happy lifetime I walk into the park—and the workers boys with transistors pass on the red tiled footpath with the tinkle of guitars and the hurp of buses' harp machinery on the busy street, the night's quieted us all to a calm smile.

Lovely the colored tile houses set up under the snaky boughed palms. And that light in the trees transparent green trembling sharp leaves.

Coughing fatigued[5] walked to Calle Guerrero, like College St. Calcutta—Bought codinettas and ate a sausage with tacos and walked on to a bright lit chicken soup all-nite restaurant, and stopped also for 8 cents huge glass of Papaya juice. Then to Hotel Ibero near an open air carnival and taxicab whore bar, and washed and slept.

3. *Naked Lunch,* by William S. Burroughs.

4. William Garver, friend of Burroughs, Jack Kerouac, Ginsberg, and others, who lived in Mexico. Addled by drug addiction, he died young.

5. Ginsberg arrived in Mexico City with a case of grippe, for which he received an antibiotic after his arrival in Cuba.

Cuba

16 Jan.

Museum Modern Art Chapultepec Magic surrealism Frieda Kahlo, combines Alberto Gironella, big black rat by Coronel, Alchemical math by Carrington, black sweater selfportrait Montoya then 13 funny historic gems by Antonio Ruiz (El Corzo) 1897–1964.—Turkey selfportraits, the paranoias, soprano. Singing chickens out of her mouth, whores heroes parades revolutions and a weird still life of precise goofy imaginary solids. Then Juan O'Gorman panoramic.

Life is too short—I want to go back to Mexico and live in Oaxaca like a peaceful bearded sage and eat tortillas for a year—I may go to Russia, China, but will I have the days to return to this small and happy solitude among rotten old churches and life the same street it was ten years ago?

New Chapultepec Park Museum of Anthro/Archeology—walking to it across street 2 bearded boys stopped me, Ginsberg? They came from Acapulco, Ron Rice died suddenly, in four hours, shooting Amphetamine long time, walking pneumonia, vomited blood and died in hospital. Was thin and pale. In their car in park got high on "Acapulco Gold" they repeated—

Then entered amazed vast beautiful new museum—colossal like Aztec pyramid the most beautiful building except the Taj Mahal, for a museum—Coastline and sun Stone set like jewels under giant teahead ten or four story slabs of polished marble, lit like Cartiers on Fifth Avenue—& stood eyes closed in high trance in front of plate of Magic Mushrooms, listening the recorded Curander chanting Si, Si, Si, S,/so, so, so, so, Si, Si, Si, Si/So, So, So, So.

Dream   Sunday 17 Jan. *6:30*

In a big house with long marble halls modern rich living style, the huge family has gone away—I was with the little sister who loaned me her tooth braces to try on—I put on the silver bands over my upper and lower jaws—then I find the elastic parts—just like my own rubberband childhood—and put them in, pulling my lower jaw forward—I open my mouth to take them all out at once and it gets a little tangled—I may crush them taking them out negligently like that—

Sometime I have closed a huge wooden door on a house corridor upstairs like in this modern house where I stay. Mondragon Mexcity but in closing don't get the hinges properly attached to the wall—we all are going out for a ride. I'm in a hurry—I messed up the tooth braces and the door—

Meanwhile we are alone in this place with Fidel Castro and the 12 yr. old girl—Everybody else has gone to the big meeting conference—Fidel is in the bathroom dawdling, taking a pee or brushing his teeth—he'll be out in a minute—I wonder if he is going to give a big speech at the meeting—I call out "Hey, are you coming too and are you going to talk much?"—but realizing he's finally alone in the house, should I bug him?—a child is pushing open the bathroom door and he cries out in a high voice "Not yet minuto esperate tu madre viendra para take you outside to the stadium"—His voice is childishly high, a little impatient but nice to the baby girl—How come he got no guard to protect him—well it's all informal he has no life of his own even in the bathroom?—I am yelling thru the hall "are you coming to the meeting?" and wake up.

Cuba

Jan. 18

Sun. Nite in Tenampa—many mariachis & empty nite Clubs, this year the musicians in uniform—drive in car to Barba Azul, Savoy, all closed— The Venezuelan poet & his wife singing Spanish Red Songs—Stopped to ask policeman couple whether any place was open— They just smiled & said only the Houses for whores—We were undecided—They said "Shall we take you there?" Very agreeable Mexican healthy cops.

Fast morning trip to Embassy, Commercial Attache Professor of Literature Alvarez served up visa fast despite cable confusions & drove me to airport, inquiring about defects of magic mushrooms. Met Arms the Ambassador briefly at Airport, shook hands, he'd given me fast courtesy visa that morn sight unseen & remembered at airport
   —"No need formalities."

Above Mexico in plane almost empty remembered earlier car trips— wasn't a dream—above a vast canyon on way to Vera Cruz—or was it on way thru Israeli desert to Elat—or above San Francisco the Sierras?— Some dream cantina perched on a Barranca of yore. Leaving the Coast —snow of Orizaba I never seen before 3 trips—still visible as above Mex-city—And free Daquiri—and little cloud puffs hanging over azure water almost shadowless—A vision of the   Earth I once had 1945 passing in tanker offshore Cuba, the mountains rise gigantic planetary cragged out of the dawn sea. To "Cape Verde's peaked cone." Smoking Delicados again.
   I slept on the plane NYC–Mexico City hardly remember the light of Mexican towns below. Steady rocking & buzz of plane over sea of white fluff cloud spread. Mountainpeaks of clouds far ahead. Schools of porpoises surfacing tiny in gaps of water below.

Cuba

I'm flying like an old poet, my head filled with fantasies of being met at the airport—Got grey in my beard.

Over the Clouds, thru gaps in the blue Carib, toward that portion of the planet which is Castro's communist Bastion—Wagnerian Echoes in the airplane—Whilst I was singing Hari Krishna to myself aloud and thinking about Paul Engle in Iowa City. Will the mail get through?

Air pressure hitting my ears, with a cold, won't be able to hear for a week.

Plane Steward asks me, among nine passengers on huge jetprop where I from—Yankee I say De Nueva York—He shows me Cuban money "patria o muerte."

I come flying so solidly myself singing Gopala Gopala Devaki Nandina Gopala and what thinketh Blake—The plane wing dips in the long yellow sun light over Eternal beds of cloud to the Horizon.

Mental Jerusalem flying to Havana.

Ginsberg had visited Havana very briefly in December 1953, when he was on his way to Mexico.[6] He had been disappointed. Havana, he complained, was a "kind of dreary rotting antiquity, rotting stone, heaviness all about," and not the freewheeling environment he had envisioned. Now, in 1965, he expected to find a changed, better city. He'd romanticized the revolution that had freed Cuba from the corrupt Batista rule, but, as he would discover when talking to Cuban street youths shortly after his arrival in Havana, Fidel Castro had imposed oppressive rules of his own.

6. See "Havana 1953," published in *Collected Poems* (New York: HarperCollins, 2006). All citations from this book will hereafter be abbreviated *CP*.

Havana Rivera Hotel 2 a.m.—Out walking with serape & took Wah Wah [bus] to center of nite life La Rampa & talked briefly with some kids 13 who admired my red & black Cambridge scarf, and was headed toward big hotel when Bam I saw 3 boys, one young with scar tissue all over face, stopped me asked was I Ginsberg and told me they were trying to reach me all day— we went off to a street corner blocks away to join the other five youths & a girl wife and with rum bottle passed between, took bus to obscure nightclub in Vedado completely empty, where they complained about crackdowns on homosexuals, crackdowns on "los Infermos" arrests in the street of sick or Beat types, they had a magazine "El Puente" & publish books of 17 yr. old poetry, are bugged by the right wing Xmunist literary dialecticians who give them not so much money,—all the arts organized into Syndicato's groups of "aficionados" and they left in cold but create the poesy now—we drank "cocktails" in the obscurity & the rum bottle dropt to the floor broke, but no hassle, they liked the revolution and I said let's end capital punishment, they said yes tell Castro—am I going to meet Castro?—They said sure—an underground of many youths, their One Eyed Cat meeting place changed management, they have no official status since everything's officialized—not a bad scene they spoke freely said I'd not be followed—

and there is a new style of music called "feeling."

Jan 19—Out driving with official ladies—to Palace Aldama to look for spot where 3 a.m. 1953 I wrote a poem—ate icecream instead & couldn't find the exact spot—Then to Cathedral Place where I wrote other poem—More beautiful little daylight cobbled square than I'd remembered—Old Paris restaurant'd become a bank and after revolution reconstruction to restaurant again—no place to sit down as before—

Cuba

Then to apartment of 2 old hermetic painters, lovers? where drunk on rum & shy before the lady aficionados. I kissed the retired hermetic one in his mathematical chamber filled with Hegel & 16th Century poets—he looked like a laborer joker but turned out to be an old cultivated queer—no telephone—they obviously know the underground City. Visit started dull cold official but with rum & embarrassment of crosspurposes the humane recognition broke through—he kept stroking my long hair.

The Hotel Havana Rivera restaurant—baroque—Miami style diningroom with complicated Chinese modern chandeliers and stylized simplified "old Spanish" murals on new silver leaf walls—in the center a woman in highclass pink colonial dress with a black mask on the right side of her face, where a sea captain in braided uniform & mustache stares at her—on her left a plantation cat with brown elegant jacket & cigar & big round hat suavely rests on his cane—she stares straight ahead half washed like a soap opera Dimestore heroine—the rest of the murals have ships, lovers, capes, negroes dancing & flying kites. The ceiling is stucco'd gold. An air of quiet, the large room with spotted mirrors giant at each end almost empty at tables.

A group of 6 Chinamen and one woman in red sweater eat & drink single beers mostly silently, three in plain grey uniforms.

To Mr. A's house bringing Ray Charles and Bob Dylan records—which they had never heard, being heads of Culture. To have them broadcast over Cuban radio.

Cuba

Dream Jan 20, 1965—

Being treated as guest is subtle form of brainwash. Whether by psychoanalystic in Washington, Lowell House Harvard or Cuban liberal communists in Cuba. Don't want to offend anyone however ugh they are. The selfconsciousness of writing for public. Still Grippe & dry lips at dawn in bed; huge hotel room with big window overlooking greysky and tops of balconied apartments.

Dream—Going into big apartment hotel—place I'm familiar with—with a lady friend guide very busybody—She wants to introduce me to and I am eager to meet Sartre[7]—she's old friend, knocks. I follow at the door but hesitate—she goes in, Mrs. Sartre at door a buxom woman welcomes her and door half closes on me, I stand there outside not moving to come in until invited—the woman opens the door after a moment of confusion, I enter & look around see he has the best suite in the house—

On the wall to the right and hung along the ceiling are two large complicated black [?] tibetan shield-like scalloped hangings of brass—I mean 7 feet long or more & curved to fit edges of room—I know those, the room was furnished after Mrs. Bede's Antique Shop in India was broken up—the management of the Hotel Chelsea/Havana Rivera/Delhi Shoke Hotel. I'm amazed he got such an artistic deal for a hotel room.

Meanwhile I see with his wife & a kitchen & pipe he's living a real settled domestic life like Herbert Marshall whom I met in NY a week ago translator of old & young Russians Mayak[8] & Voznesensky[9]. Bathrobes & fruit on the table.

I open a book & see some very small, microscopic drawings from a

7. French philosopher Jean-Paul Sartre.
8. Russian poet and playwright Vladimir Mayakovsky (1893–1930).
9. Russian poet Andrei Voznesensky (1923–2010).

Kaballa book or I Ching (in style hermetic like those of old queen painter I met yesterday) a paradigm of a pyramid with select Chinese fortune cookie moon-poem above, it's all un-interpretable, I suddenly realize that the merit of such art works is cosmic and secret & incomprehensible like a Mantra, one copies them & sends them as Xmas or birthday cards merely for the merit of sending a mysterious message.

Moon over Abbatoir

King takes pleasure in water

which is not comprehensible on any Conscious level but which does make literal sense in some mathematical/astrological Inside-God play or relative futurity or antique world-egg architectural plans.

The design rather a petite pyramid needed a ruler to copy correctly with a fine drawing pen & many colors of ink was a bright round orange sun over accompanied by as it were an I Ching model fit for Bill Heine's altar in Huncke's[10] pad in top floor of Amphetamine universes New York.

Gary Snyder[11] is there, we're discussing initiation with Sartre or a disciple "But you have to be a good Demon" says Gary to both or us, shyly & with a wise rueful smile—He's busy whittling away at some Japanese antique wooden fish—or transcribing some Mahayana Ideograms in a schedule book—"Now I got my initiation from Ginsberg here in that he chose to appear as a phantom both male and female & Neuter —Probably didn't know he was doing it that consciously but definitely a

---

10. Herbert Huncke (1915–1996), author, friend of Ginsberg, Kerouac, and Burroughs, and Times Square hustler, was a model for characters in Beat Generation works.

11. Gary Snyder (born 1930), poet, Ginsberg friend, and model for Jack Kerouac's Japhy Ryder in *The Dharma Bums*, was highly influential in Ginsberg's study of Buddhism.

Cuba

secret projection of his Boddhisatvahood—but you have to be a good de-
mon to that without creating bad karma in the soul you are initiating—
simply as that—if you split up three ways you still have to do it with good
intentions, magic powers themselves & trinity phantom appearances
don't work right unless you have a good heart."

There seems to be a teaching dispute in this room—I'm meanwhile
impressed with Sartre's V.I.P. family simplicity—he sure doesn't get tan-
gled up in politeness to petty bureaucrats & hang-ups on streets visiting
elementary school principal's offices & bureaucrat bathrooms like I do—
Has this big settled family suite in the guest hotel, decorated with re-
mains of a nationalized antique shop's best Tibetan wall-shields.

I wake up & still wonder how deal with this problem transcribing
Cuba. Dry lipped & throat sore, still coughing and smoking.

---

20 Wed—Morning visit architectural spectacle arts school with gran ar-
chitecto who explains his stone moods, later I find is another queer
artist.

Afternoon lunch with Mr. Cohen, the English translator of Cer-
vantes, a charming character actor from the British movie dream world
with mustache & all sorts of scholarly in-jokes like Alan Ansen.[12]

Then Miguel Barnet[13] all afternoon till supper in my room explain-
ing Yoruba-Bantu-Cuban Local yoga with songs like mantras & plenty
drum excitement.

Some time old Chilean journalist acquaintance with mustache sub-
editor of "Cuba"—I complain about the Lacra Social Dept. (Depart-

12. Alan Ansen (1922–2006), poet and playwright, worked as W. H. Auden's sec-
retary and as assistant on the editing of Burroughs's *Naked Lunch*.
13. Miguel Barnet (born 1940) is a Cuban novelist and ethnographer.

ment of Social Undermining) last 2 years social policy on homosexuals, marijuana, fumistes & "los infermos" the Sick Sick Sick style youngsters of La Rampa social street—lots of people busted wrongly suspected of homosexuality because of bluejeans tight pants crazy beards—Castro now somewhat *sick* style because of *his* hair—"They've forgotten the revolutionary beards already" said one 17 yr. old poet of the Puente Writers & Artists Union group.

Cuba so far enchanting like Marx Brothers Duck Soup revolution.

The "revolution" an obsession in everybody's mind, like the hallucinogenic drugs in mine, a change of reality itself. Everybody smart enthusiastic, but that it go the way *they* want. The architect lives cheap, builds big domed art schools, the scholarly ethnographer gets money to study voodoo—"culture folklorica"—the Casa De Las Americas[14] like liberals from the Bronx a bunch of ladies running left wing culture for idealistic Hope, the young Sick muchachos complaining & fighting a bureaucracy of bourgeois old dogmatic mediocrity Marxists—Guillen[15] and another poet (Retemar) secretly visiting one Ramiro Valdez the Minister of Interior to complain about persecution of faggots in the streets by Lacra Social—they dissolved Lacra supposedly, but the whole "problems"—"contraversio" about Departments of Social Undermining never made the papers—Blas Roca is editor of *Hoy* and has no beard—Haydee Santamaria, head of Casa de las Americas, a lady humanist from the Hills supposedly a generous soul with power.

"At the height of my troubles with the bureaucracy Castro came out of the fine arts school and said it was great, if we spend all the money in Cuba & create something beautiful that is enough," said the Architect.

14. Sponsor of Ginsberg's Cuba visit.

15. Nicolás Guillén (1902–1989), Cuban poet, journalist, and political activist, served for more than twenty-five years as president of the National Cuban Writer's Union.

Cuba

"But what if Castro drops dead & you have no protection in the bureaucracy?"

"Don't you believe in individuals?"

I stammered "It was individuals in the State Dept. didn't want to validate my passport for trip to Cuba—If I didn't have a sharp lawyer to protect my legal constitutional rights I wouldn't be here."

When "Feeling" music came in it was attacked in the newspapers by the "dogmatists" as causing social dissolution, American influence a la Billie Holiday. But the albaniles heard it & now it's the style—I not heard the feeling singer Elena Bourke yet—

So supper and visit interview bearded well drest tie suit reporter from *Hoy*, & ring the phone 2 boys from the Bridge Sick gang bringing translations from Kaddish,[16] the Hotel Management Havana Rivera wouldn't let them up—I was told by IPEC [*sic,* should be ICEP[17]] guide No Visitors in Hotel Rooms (on account vast hordes of whores hanging around for visitors and farmers bring huge families of cows up the elevator if visitors allowed—Bridge boys & others said it was just puritanism.)

Tho all

day a stream of Quasi official editors and Folklorists—But they stopped Manuel Ballagas & little effeminate Jose Mario poet—So I went downstairs trembling to confront the octopus police State—Met them in lobby (dragging Hoy reporter beard along for witness) & started in elevator—was asked to consult ICEP guide Friendship Peoples office *Mario*—who also embarrassed, asked the boys for identification—which they had, members of Govt-sponsored Puente Publishing branch—Jose boy even had a neat little official Bridge card d'identite—

16. See *CP,* 217.

17. ICEP—International Cultural Exchange Program.

"Well, as long as they can identify themselves. . ." and as for the other who had no card but typewritten pages of translation of Kaddish—which I clumsily seized and thrust in front of poor Mario guide's nose—"That's his identification he translates some texts of mine"—But by this time everyone relaxed it was embarrassing since they obviously *could* go up—So I added—as Mario Guide smiled in relief

"Besides the Doctor told me to stay inside & not go out for Grippe so obviously I have to receive people upstairs, journalists poets etc."

Thus ascended elevator & sat smoking & talking till midnite, correcting Kaddish translation by 17 yr. old acne-faced cute Ballagas, getting lowdown on Lacra police—

They busted a 14-year-old boy in a john & held him 3 days because they raided the bathroom when someone passing by outside said "something funny's going on in there."

And their tall friend I met the other nite was rejected from University suspected of being queer for hanging around with Infermos of Puente gang on La Rampa Street—Explanations asked of the admissions committee "We cannot accept homosexuals in the University"—Tho, as it turns out, 2 of the three on the judging committee are big fairies, & a third "Una terrible Lesbiana"—under the thumb of Lacra at the time so afraid to come out too liberal, they finked out on the kid who as it happened wasn't even queer.

And by closing the whorehouses made sex more difficult, now homosexuality is on the increase & becoming a "social problem."

I told them how in Russia (according to Ylena Romonova[18]) there was a huge lesbian problem on the collective farms—all those muscular isolated hard working bull dykes a product of Marxism.

18. Chair of Western Literature at Moscow University.

Cuba

So various poets and anyway the head of the Dramatic Arts school and Portocarreo the best "accepted" painter are all marvelous homosexuals—Porto in his house all day with old painter Boyfriend I visited, living in domestic bliss & timidity upstairs in apartment overlooking the sea—And maybe Che Guevara or Raul or someone else likes boys too anyway—who knows or cares—So nobody expects the Puritans to take over in the long run & it's a charming political-psychic battle for "more ample standards of behavior" like it said in the Harvard Crimson, when Peter & I got kicked out of Lowell House last month for talking about cocks & coming & typewriters, his reading aloud "Sex experiment #1, Peter jerking off Allen."[19]

Meanwhile dictated to Hoy correspondent page long appreciation of Revolution mostly sympatico and complaining about Lacra persecution of fairies & infermos, paraphrasing Whitman on tenderness between men "with all it implies" as bien, the adhesive element in democracy & Communism, Voznesensky "Communism comes from the heart"—Also in answer to question "What wd. you ask Fidel Castro if you met him"— give 3 point Salaam 1.) What about fairy Sick persecution 2.) why not legalize marijuana, with reasons 3.) Why not end capital punishment, suggesting Magic Mushrooms & job as elevator men Havana Rivera Hotel as sufficient treatment for bomb throwers. Said, tell Blas Roca if he won't publish interview I'll write about it in Evergreen Review[20] & they'll translate it in some Sartre magazine in gay Paris.

19. See Allen Ginsberg and Peter Orlovsky, *Straight Hearts' Delight: Love Poems and Selected Letters,* ed. Winston Leyland (San Francisco: Gay Sunshine Press, 1980), 94.

20. Literary magazine founded by Barney Rosset, publisher of Grove Press, in 1957, *Evergreen Review* regularly published Beat Generation writers and poets, and devoted an entire issue to the San Francisco poetry scene.

Cuba

Saw young kids 3 blocks downstairs—touched their necks—& returning met poets from Nadaistas de Gloamulea—a cat named "El Mouilencia"—and a couple from group "Roof of the Whale" from Venezuela latter I'd seen in Mex City.

Nicanor Parra[21] due on Thursday. Still got to see downtown Havana which from car the other day looks the same lively, except daylight groups on line inside shoestore arcade to buy rationed shoes.

Milk scarce. Series *Marilyn in Memorium* playing at the Cinemathique.

Morning better than terrecmayjacin—and to visit national schools, Blakean school children doing exercises in tennis courts neatly arrayed pretty architecture dorms for adolescents, Edgar Allan Poe & Russian histories of the Middle Ages in the bookshelves—bulletin boards—at the end of corridor with school drawings: "Yell at teacher absent from school, don't study communally (pupil hiding under bed), keep your room dirty & you are friend of the Enemigo"; a drawing of Uncle Sam in Top Starry Hat & flag-striped tails finely crudely drawn, it looks like Uncle Sam fucking Cuba isle up the ass. Huge Cafeterias and general utopian sensation of the vast campus, ladies like Aunt Elanor busy leading the meek tiny children in long single files along the street to the Central Corridor outdoors—covered with modernistic red roof but open at all sides; 1000 infants with trays eating.

"We all know each other."

When taken to jail, in "the persecution of homosexuals," they are photographed with Number & word on their chests like 70479/Homosexual.

21. Chilean poet and professor of mathematics.

Cuba

Union Jovenes Communists denounces fairies. Their convention of Eskol of Art Instructos issued a declaration against decadents, existentialists & homos. A special brigade of pure untouchables created to work with laborers—Nov.–Dec. See "Mella" mag, their organ.

Lunch with Mr. Feo of Writers union: a mad novel about Lacra Social Police with say the head of Lacra a faggot could not be published without referring it up to the Party first.

No free Press, says M. Rosa's husband later that night, but so what, everybody knows everybody, you can always complain to Fidel or take up a grievance personally with someone in power.

Castro on TV—Hotel Havana Riviera—Sitting, over notes, talking, hand to his mouth, then pointing, hair black on the television screen— Grabbing microphones to adjust them—riffling thru piles of papers sitting at end of table—talking about airplane bombs attacking the sugarcane—drinks cup of coffee—"The counterrevolution doesn't even know where to tie the ropes"—his hair is mussed, he's paranoid? about "enemies?"—5,000 workers will get prizes—trip abroad—1000 motorcycles— like a vast church raffle—refrigerators—small details, what kind of refrigerators go to what cities—He gets lost & is silent a moment looking at notes—a disc jockey—Der Fuhrer Gorilla—a pop art poster—lovable friend—Television giveaway program—A real hairy creature for president—Ten times more natural than Johnson in fact human, the numerous spontaneous changes of face & gesture in course of a speech like a man over coffee at night in a Mexican café, tapping the table with 3 fingers at once—a wristwatch & open neck khaki shirt & jacket—We have to incorporate the feminine half of the population into our Social productions—Women important for [?] production also—one finger up—talks rapidly like Cassady[22]—Trapped in the world's descending sugar prices—projects for producing oleomargarine, in detail, by what river—worries about Manteka—eggs—the black market—increasing fish consumption—the *sadness* of him struggling to achieve substantial fruit in the threadbare state of hostility Cuba sits in—USA on their conscience—Why Govt. sets high prices in restaurants? To take in loose change from the streets.

He's too facile with his gestures of amity, comradeship & kindness, as I am, for the same reason, a fantasy of idealistic preoccupations moving too fast in too much detail to really attend totally to anyone.

"Gentlemen, things aren't easy."

He talks for hours, and tomorrow we can all exchange notes & perceptions about his ideas, his mood, his performance like a World Champion prizefight.

Communism/Socialism/Revolution constantly under discussion. I'm obsessed with Lacra
Social.

Regio Guerrero

Earlier this afternoon young boy from poor family came to see me with handscript poems—secret humor seriousness in his eyes.

"my vast penes
al frente del fabricas

22. Neal Cassady (1928–1968), Ginsberg lover and central character (Dean Moriarty) in Jack Kerouac's *On the Road*.

Cuba

Confronting factors
Confronting Cuba
Confronting the revolucion
Confronting the ocean"

           —made date

to telephone him later. Nineteen friend of the Architect, his pants seam home-sewed back together with white thread. In hotel lobby, interrupted by lady reporter Nate Gonzalez Frere from *Revolucion.*

Started to go up elevator but as usual, had to get permission from Culture Friendship office. I got mad upstairs when she said system made sense because whores cows robbers—Especially counterrevolutionaries might come to hotel upstairs assassinate me. Explained U.S. prosody change via W. C. Williams, tone of Lower East Side, general sympathy with revolution, Indian Mantras, relation between breathing/physiology/ rhythm/prosody/self expression of "feeling." Thence to Lacra Social, yakking an hour about that, complaining. She said she couldn't report that as she was interested in "literary" matters. Anyway, Lacra, which was terrible, was dissolved—I said O no they arrested a boy on La Rampa last week, relying on gossip. Loaned her books.

Then down to lobby to meet Umberto Norman—the boy rejected from University for being called homo by the young Communist Union. Because several years earlier he'd left the Union bugged. Now writes poetry. Believes in constant struggle for Revolucion against puritan dogmatist mediocrities, & isn't queer, but unshaven and rather meek. We walked all over downtown Havana with Mario Rena (met first nite with La Puente group) who also was kicked out of teaching art in Oriente with letter "Get job elsewhere, no faggots here." Also done in by Union of Young Communists. They had no proof, he complained; & anyway his teaching was O.K. Both Critical of Press—"mediocrities is the trouble" said young Ballagus yesternight – picked up in jail several hours by police who examined their writings—I don't remember Old Havana Streets, a bookstore where I bought children's: "Abajo El Imperialimo" coloring book. Newspaper politics cartoons of USA Sam top hat money in hand buying off "Gusanos" or as puppeteer on OEA Stand pulling strings on fingers of doll dictators Somoza, Ydigoras, Romulo, Stroessner, Prado etc. Red pop art. Saw afore-recorded Castro TV speech later at Maria Rosa's[23] house & with her husband entered dialectic type discussion of dictatorship—he says no free expression outside of revolution because it's the chance everyone willing to take unity in "difficult" time. Anyway can always complain to friends upstairs. Anyway US free expression (Supreme Court Art Decisions) only support oppressive system not change it; by providing escape valve for otherwise revolutionary steam.

I said U.S. back to Atomic Apocalypse wall *was* probably changing toward accommodation, Vishnu's "Each time I rescue you this way."—i.e. an assertion of unconscious body of desire to continue evolve race not die suicide Hydrogen; and that forces the accommodation to Communist Revolution. U.S. Art part of that psychic change & not therefore a flower ornamental on Capitalist corpse—because no death war, no corpse, but living changes.

But the general acceptance of original sin—Marxism ruling like Catholicism over erratic individual intentions—bugs me more & more; however sophisticated & sensible the argument. Elimination of irrational public prophesy; as if it were not *functional*. A sort of hypocritic lip-service to art if is on "our" side. Human prince Castro—and the bureaucracy— set above dream knowledge—"because the revolution and the material revolution must succeed"—And true enough the guilt of

23. María Rosa Almendre, director of Casa de las Américas.

Cuba

the U.S. is fucking it up—Creates an unresolved contest between centralized organization and individual deviancy. That tolerant deviancy being evolutionary Life-kicks *itself*, Atman-Brahman goofy, the Me-Knower. Well, philosophy never goes anywhere. I'll take off my clothes in the Lobby of the Havana Riviera if I get into trouble.

Hard to judge others. Creepy small town in-group police state, I'd say, with conditions.

22 Jan.

Guerro the layout man from "La Cuba" Mag—his letter to Dorticos[24] & Guillen after his arrest—"I'm a workingman & I got a right to drink to go with girls & hang around La Rampa."

Penilla Sub-Interior Minister in Charge of girls.

Morning rose late and then to Hemingway's house out of town with a gang, lunch & long explanation of difference between surrealist spontaneity and 1960 unedited in "corrected" composition motives to Arey, young poet of Venezuela "Roof of the Whale" group.

Old Man of Sea bay small not as imagined, just a little busy bay-port with no docks, small beach. His restaurant, "drove into that part of town old ford stationwagon with chauffeur."

A big "house on hill, a finca lots of land with great row of trees to the fence—inside a museum, really sad, the skeleton remains of his grand domesticity with the Person gone—all favorite chairs noted, the table set for three, a bathroom with a bottle of [?] grease & by the scale neat penciled on the wall a list of his daily weights—one with a note "trip to N.Y. off diet & 5 days drinking."—then Cancer?—odd dreamlike effect

24. Osvaldo Dórticos (1919–1983), served as Cuba's president from 1959 to 1976.

With English publisher Tom Maschler,
touring the Hemingway museum in Cuba

of the African stag heads jutting out of the wall around the sun table, as if a corner of a Buddhist extra-world where such creatures as jut out of walls do stare dead—And an old house in Rutherford, N.J. where unbalance-footed Mrs. Williams guards the last dream remains of domestic decades flitting by into the shadow—Great collections of tender memorabilia, horns, knives, John Hermann's *The Salesman* among the 1950's books in the many book cases—Folkways Records Sioux Sun Dances among the wall of old L.P. albums—How fast it all grew old—His typewriter on bookcase propped on Who's Who in America—The Editor of *Cuba* Mag overly young but erudite about the dates of his Cuban writings—A desultory group impressed by the traces of Character—He used to go occasionally fishing all day with Castro & once on return kissed the Cuban flag—I drew in book a Jewish star with skull in center and sun flower dependent from the teeth. Great sadness all around, as if of an immediate death, the new death of the day before, yesterday; preserved as a museum.

Ride back thru old Havana—great fragment of 1961 [?] exploded French armaments ship standing in the middle of the Malecon like a giant John Chamberlain statue. Numbers of hands & heads were found scattered among the pieces of ship iron in the waterfront, said Liceo the driver. Ambres Mondoo hotel small like a Paris side street hotel—"To Have & Have Not"—The room preserved, but couldn't locate the guardian of the key—now student hostel. Past *Floridita* Bar, old soul, and around the trees and colonial edifices thru Columbus Square again & back to hotel.

Inquiring more from Liceo he also says the mid-1963 raid on homosexuals in La Rampa resulted from Castro speech denouncing fairies, & continued the arrest of one Guerrero of his magazine, who after several hours suspicious detention wrote Carbon'd letters to Dorticos and Guillen Pres. of Artists & Writers Union—private protests & telephone

Cuba

calls were made, the old people were not used to this—Nothing ever in the papers about Lacra Social, settled out of public court as it were, & Lacra dissolved Says he. Seems to be general Establishment opinion.

Lady in Hotel lobby, [?] member from Chile now 3 years in Cuba ex philos. professor; presently on rich leave from work reforming prostitutes (morning lectures to soften up instructors, afternoon Social-Care-Working) had nervous breakdown overwork besides being herself unmarried with older editor Dario—Complaining about a general Spanish puritanism overhanging the Cuban virgins still—She lost her 4 children in Chilean divorce & she's the fifth girl for this gent who himself had 5 children, and her mother in Chile locked her out of house & money & called her a whore—so she was advisor to reform of prostitutes, under Ministry of Interior.

Fantastic optimism in pushing people around.

Everybody seems to agree illiteracy abolished & Health services improved. Probably the average life-expectancy figures now gone up, were there any reliable figures.

Supper with Tom Maschler[25] & Jay Colon & walk on La Rampa first time at night chic dark Boites almost empty, Russian restaurants $6 a dish $1 for baked apple, quite a few people eating.

Dorado Cigarettes $.25 a pack everywhere even from night club service girls, no tipping anywhere.

But no action anywhere I could leaving see except some interesting looking people & sitting around on the edges of buildings concrete or marble projections. No big mad cheap poetic café. Reuters man a cute young kid with exquisite mulatto girlfriend we met on later streetcorner, stopt me & took us for a drink at small livelier "21 Club" He said

25. English publisher and editor.

Cuba

he couldn't fit any theory to Cuba. No reliable statistics, among other problems.

Story of French Grass expert Andre Voisin invited Dec. '64 here, exhausted by all night conversations with adoring Castro, died in 6 days, was buried in State funeral, after days of TV lectures, his papers published still today serially in all newspapers—monographs on grass alkaloids and viruses.

Reuters Man watches thru spyglasses lovers copulate in many of adjacent [?] hotel—Saw rooms full one night when loudspeakers were blaring universally in the streets a Castro speech—the couples bouncing in all their beds to the ecstatic rhythm of the moving Voice.

-----

23 Jan. 12 pm.—Just washed shirt sox & large blue handkerchief Maria Roca's husband gave me, showered, spent minutes brushing teeth with new broxodent electric toothbrush plugged in wall, chanting OmO-mOm/Sa'ra wa bu da da ki ni yeh/ben/za/wa ni yeh/Ben zo Be Ro T's ni yeh/Hum Hum Hum/PHAT PHAT PHAT/SO HUM. Tibetan mantra Maretta[26] taught me for raising electric heat exaltation solidity lightningbolt in thy corpse, Felt animalesque heat chanting looking in the mirror, swaying my ass body to the beat. Williams in his North room.

Took off 8 a.m. in train of black Cadillacs thru North shore highway past Matanzas, thru towns & hills but hardly looking at the fields & houses of Cuba talking rhythm—rhetoric—histories with Nicanor Parra. His English now more hesitant after half year in Russia trans-

26. Maretta Greer, Ginsberg friend and occasional houseguest, taught Ginsberg Hindu mantras.

Cuba

lating a hundred poems into Spanish. Met all poets & was friends—says Yevtushenko declared that 20,000 were deported or disappeared & 5,000,000 killed in Stalin's time & thus now Nicanor after years a Marxist is more relaxed—The politics metaphysic arguments we had 4 years ago all vanished like mist & both of us later sitting by Cienfuegos hotel swim pool exchanging gossip & amazed to be in the same amiable place in our bodies in Cuba. Gossip about Neruda, pushing him out of Argentine anthologies & stealing his (Parra's) style, he met Laughlin[27] in Yucatan, Yevtushenko crying infuriated about the Chinese—"What can you expect from a people who don't even see what they eat." (Rats?)

Parra's old dream poem line: "Te por Mariposas, estrellas, etc."

So Parra declared himself for liberty of expression anti dictatorship—he being so intelligent & his Chilean anger years ago preoccupying me all this time I felt relieved that my sense of emotional reality was re-affirmed, the same thing came into focus for both of us. Gossip of Raquel Signoret, Baulio Arenas, Theofilo Cid, Pablo de Rokha, Neruda's Western publishing "bubble," local characters from Santiago, Parra has a Lolita now is happy. Expect in Newtonian mechanics, which is probably a large abstract incomprehensible specialty totally Void of anything but signs & language for him nowadays?—Should ask.

At dinner huge conversation with Colombian Elmo Valencia leading "Nadaist" Escritor—Description of Burroughs, Celine,[28] Pucallpa & explanations of Cuban local *Infermos*. Next to him leading *Roof of Whale* Venezuelan Escritor, and Parra described new Chilean youth literati the *Energumenos*, All post-Atomic kids. As I described Infermos, (oddly enough Elmo had not yet discovered them) the tourist IPEC guide lis-

27. James Laughlin (1914–1997), founder and publisher of New Directions Books.

28. Louis-Ferdinand Céline (1894–1961), French physician and controversial novelist/playwright, author of *Journey to the End of the Night*.

Cuba

tened & agreed. Asked me about homosexuality & I launched into half an hour's talk with him about Tenderness—>feeling—>physiology—>reality—>political communication—>anti-Paranoia—>anti police-state.

Boat ride to old Spanish Pirate fort across the bay, taking photos, everyone with cameras, at fort raised mine to picture Parra engaged in dark glasses conversation in his suite on hill in front of Bastion now a postrevolutionary military installation—NO Photos, the guides & soldiers intervened. Long conversations about that—there was nothing to photo there but a picture postcard fort with some sloppy new soldiers hanging around a rampart.

Evening to house built Moorish style by eccentric millionaire, died broke after importing 200 Moroccan artisans? Now an art school run by naturalist/poet/humanist/guru/art scribbler Crank provincial genius once of Harvard —Ficaso?—Anyway clay leafy Hui-Hui's (river trolls)—Later at his house a display of primitive work by local painters, excellent nutty Hui Hui fruit—cabbage ghosts who drag little children to the river bottom to disappear forever—his man genius.

I'm sleepy.

24 Jan '65

I made a mistake, I should have written daily descriptions like this years ago. On this planet I haven't much time—combing my hair in the mirror saw the spreading fields of white in my beard; never noticed so closely before. That's one thing beards are good for.

Began day early sleepy vast hotel overlooking Cienfuegos bay from 6th floor at the end of a map-like peninsula, sunrise over mountains on mainland—in car to Playa Giron where there was once an invasion from US-Cuban types—now a fishing school with scores of half-naked mulatto boys bathing with snorkels—tired, wandering around looking at a

few bombed Cabanas—Had stopped at ruins of a US plane shot down,—
I climbed aboard the rusty motor for a photo Yipieytayay!—A sacrilege
to all sides—(oddly enough Terry Southern[29] came up in conversation
the day previous with Tom Maschler in a red sweater the editor for Jon
Cape)[30]

On way out told Parra long story I'll be waiting to relate to him of
saving the shit bestrewn beggar fetus in Benares' Dasaswamedh Ghat—
He explained his 25 years work on Newtonian mechanics arrived at
M=M. Didn't clearly understand more than that it involved definitions
of a priori propositional figures like Mass & energy. Took decades to re-
solve & says can teach it now in a year.

After, to a Crocodile Isle—Swamp reclaimed & built up in fine style
w/green isles, coral waterways, and a variety of wood-thatch edifices—
museums, restaurants, towers with circular stairways and hay roofs—
Pleasure resort & Alligator Farm—Stared at a huge dinosauric creature
a long time till it opened its eye—   Slept on the grass tired in shade of
new tree—back & forth on long slow ferry-launch rides.

Days ago Reuters Michal Arkis remarked on lack of logical statistics,
& was curious on the fact that once there was surplus of eggs & beef
here, & now rationing & shortage—6 eggs per month per mouth & a
liter of milk a day cheap, but that's all. Restaurant prices mostly high—
$3.50–$5.00 for a truckdriver's diner lunch of rice & oxtails & desert
& soup & coffee in say a bus stop cafeteria. On TV Castro says to pick
up inflated loose change on streets prices are so fixed. Syndicate factory
& school meals free or cheap, store prices low, rents low, health services
medicines free & cheap, but restaurants double U.S. prices.

29. Terry Southern (1924–1995), satirist, novelist, and essayist, author of such
novels as *Candy*, *Red-Dirt Marijuana and Other Tastes*, and *The Magic Christian*.
30. Jonathan Cape, English book-publishing house.

In crocodile restaurant I inquired why now short on eggs meat? "Because everybody now can afford & eats them." The original question troubled me & the answer made sense. What appears to be lowering of production may be actually increased consumption—The Reuters man was mystified & obviously lots of Cuban analysis is mysterious & off color because of lack of information.

The young guide who I gave big lunch lecture on Maricon faggotry has been sweet & attendant all day, took me off alone to Swamy museum to see Mickey Mouse-eyed pre-Columbian Indian crude figurines, being around with me all day, I kept looking at him feeling good & sizing him up for love but both of us too pre-occupied & shy to make a move & the unconscious Spanish Revolution police state paranoia still too much on my awareness like a wet blanket to relax.

The Launch ride, lunches etc. all of a superficial Summer camp bourgeois distraction like an official young peoples Club or something and tho not oppressive, no sudden attacks of mass gaiety or mass sexuality or mass drunkenness or mass communion of any kind except the one Common slightly ambiguous Consciousness of La Revolucion. Affecting material culture in every way like a big dream drug everybody's on like Amphetamine, but still no basic revolution in the Nervous System itself—so that the humanity here not yet sexualized nor myself except at night in the hotel Havana Rivera I masturbate moaning please ... please ... please ... please to the pillow.

With the guide 2 a.m. in night club at Veradero Beach old hotel bought me a drink & for first time saw new Cuban wave dance the MOZAMBIQUE consisting of shifts to right and left open hip-leg & distant *Stop-rest-tune-gap*. On every fourth beat or something like Newtonian Mechanics, both I don't understand enuf to explain.

Earlier 12 AM–2 AM I'd sat crosslegged on dark beach in front of the thin hush-roar of baby waves & looked up at Orion's belt in the black

Cuba

sky, pleades, Venus m shaped Cancer?—Singing O M A Ra Ba TSANA di de de de om A Ra Bat sa Na D E D E D E D E etc. in round, breathing from belly & chanting silently on breath intake & loud on exhale— shifted with finger cymbals to Hari om Namo Shiva & discovered right cymbal rhythm, opened my eyes to the star field, sang to the entire universe till happiness came. A few teen age Cubans appeared at my side to listen & one asked for the words written down—I also gave them a big red rose I had in the dark to smell their noses.

Tues 26th Jan—Woke at Veradeo beach, swim & got sunburned & sang Hari om namo shiva with cymbals, for five to ten minutes—I'm sleeping 3 AM—Lunch, I sat next to big huge heavy bellied Richard Latham, former pres. of Chilean Soc. Of Escritores who had published Howl in Chile. Didn't talk much but asked him why not relax bathe not rush back to—

Tired broke off slept—

Not rush back to Havana, he was unshaven and sweaty, huge bellied tall old grey faced official man ex-ambassador to Uruguay—"I have appointments to keep . . . meetings . . . telephone calls"—So he went back to Havana early.

We went to visit in string of 6 black Cadillacs on the Cuban roads east Maguey & Sugarcane fields to visit a small shipyard, I got hung up talking to a toothless gentle old man in the Workmen's Cafeteria, where they were all standing around a blackboard studying ship-blueprint geometry—He said he was collecting Friendship buttons Russian Chinese did I have any? I thought in bad Spanish he wanted to buy my shirt (from his gesture to lapel) and said this was my one & only shirt till I got the idea straight & showed him my belly button.

Cuba

All the time discussions with Cubans about the Revolution asking ship workers about Police State possibilities & they all saying, well, it's a problem but we trust Fidel and anyway you have to live here to see how it works—

In the evening a delegation of Local Culture Committee and I began giggling hysterically listening to the conversation between Interchangeable polite Uruguayan–Colombian–Argentinean–Cuban Delegate Types saying:

Delegate: "We have a Cultural Organization here in Matanzas province."

Visitors: "How many such culture organizations are there in Cuba?"

Delegate: "Oh for every city—it's divided into etc. etc."

Visitors: "How interesting—& what kind of work do they do?"

Delegate: "Hold conferences, give exhibitions, this year we had a conference in the library on 6 Jan anniversary of the revolution."

Visitors: "And how many members are there in your group?"

Delegate: "Well five here with us to visit you & Steering Committee of 7."

Later a big bearded spade painter & beautiful dark chic Cuban wife came in & looked so classic & alive I came down & got interested. She's reading new Cuban edition of Kafka for first time & thinks the revolution is a great existential scene.

Tom: But there seems to be no organized govt.—

She laughing: I grew up under Batista organized Govt. & now we all breathe a sigh of relief & don't want *any* organized govt. At least nobody has any idea how to organize one yet & who cares? For five years it's been a pleasure.

I launched into questions about persecution of faggots & Lacra So-

Cuba

cial & How come always making big decisions of diversify sugar or impound the fairies & nobody yakks back in the newspapers, no argument, everything settled by telephone gossip in private so to speak—

At which point a sort of angry battle began between me & a Cuban writer jewish polish cat who thought I was exaggerating obsessionally about the fairies & anyway "It's awful, you met that gang of El Puente the first night you were here they're all fairies themselves & filled your head with hysterical gossip—anyway you're corrupting them with your irrational preoccupation, nobody's persecuting no homos here. I have 50 fairy friends in the govt. As them they're more mature."

At which point "I got the Fear" and began worrying if my continual babbling was going to get El Puente Bridge cats into real trouble later— "This poeta Norteamericana came & they took him aside like a little Cabal of maricones & made bad propaganda ? ? ?—and so told the pole my worry over that & he cooled *his* hysteria a little—

Bam in walked the ICEP guide to say that El Senor Latham died suddenly in his hotel room in Havana after he got back—sudden stroke—Everybody silenced—and immediately by some ant-heap telepathy all the Spanish ladies jumped up & gentlemen declaring they were returning to Havana immediately. In hushed voice the guides rounded everyone up saying the cars would be ready as soon as we packed our baggage—Tom Maschler protested he saw no English reason to rush off to Havana at 11 p.m. at night, it would be of no avail and anyway he hardly knew the gentleman—But somehow everybody afraid to say Fuck it Let's stay on the beach another day like we're supposed to—Even I caved in, rather cowardly, as Tom was looking around vainly for support—and as it turned out when we returned to Havana 2 a.m. that night, there was no reason to fly off like a bunch of chickens—Absurd in fact the line of black autos in the middle of the night speeding through the countryside & no one clearly knew why we were demanded to return except the young ICEP guide thought he was supposed to do that—Bad publicity for Cuba a literary delegate kicking the bucket in the hotel I guess & last month Andre Voisin dropping dead the same way—So, concerned that we all take it serious & sorry, and act like it was important—We arrived in the pitches of the night by the palmtree fronted Govt. Nationalized Funeral home & went in upstairs to look thru the glass at the huge rotund jowled bulge eyed grey familiar face in the coffin—a froth of bubbles slowly breaking, that had built up around the lips—I stared a long time at the "old Sofa" & hummed ram Ram Satahay Ram's name in the Truth an old song from the burning grounds. Back at hotel too tired to write, slept.

26 January 1965

Gomez and Aldama

that night the Cuban Cab
Calloway rushed up and embraced
The cop—
Fatnose forgotten—
11 years later.
The honk of a bus turning the corner

A searchlight penciled in the black sky
(from over the cloudy walls of the Moro Castle)
The great Mariachi Corner has Descended
into the dust; the guitarinos dispersed
to groves and ageless back rooms,
The corner swept clean by time's broom
of workmen and wrecking machines (bulldozers)

the palaces stand & the domes, the green
trees let in the park, the clatter
of schoolgirl's feet on the pave,
the yell of babies in balconies—
8 P.M.—with 2 young poets of Havana with
[?] and scandal,
sitting quietly on the old step of
   the Invisible—
gone Crazy I don't know what to do self Conscious
in the Solidity of a City gone Communist
with its long hair & negros—my beard
grey streaked & a cough in my lungs
from 11 years of Cigarettes and
the deaths of Mothers in Madhouses—
feeling calm—anxious to recapture
   the catfish sandwich
      now 35c
But the corner's changed from a bright
lit borracho café with policemen
   in dust streaked uniforms
   and fat whores dribbling blood & tears
      from stupendous ugly busts
changed from the great night city gallery
   to a market of flowers
   a market of flower, a market of
      flowers—
With little neat brick shops like Walt Disney
and a bicycle rider poster on the door
  "Second Vuetta race in Socialist Cuba."

Cuba

The old pavements about the same, this time
the eroded squares of concrete overflowing
   with Cactus & huge yellow
   flower eyes staring thru plateglass
       in dead silence.

—Thus up late fast lunch & met Manuel Ballagas who gave me his dead father's poetry book. Parra there in hotel lobby said all that night the curtains in his room rustled like the funerary curtains over Latham's coffin. He was terrified, I myself had only a split second of terror sometime last night.

Went with Manuel and Tom & Cohen & the boy refused University for being queer to the University to meet little bright-eyed funny face negro Nancy Moreno poetess between classes. Sat around discussing Revolution with crowds of young poets. They all say don't worry, the extremists will all die off, mistakes will be made & rectified so what. I keep probing & getting optimistic answers.

Manuel & all then to Art Museum—vast halls of old historic Cuban scene paintings & one modern primitive Matamoros with a midnight-rousseau country road so dark the little blackhorse in the moonlit field was almost invisibly set in tiny black paint. Like Iris Brody but black.

Then walking on Prado with young boys—stopped by odd huge American in dirty sportshirt, sockless sneakers, hat & white beard "You don't by any chance speak English ... I married a Puerto Rican & had children ... my brothers are Texas lawyers & would put me in the madhouse if I return ... The F.B.I. came to see me & said get on the first plane out ... I been here 5½ years ... They kicked me out of the Communist party in N.Y. ... A Puerto Rican was jealous ... They have my number in Texas & Miami ... Now the Cubans arrested me but I told them where to get off so they let me go, I'm not afraid of *them* ... I inherited 18,000 but

Cuba

my sister only sent me $600 ... I'm going to the Russian Embassy to-morrow to ask them to send me there... I play a one-stringed violin & my dog does tricks ... on the street ... My room $5 a month across the street above that's the only place they make coffee on the Prado ..." The Ancient Mariner, we sat on granite smooth bench & he talked on, till I bid farewell & broke off ... & then walked all over old Havana to the docks, tired after a $1.00 pizza, & bus home at midnight. Dead quiet in the streets & bars mostly except for rare oases.

27 Jan:

Big meeting at Casa de las Americas Haydee Santamaria Chief "Give praise best work outside of politics & go talk to anyone you want." All sorts Spaniards Cela Barral & I met a Chinaman reporter who talked Spanish & listened to long "dull" liberal speeches.

Lunch at hotel, handing in usual meal ticket, cooked smoked pork, too salty so I didn't eat much—Companions were Elano Valencia, short grey faced Nada-ist & painter friend of his from Colombia, and courteous excellent elderly Argentinean literary professor. Elmo said why they were Nadaists—usual explanation of a decadent literature old themes old meters in shadow of a disorganized hunger-nightmare variety typical of S.A. I gave long discourse relating Pound Eliot Williams Gertrude Stein Apollinaire Artaud Celine Genet to present U.S. poetry composition, wound up expounding from text in this notebook on Aldama Palace—broken lines passing back & forth between prose & poetry to graph the excitations of breath or mind during the time of instant composition, Kerouac's spontaneous prosody or W. C. Williams variable measure, a concept that theoretically at least the Latins haven't arrived at inasmuch as their idea even the Nadaists, is still, for avant garde, merely post-Eliot.

Cuba

Cela a Spanish novelist looks like a diplomat earlier had said he thought Bagatelles for a Massacre Celine's best book, which made me excited since everybody else Jewish put it down for politics, which means there is still a grand Celine explosion ahead in U.S.

Young poor poet didn't show up for date so I fell asleep looking at an anthology of Nadaist poetry which oddly was quite lively.

Dream: Some long conversation with Karl J. Shapiro[31] about revolutionary politics, wherein I stirred from my sleep to write it down but ashamed of such a literary dream rejected it & fell asleep again to be in the middle of a publisher's or Casa de Las Americas party with Jean Genet who looked much younger than I thought or in more robust health a little like John Ciardi or Sarewsky the Pole I argued with or Parker Tyler of yore, we were on a couch & he didn't pay much attention to me & I was never sure it was him since I didn't recognize him from that whitebroken nosed photo on books, as he turned to go down elevator I said "Adieu Jeannot" an intimate diminutive from Books & he sat down on couch, we began talking & putting hands all over each other & finally kissing each other on the lips, I got happy to be so close to him & he so open, looking at me in the eyes & talking, but I was anxious since I wasn't still sure it was Genet or some old queen whose name I'd mistaken—shameful dream camp—so asked why he didn't look like his picture—had all his hair, dark—He said, so sweetly, he didn't know, he *never* seemed to look like photos of himself—we went off, down to go out to City Havana together & the dream went off somewhere else. I've forgotten this half hour later on waking.

This result of various half-embarrassing conversation I've had with

---

31. Karl J. Shapiro (1913–2000), Poet Laureate, 1946.

unattractive middle age journalists now, on my complaint *Hoy* won't publish my interview on "socialist" social acceptance of homosexuals want to know why I propose such a strange subject, am I serious? Am I saying it to "Shock"?—And having had this interview already over & over it's become an obsessional subject of explanation like I'm sick of it & my own opinions except the whole lack of communication on the subject indicates either I'm a neurotic special case out of step with the universe or they're just plain insensitive—so I have to go into long painful explanations of why I have lust for boys & men & that gets sticky, wound up trying explaining my early image of women was affected by my mother died in a bughouse, the journalist very sympathetic, but altogether the point was lost, & when I get by myself I realize these people are just straight laced minded & in some sense inhuman, haven't got the sense of a Whitmanic Jean Gabin dockworker or peasant who fucks sheep, and I become some sort of idiot rational explainer of passing realities. I don't even get laid, overstating the "case" for homosexuality. Genet in the dream at least was real I mean the rapport glance of intelligence & human presence made "gratifying sense."

The socialist revolution doesn't understand anything "intuitively" as far as its explainers & thinkers are involved but that's the same as Joan Konner on Channel 13 N.Y.C.

Even this Notebook begins to be explanatory, a journalistic mode. Fuck it. Socialism turns Everybody into polemic intellectuals—as a defense against invasion of imaginative instinct by collective bargaining boards.

Plus letter via Mexico from D. McDonald[32]—I woke up from dream

---

32. Dwight Macdonald (1906–1982) was a writer, critic, editor, and political writer.

Cuba

realizing he wanted reassurance & was sincerely wounded questioning why I so angry grabbed his lapels in fury when he wouldn't defend Flaming Creatures[33] or even principle to totally free sexualized movies, & why later Leroi Jones[34] cursed him out as white liberal creep bastard in front of Dakota Chic apartments months ago. Old wounds.

Only answer Leroi Jones go to bed with Dwight McDonald under a blue Carib wave.

Cathedral Square—

    The beautiful house of the counts
        Bayona
in the midnight silence now
with a dark lone palm
in the courtyard overhanging
        the roof
and the scratch of leaves on
        Cobblestones
with a few yellow lights under the
arches—the blue neon
        gone away—
absolutely dead but for our
        four voices
and the heels of a couple clicking
across the square

33. Experimental 1963 film by Jack Smith.

34. African American poet, editor, playwright, and activist; later changed his name to Amiri Baraka.

Columbus Cathedral stands
more solid than my watery
      mind
weatherbeaten tho may be
and emptier now of painful
Sacred worshippers
The Spanish masturbating priests
sent home by Revolution—
the palmtree's waving its arms
  in the moonlight to say goodbye
 to me and the priests
and I have not much more time—
than before to return again

When the lights are on in the
Paris restaurant
and the mariachis with their
violins play another ghostly
     tune
and the water comes forth from
the ancient holy okker door
between the potted greenery trees
under the antique porch
To serve the lone wine
I drank to make my
   breast alive more warm

To see the stone square burst
into music, and boys
   dancing hand in hand with

the back of dogs.
A motorcycle moves by Malecon down the street
and one invisible beggar
Coughs his *arm!* by
the Cathedral's grey pillar
    old & asleep.

To Theatro Marte a vaudeville show the Last in Havana (or N.Y. or
London for that matter): the stock characters are a handsome boy, a
blackfaced spade who dances, his wife the servant mulatto, an old
creakybacked impotent lower class husband and his oversexed wife, &
a Chinaman who I didn't see. Funny sexy popular sketches about Jeal-
ousy at the beach with some crazy dancing in the middle, in an old
baroque rundown theatre with balcony windows open to the balmy
night breezes & streetlamps & bus noises.

Walked to Cathedral Square and sat down on steps & wrote poem,
and then wandered around with Uruguayan actor—the streets empty
mostly, a few bars with scarce customers, no night life much—the revo-
lution lacks imagination for Megalapolitan excitements—Found a taxi
corner with some open restaurants, prices $1 & $2 a plate, I ate some
"Mariscos Fritos" which came greasy fried doughballs with invisible
slivers of fishiness in the yellow middle, 60c. An argument with the wait-
ress started in the corner: *How Politics Got Mixed up in the Soup.*

The waitress brought soup slow & late & apologized. A thin nervous
mustached fellow began yelling & arguing excitedly "I didn't fight for
a Cuba Libre revolution for this kind of lousy service." He went on ir-
ritated for 10 minutes. She said "Well I'm for Cuba Libre but it would
be a happier Cuba if everybody learned some manners & had better ed-
ucation." He: "I don't want my soup It's too late, this is not revolutionary
soup!!" and she was real mad too. He left & the argument continued

Cuba

with a short Juvenile Delink. Looking cat on the stool reading *Hoy*: "Why bring up politics, we have a free Cuba now." And she got mad again, saying I didn't bring up politics, he brought up politics, all I did was bring the soup slow, I'm not an electric choo choo, and he should be better educated than to yell at me." The young kid said to herironically "Well you have some reason on your side" with his eyes to the paper headline Vietnam Govt. Changes, shook the paper (as she walked away) to cash register & said "Cojones! Balls!

So that's how politics got mixed up in the soup.

"There's one central very big scene going on and then the side scenes are harder to get into & not so interesting." Marcia Overton.

Thurs. 29 Jan '65 *[sic]*

[...]

Stayed home all day began to read mss. for poetry competition, 91 books in carbon & I can't read Spanish.

Young American girl here five years came by hotel to invite me to meet the American Colony—said she wanted to go home now, too much isolation from the latest music, mouths, movies, U.S. anonymity relaxation Said: Manuel B. came to help me read the mss. & stayed all day, after trouble at the elevator getting him upstairs—young kid with acne'd face son of an old poet, now 17 years with little cute beard and lively friendly intelligent sexy manner, in sweater & tee shirt carrying a few books of young friends to leave with me. Has been a writer four years, & registered with Union de Escritores as writing since 1961 so has one year to wait till he's received as a member of the Union—Condition being 5 years active practice—now works as an Editor of govt. sponsored El Puente publishing house—He once lived in N.Y. so speaks excellent soft English with perfect sober understanding and—I feel more love for

Cuba

him than anyone I've met here, or feel trust, in his affection & his judgment. Gave him $10 pesos to get some tea to turn on Parra & the other judges.

Sat all afternoon reading & making phonecalls & gossiping. Seems that after dissolution of Lacra Social the problem of homosexuals, beards, existentialists, infermos, social delinquents lesbians & eccentrics moved to another level & the pressure became more conventional & subtle. This month, I gather from vague gossip, a professor from the Arts School was removed from his post because of being homosexual, & several students from dramatic arts were also expelled. Sometime in the last weeks a group of Establishment deviates visited Pres. Dorticos & were reassured that the social revolutionary planning would leave them—as professionals, and artists— untouched & unmolested for the most part—but, as deviancy was becoming a serious social problem, or, at least a serious bureaucratic consideration, a board of psychiatrists (Pavlovian?) was being established to make investigations & plans on a national scale—and as far as the younger element the nonestablishment kids, something had to be done about them, so henceforth (I hear as rumor so far) a series of "psychological" tests for sexual and other deviancies would be established as preliminary to entrance in the plastic arts schools—go weed out the social creeps fairies etc.

So passed afternoon pouring over odd Latinamerican poetry texts. Got extra ticket for lunch with Manuel—he had brought letter, on Writer's Union stationary, saying he had work & consultations to do with Senor Ginsberg in behalf of El Puente. Signed by young Jose Mario, chief organizer of Puente group. A sort of slight-of-hand bureaucratic style, since Puente itself probably has no stationary of Hotel status.

At Elevator when we went in, old whitehaired man said "No visitors upstairs, orders hotel regulations." We went letter in hand to ICEP of-

Cuba

fice,—they said it wasn't their responsibility but that of the desk clerk. At desk the clerk told us to check with ICEP, & as we turned back to ICEP the guides there were waving us back to the desk man who was saying "No visitors hotel rule" Tho Manuel after a small discussion had been admitted a week ago—as well as a stream of official journalists. Finally we produced the letter, the clerk took it indoors office labyrinth to manager, came out again saying OK, go up, & on the way up the elevator man explained "We have to have these rules to protect our guests from being molested, counterrevolutionaries or robbers or assassins might prowl the halls if we let everyone upstairs."

Later in the day Mario my ICEP guide, looking fatigued sat down with me & said, Maschler & J. H. Cohen were complaining about the food; & the service, & said I'd complained.

"The food is say not so great I could cook better but I'm not so preoccupied with food as the problem at the elevators with guests. But you might as well listen to Tom he's a big international editor & knows hotels tho his tendency is to hysteria when the service is low grade & food is dreary."

Then I recounted the day's elevator adventures, for Mario Carmona, in mid afternoon had met me in the lobby and we decided to go upstairs to visit Latham's widow. Carmona's sub editor of *Cuba* magazine, a big wheel always in and out of the hotel visiting VIP's and knows everybody in ICEP & had been up to my room to see me with his subud-nervous breakdown wife & their puppy Lekula a week ago. We'd got on elevator to go upstairs & the elevator man prohibited Dario Carmona. Now, Dario's wife had been assigned to company & sleep over in hotel with Dame Latham so it was really too much. Dario said he never heard of such a hotel rule—we went to ICEP office & chief there immediately escorted us back to elevator, & winked at elevator man "Senor Carmona was with Fidel in the Sierra Maestra"—so we went up. The Lady came

Cuba

out dressed in black, very staid & sober but lively, spoke well of her husband who had died as he wished, active and traveling—died in fact in 4 minutes from a total stroke all at once as he was preparing to leave hotel room—"What's life seem like?" I asked "Not worth all the trouble" she smiled.

So talking with Mario of ICEP I explained all the contradictory elevator experiences & he said it was confusing him too, would I please write a written complaint. I told him, so far I'd heard half a dozen reasons for the rule from clerks, elevator men, ICEP guides, journalists— 1. The old days the hotel flooded with whores. 2. The old days peasants country people brought their relatives cows & chickens. 3. No hotel in the world allows visitors upstairs. 4. Counterrevolutionary assassins might molest the foreign guests. 5. Everybody has to be identified. I said I'd write a diplomatic note suggesting simple system that if guest in hotel identifies visitors & asks him &/or accompanies him up, that resolves the issue & simplify confusing decisions on part of the employees & ICEP guides. He said it might work. Meanwhile Carmona said he'd try to find out the real rules.

The hotel is run by backroom bureaucracy & so the service in the diningrooms is over-rigid & unenterprising. Cohen couldn't bring out dessert to Tom at swimming pool tho he had Tom's ticket, & if you forgot your ticket, even if they know you're an invited guest with a book of tickets in your room, you have to go upstairs & get it, they won't wait till supper or later. Have to present it in the kitchen or something. So the waiters are not very "macho," I laid that word on Mario—he agreed in principle that over-rigid systematization was lowering the tone of the trip.

I guess now I'll have to write a big complaining letter to the management to improve their Socialist revolutionary efficiency.

Meanwhile according to Manuel, the reporter from Revolucion Nate

Gonzalez Frere had run into Jose Mario (young faggot *Puente* editor) and grey cheeked young Heberto Norman—the kid not admitted to the University school of letters suspected to faggot finked on by Union of Young Communists—

Thereby hangs a tale. Turns out he really was sort of faggot at least him & Mario were making it—lovers—Mario had also a Peruvian boyfriend to whom he wrote book of dull love poems submitted to the poetry competition I'm judging—Well anyway, when you apply to the University you get an oral conference exam wherein they ask you what you think the attitude of a writer should be towards the Revolution, & this & that, and apparently Heberto must have argued with them—the examiners being loaded with doctrinaire Communists—So they discussed him & turned him down, he's not politically mature & "besides why should we put a homosexual in the school"—The secret discussion was reported to him by one girl Joven Communists on the board—who was later expelled from Young Communists for telling tales like that & leaking secrets to fairies.

Mario himself had been school & been questioned or given so much static—as he's an obviously slightly effeminate type, he'd finally left voluntarily rather than take more shit— Well anyway, Nate Gonzalez Frere had run into Mario & Heberto at the Writer's Union & warned them against my influence "You're young & he's very corrupt & wicked—he has a suede jacket & it has holes in it that he cut purposely to look strange & make sensation."

Now this lady journalist had visited me & we'd argued & talked as I wrote pages back & she did ask about my coat & I explained it was a handmedown from a dead friend—romantic sensation like that. But she invented "a pair of scissors" for me unquote. Besides she'd borrowed books overnight & not returned them for a week. So I phoned her &

Cuba

yelled at her on the phone for being sloppy with her gossip & her given word. Then got limousine, went to her house, drank wine with her husband, complained more about recent arts school crackdowns "You're obsessed with this subject ... it's unimportant ... food for the workers is the real achievement of the Revolution ... besides you rely on gossip too much. Besides if the homosexuals make a spectacle of themselves on the street ... mind you some of my best friends etc." Difficult to control my temper. The same piggish bourgeois cowardice & stupidity & rationalizations as New York or Saigon or Benares—The same stereotyped arguments 1927 Russia 1945 U S McCarthy the same journalistic evasion Time magazine Pravda Revolucion New York Times 1965. Left with chauffeur & books.

Spoke to Spanish publisher Barral & asked him to think over doing Spanish translation of my poetry—circulates all over S.A. Left the books with him.

Nobody here's read Burroughs yet.

Supper with the Argentine courteous Professor Fiejoo & Argentine-Englishman Blake translator Enrique Carrisiacolo & gaunt goofy Miguel Grinberg & big mustached Mexican poet Jaime Savilla—explained Mescaline effects, Tibetan Book of Dead, then conversation turned to comparison of Spanish Mystics & Indian Saint poets Kebir & Mirabai—I thought Blake & San Juan coincided rhythmically in intensity—

Este Saber no sabiendo
que me queda Balburiendo

Everyman to every night
Some are born to endless night

Late evening Manuel didn't call, another reported to me, did he get busted scouting for me?—Went over to Writers Union with Ray Charles & Bob Dylan records—

Met young poetess there who'd been taken to jail, sent to hospital, given 14 shock for staying out late all night & acting excited—She'd kept journal police confiscated for evidence & never got it back. I suggested a lawyer, she explained there were no fixed laws, courts, or constitutional rights established yet to work from. I told her to write a novel out of the story—she said it couldn't be published, the older writers were too chicken to really protect the young in really difficult situations—Guillen helpful but would wash his hands of an ambiguous case like hers. "Typical hung up chick" yet with great softness & humor & obvious sensitivity—reminded me of suicide Elise.[35]

Discussion & more gossip about the fairies meeting Pres. Dorticos. The established professionals reassured nobody would molest *them*, so they feel safe but don't want to rock the boat, so the younger unprotected kids get the shit—expulsions or difficulty with schools, McCarthyite gossip from the young Communist league.

I still not seen the leaders of the Joven Communista, nor *Hoy's* Blas Roca, nor Ramiro Valdes, head of Minister of Interior including police—and the Conseja Superior de Defensa Sociale—That's probably the infermos juvenile delinquent department.

You're all right in this bureaucracy if you have pull, friends, or are on the Revolution Grapevine. Otherwise no structure for protection.

Manuel not reported in all night & I began to worry. The boy said he's probably alright. "Is he in jail?" "If he is we'll get him out."

---

35. Elise Cowen, profiled in Joyce Johnson's award-winning memoir *Minor Characters,* was a friend of numerous Beat Generation writers, including Ginsberg.

Cuba

Jan 30 Friday *[sic]*

9:40 AM phone rang Manuel calling—said he had trouble last night—after I left him off in car (on my way to Nate Gonzalez Frere), we had been followed & he was picked up by police. Said he couldn't come to hotel & I said where meet? He said Writers Union 3 p.m.

Breakfast, Tom & Cohen all going to write a letter to ICEP complaining about Elevator Molestation of visitors. Couple from *Hoy* newspaper stopped me—a young poetess & her husband—and with photographer & sketch artist tried to get up to my room—stopped again & we went to desk clerk who sent us to ICEP, Lady there telephoned downstairs and up came a new personage, swarthy & intelligent looking in dark glasses—Romero Vailladares, who glanced at their card and approved them. I asked his name, as he said "Perfectly allright." Maybe he's the Chief Spectre.

Meme Solis
   quartet
Blue dresses—Feeling music,
  Amadeo Rodon Theater
"The Chinese don't make fools
of themselves in the theater"
    —Parra

If you keep playing with that Straw
Machine you'll have to send it back to
Czechoslovakia for repairs

   * * *

Cuba

Pieces of ice in Bob Dylan's coat
one after the other: Scene in Movie.

Fri. 30 Jan *[sic]*—12:30 P.M.

Early up from phonecall from Manuel—went in, talked to Tom, schoolboyish conspiracy glee about Manuel's arrest—since the police are so inept they be easy to entrap. Accosted by more reporters from *Hoy*—a lady Puente poet and her husband Callejas—some problem with ICAP[36] getting them upstairs. Later found that aforesaid swarthy Romero personage was just the Chief Carpetiero or floor Clerk & not secret police. My paranoia same long interview mixture of literary discussions of prosody Williams poetry a la Voznesensky an exploration of consciousness via association rather than metaphor, thence to I am a maricon but also like girls I smoke marijuana. What about persecution of homosexuals—the same stereotype answer "you must understand the revolution is more concerned with basic issues raising production feeding & educating people cutting sugar & defending ourselves from U.S. pressure. Later on these aesthetic issues can be discussed." However by the time interview was over they did say Blas Roca, *Hoy* Editor, was a humane gent, married with children, *but* the Press in Cuba was not open enough & there was a shut-out of discussion of basic issues. Said they'd report what they could.

Lunch with dyke looking intelligent shy young lady prose writer Evora Tamayo & young swarthy painter from Casa Americas talked about Melville Saroyan Bradbury her favorites, Bartelsby especially, I told her plot of Billy Budd casting Cuban Enfermos as Billy & Claggart as Blas Roca and Captain Vere? The Revolution of Fidel? Nah. But Billy

36. Cuban Institute for Friendship with the Peoples.

Cuba

Budd suddenly fit into the scheme here—to Cezanne & Strobiscopic lights & Gysin's[37] dream Machines—

Rushed off with Ray Charles & Bob Dylan records & Japanese finger cymbals & Howl & copy of Guillen poems & a tie & clean shirt & suit to Writers Union to meet Miguel—who sat on couch & told me finally what happened—arrested after I left him off in car on way to Nate reporter's house at 5:30 p.m. & then to 4th precinct—we'd been followed by ICEP car—They picked him up a block from writers union & kept him until that morning in a room—Grand-fatherly cop (official de Guardia named Jose de la Pas Moral Valdez) asked him a few questions and took him home at 5 AM to his mama to sign a paper saying he'd been arrested, "Was taken to Unit for having talked with strangers." She has to bring him in anytime they call—probation.

Went up to see Nicholas Guillen, with Manuel & Herberto—Sat on couch met learned Journalist who'd written account of my texts for El Mondo—had rum—Guillen whom they call avueleto little Grandfather very friendly—I explained the situation, told him I'd been going around calling myself a pot smoking fairy & complaining about Lacra Social & persecution of homos—He said he'd call Haydee Santamaria & asked Manuel to write it all up on a piece of paper typed, to present the situation to Dorticos. Made date Monday night & listen with him to Ray Charles & Bob Dylan—he looks like big frog—Cheery manner & sympatico—told me to go ahead & blabber away, might do some good here & keep notes, which I'm doing. Then downstairs drank beer till 5 in Writers Union restaurant explaining W. C. Williams "No ideas but in things"—Pound's Chinese Written Character to Jose Mario lovesick

37. Brion Gysin (1916–1986), painter, writer, and performance artist, whose cutup method of writing influenced Burroughs and Ginsberg.

Cuba

vague poet—Then back of Union a huge dance studio with toccodisco phonograph—Huge noise of Charles What'd I Say and Drown in my own Tears—

Lift by cab for cocktails British 3rd Consul who wasn't home called away talked with his wife & mother-in-law briefly—they moved their lips in high teacup tiddly fashion staring in each others eyes like childish madwomen—"Won't you have a little droplet of gin, mummie?"

Limousine back to Hotel Supper yakking with Mr. Cohen, "I realize you & I are compulsive talkers" & he seriously agreed. His wife does most of the talking at home.

Thence to Theater Almadeo Roldon with huge gang Parra Tom the courteous Prof. from Argentina, Arrey plastered & shouting cheers up —Animo! Mr Feo of Writers Union to whom I gave a flower as he told me the big gay scene was Sat. nite at the Ciros Hotel bar—"I didn't know you were interested" said he—"You haven't asked the right people"— and Elmo Volente was there in the free box, and a friendly sweet ICAP guide reading Crime & Punishment on his night off (he has trouble con- centrating studying law)—Also Manuel and Heberto showed up & sneaked in on our invitados box seat tix—and Jose Mario too came late and Nancy Moreno lively eyed colored poet 20 yr. old sensible girl down- stairs unbeknownst—

The *feeling* singers one after another in style derived from Billy Hol- iday & Kerouac's Frank Sinatra slow meditative speech song—almost prosaic Creely-like deliberate statements of existential Self—one mad quartet in blue led by pianist Meme Solis—and he sang alone his own alas song La Distincia which was so personal it was almost Mikastonal Indian style—but later the whole dark cabaret style intimate cool self statements got boring—"The Chinese never make fools of themselves in the Theater" said Nicanor Parra, bored, anticipating the stereotyped rhymes—but something was going on in the *Feeling* as a statement of

Cuba

personal slow expressiveness that you have to listen to calmly without rhetorical displays of mad music—Animo! Animo! muttered Parra & also Arey shouted at the end of songs from the dark boxes—their Elena Bourke the heroine of the whole group of composers stept forth robust & sophisticated in short blue dress with silky blue drapes arms, her dress almost above knees, & *pronounced* the casual intense songs with more authority than the other singers, they're like little sketch-dramas fit for a Supper Club in time melancholy AM philosophos—Ball of Snow on records I heard had some personal English in his husky weary fag voice—too many cigarettes—

We left & walked
to hotel stopped for beer, Tom playing with automatic straw machine like flipping up straws for a one armed bandit game—"You better stop or they'll have to send the machine back to Czechoslovakia for repairs" I giggled—

I got home started writing & bring bring the telephone—Heberto downstairs, Jose Mario & Manolito arrested leaving the theater. Went downstairs there was Nancy Mrejon & other poetry girl—all the Cuban literary girls a little shy, and sweetly brave—in Lobby—we talked strategy—They'd called Writers Union & told Guillen, he said he had date morning with Haydee Santamaria—wait till then—We went to Maria Rosa's house—She was a little insider bugged with me—Said well perhaps you don't understand how hard we have to struggle to keep the revolution clean—You have to understand the stupid ones the squares here think it's bad for us to have the young ones washing our dirty linen in public, discussing problems with foreigners—after all *we* have to struggle with the conflicts & worse with threats from outside, not you—but as far as I feel your work here is 90 percent destructive & perhaps that's as it should be—

The younger kids afterwards downstairs thought she was "playing her papel (role)" as official in the Establishment. I don't know what forces she has to struggle within interior politics square dogmatists against revolutionary liberals. Maybe the squares are stronger.

Meanwhile problem left till morn, she'll call Haydee Santamaria tonight—H. S. works all nite & sleeps—"God knows when."

----

30 Jan Sat.—[...]

At Conuunco Folklorico—simple step-dance shuffle, arms falling down sideways like fishing poles everything pelvic from the waist down & relaxed—terrific drums, tradition of Santera. Then the ecstasis Nanigo man dance, individuals with sticks & handkerchiefs improvising to each other around the huge room—to such depths of freedom of the body they were like black meat gods in wooden heavens & tears came to my face.

I thought people were watching me too, as the dancers came ever bounding & kneeling & touched my brow. The ecstasy seemed a justification of all previous intuitions about what's wrong with Cuban politics.

This group organized post revolutionary folklore revival of Santeria—Had to leave early to Casa Americas see Haydee Santamaria.

Long tangled conversation, at first she was mad, Usual vague theories about need for society to deal with homosexuals making spectacle in public & seducing youngsters & these El Puente kids filling my head with juvenile complaints. I had to finally interrupt her & said she was talking too theoretically so I should explain practical problem of boys in jail & so step by step for 15 minutes gave her clear drama description of when met, what said, how said, when & why arrested. She bluffed a little & said oh, she misunderstood *who* was arrested now she realized it was a stupid uneducated police mistake, she thought, she said, it was

Cuba

one of another group of pro-americans who thought they could black-
mail the Revolution by taking refuge at my famous poetic side. I said I
hadn't met this group, who were they & why mightn't I meet them too?
She said she see Guillen that hour, later in day visit Valdez Minister of
Interior & investigate exactly how such bad orders & bureaucratic stu-
pidity came about, & boys be released & safe for me to see all I want. I
left relieved but later thinking it over she seemed stupid & full of Au-
thoritative Bullshit, as if she was doing, or the Govt. were doing anyone
a favor by leaving them alone. On the other hand the Revolution has
"problems." The more I think of it the more I think this sort of problem
is their (her) own making—She's in charge of *Berudos* (Scholarships)—
as well, it turns out, as Venezuelan projects. She said 23 ruling members
of Council all have different opinions on art, but don't consider it their
business to promote one kind or another ("abstract realist, impression-
ist") as long as whatever kind it is, is "good" art.

God knows how they'll ever recognize a new innovation in art. Run-
ning art by bureau presupposes preconceived patterns of good & bad.

I said I thought any good art was invention. Probably not communi-
cating much.

I brought up Parra's 20,000,000 arrested Russians & she said they
were aware of Stalinism ("not that many?") and were fighting to pre-
vent it, sure it could not happen here.

I slapped her on the behind as she left the door. She talks too rapidly.
Said she was *also* a "Biche Rara"—Weird or strange type & I said so was
the Revolution itself. She thought artists were also Biche Rara.

All day long—visiting with Yoruba derived Congadrum Ceremony 2
—Midnite chanting Dancing event and people collapsing in possession
—mass cooperation in establishing cosmic body-drum dance rhythm to
point of flip-out faint & ecstasy limpness—great sound and powerful
people, tradition maintained centuries after slavery from Niger to

Cuba—Santero said my Santo was Change, red phallos Shiva cre-
atortype—I had Jose Mario's protection Santero beads of Yemaya,
Ochun & obstasis all lost days around my neck, surprising the elevator
boys & being quick friendly response in buses & stores—1,000,000
Cubans practice Santoria which is like Ending Bhakte, the gods being
derived in the drum, & rhythm, chanting, & dancing Devotional Yoga
the Sole vehicle for man-god consciousness—entry into the single
rhythm of one soul in one body—

All day & on ride
home thinking about how bad actually her & Maria Rosa's rationaliza-
tions were for total fear-police-state-intimidation suppression of not
merely dissent but mental style, suppression of simple human commu-
nication, stereotyping & control of mechanical massmedia, as per the
reporters all thinking of what is *politic* to report of my babbling, not
what I babble itself. Everything *edited,* including my conversation com-
munication with her Santamaria because of *fear* of what happen to
the boys if I flip out, insult, or just say fuck your egotism *you* are the
state & you think you can run teenager's sex lives & attitudes toward
you?—which is what this stage of personal govt relations in Cuba boil
down to.

What they need is adequate set of civil laws speech laws.

Senteria ceremony needs license 8 days in advance.

The govt. now older ignorant of sense of independence of young. The
older are addicted to *their idea* of the revolution, the teenagers, those
not brainwashed by elders, have their own idea of amplitude of human
nature, sex scene, night scene, feeling & probably political tactics.

Haydee looks about 45 Russian blonde buxom, talks like a woman
making a speech to high school girls, too rapidly & with too much au-
thority as if her words were some kind of governmental Policy, which
it is, which is dangerous, since she doesn't know much more about psy-

Cuba

chic life than my Aunt Clara. Obviously an intelligent & courageous soldier revolutionary & political bureau manager & a mother of a child of 4, but the idea of her directing decision making on the psychological sexual testing of scholarship applicants seems not only absurd but morbid.

It is basically a conformist scene in personal relations they're establishing by mis-management. The revolution needs an astute psychic manager, someone with executive ability for outer propaganda & internal harmony. Like me maybe. Too much—Maybe tomorrow go into details—Need fucking tape recorder.

Jan 31—1 AM

Woke early and phoned Manolo—his mother answered & said in sotto voice "please be careful" & turned phone over to him. Last time I'd called a week ago she's said merrily in excellent English, "Oh, you're the creepy Northamerican Poet" "Yes that's me, ma'm, is Manolo home?" "No he's out somewhere with those alley cats friends of his"—

This morn Manolo answered "Are you phoning from the hotel?"— "Yes"—"Well we can't talk too well"—"When did you get out?"—"They only held us 3 hours, an official from UNIAC (Artists & Writers Union) came & got us out that night"—"I saw Haydee Santamaria & she said it would be all straightened out, I talked to her long time described step by step the scene & I think she understood"—"Well I think it's better that I don't see you right now"—"Why?"—"I saw Guillen & he told me it would be better if we didn't hang around with you, it might make less trouble"—"But Haydee said"—"Well don't tell anyone I told you Guillen said so." We made date to meet at Writer's Union Mon. eve. 9 p.m. Then I have date to play Guillen raycharles and Dylan prophesies.

By this time I was up early, called Porro Architect to make another date lunch tomorrow, he said Deglo Guerrero whose cock confronted the ocean was in trouble, he'd tell me about it at lunch—"on account of seeing me"—"No, of course not."—and spoke phone to David Biegleman, who'd sent me translation of *Howl* via Gino Foreman months ago—Made date for him to come—Found note from Robert Williams & called he said he'd be at hotel this evening, we talk,—I remember story of Leroi Jones, him confronting the U S Consul Havana with a pistol demanding protection for his family threatened in (Monroe?—)—and by phone consul calling U S A & getting protection. Also had seen biographical account of his Cuban antiwhite antiyankee propaganda in NY Times, which painted fair tho smug picture of his ideas but completely left out ignored or eluded his early terror-suffering experiments in his home town which drove him to total & rational distrust of local & Federal authority in that area, to take up arms to protect himself & his group from white anarchy.—

Lunch said adieu to Tom off to Sierra Maestra on solo tour—sitting talking with Nicanor & told him arrest problem, he considered slowly & with smile-judgely humor boxer-mulatto face & told me to go slow. Called Maria Rosa, no word yet from Haydee–Guilen meeting, tho Guillen's advice to Manolo had come after that meet—made me worry more curiously how straight she was with me—

Maria Rosa on phone said can trust Haydee's word, the boys be all-right—

Then phonecall from Mario Pena who called to tell me the boys were taken, which I knew, & to try arrange a meeting some place private—I said best at Writers Union Monday & I think things be straight—he said "I don't think it be that easy,"—"The problem too deep hondo?"—"Si."

I was tired and napped. Nicanor reading the poetry books found a nice fine electronic-political-romantic quotidian poetic rant from Argentina complaining "the radio doesn't say the president is playing mickey mouse with the treasury" That probably get prize.

Cuba

Mr. Cohen who'd selected a squarer book, surprisingly openminded & at Nicanor's suggestion rereading this rejected mss. decided it *was* that good.

Woke, David Biegleman came we had coffee & went upstairs—oddly no got stopt at Elevator—& revised his Spanish Howl to Cuban shorthand syntax speedyness several pages—I had headache & was tired. He neurasthenic thin sort of nice face red splotched had lived in US visiting yearly, said he owned a big Siamese Buddha he wanted to show me at home, & several of the primitive country paintings that Fiejoo was popularizing. He sent me one I never got from Gino in N.Y.

Discussed politics, he thought Oswald was in a co-plot that had been hidden, that world *would* die by bomb, that he thought Cuba was like a lost ship but Castro Ulysses & would we ever get home to Ithaca?—he loves Castro—That Puente group worthless poets except for Ana Marie Limo, & Manolo too—That he was a virgin at 21, never having girls except once brought as teenager to whorehouse he screamed & flipped out nervous & distant—don't know about boys but doesn't like women— oddly the youth after revolution began discovering homosexuality he thought—I suspect this exaggerated on every side, they probably just talk more openly than elders—But that it was sick faggotry not Whitmanic openness—I explained my Indian Mystery version of "get back in your skin" or return to the body, that Death was a threat only if life is lived solely in the mental worlds but life opened to infinity like in Blake if lived in the feeling body—which means acceptance of this body that must die—He said that the Mystery behind the Fernandez-Ordoqui trial was that Ordoqui was a CIA agent under blackmail, even if that version sounded like another Zdanov trial excuse—he referred to Merlau-Ponty book on Russia History 1930's I never heard of but sounds very sophisticated—being laid he admires F L Wright (David self studying Architecture) the lone man whose works will be destroyed in Amer-

Cuba

ica by Bomb a tragedy—Cuba ship a tragic ship—Alas U.S.A. the huge threat hanging above like a Bomb—I said I thought everything be OK like Vishnu rescuing Earth girl from ocean flood floor with his big bestial ugly snouted boar's face looking tenderly down on her tiny femininity riding on his shoulder, a vast pig eye & aethereal voice "Each time I rescue you this way"—which I interpreted as the biologic Chakra-filled body below the neck emerging to the surface of consciousness & reasserting its Life desire, awesome Unknown human bottom consciousness body taking dominion over mind-illusion coldwar phantastikee—except maybe for a maniac or mechanical pushbutton mistake—young David spoke of "Black forces" of Capitalism & Man pushing the button.

Strange here in Cuba the Coldwar apocalypse neurosis anxiety consciousness (that dominated us US all till eyeball to eyeball confrontation & retreat from Doom & Vishnu preserver emergence in minds of K. & K.) still maintains hold over thinking popularly as if the unconscious realization that US. Russ Coldwar's over that's slowly changing US. Russ psychepolitics has not yet come to Cuba—logically since U S still threatens doom to the revolution which all here one way or another live in, for, with, confide, distrust, worry, work in, around, but is the one Big Life force here with Castro as emotional Communion Symbol everybody needs wants digs.

The women all love Castro as son or lover & the men too dig him tho they joke that all others are paled or castrated or silenced or look sick in his presence in a room, even Blas Roca who shuts up & looks on beardy locks with Beatle-joy worry admiration. But all the Cuban women have sex fantasies about Castro for sure.

Biegleman has eyeglasses & read Buber and Reich, & complained there was no communication—as he felt toward Wright—for him here, his own fault or that of society small here he not sure. I was near to

Cuba

touching him physically & resolving his isolation & felt a little sexy but was too scared by all early scandals to take on another deep scene.

All these people even old Paris fairies here all going around saying they don't think it's right elders seduce the young. They have absolutely no idea what goes on—oh, for my NY bed full of teenage boys & lost wandering Tibetan/Amphetamine girls of 20.

I explain it's my doctor's orders I sleep with teenage girls as a cure for my sexual retardation. So I said to Maria Rosa, Parra, journalists, old queens & local bureaucrats when they come on with the sexual Catholic/Marxist/Spanish/American/Cuban family bourgeois Party line.

I think there's a world teenage sexual revolution going on that is felt in the young sensitives of the Bridge, that the older revolutionaries haven't felt yet.

Only answer is the teenagers take them all to bed maybe. Then they get the beauty of it. should've taken Biegleman to bed, I told him he won't live forever & he's in his sex romance peak years now, at my back I always hear time's winged Chariot, he doesn't yet alas. He'll lose his youth, worrying about communication & making plans for Cuban Egyptian Pyramid architectural masterworks wherein the whole life history of the society is expressed like the whole history of Xtianity in the windows of Chartres.

Left & ate & met Robert Williams in the Hotel Lobby—Conversation on couch with him, he's insane, I think, says he's isolated & wants to destroy world of Injustice even if it means starting over a la Chinois with radioactive universe. But he was open to my white shit & we argued & made date late for later. I told him about Marc & Leroi activities plays in NY—he seemed impressed by Marijuana Legislation Campaign. Then that evening with Parra & others to Maria Rosa's house, Met Lisandro of *Cuba* mag & had to fend off *his* put down of the kids of Bridge—

Cuba

"They speak more kindly of their elders than their elders speak of them." He said gossip was everywhere, that they were complaining to me about Cuba & that they were persecuted & unable to publish their works. I tried to put that in kinder perspective & recounted experiences with Nate Gonzalez Frere as example of source of that kind of McCarthyite gossip. Headache, listened to Drown in My Own Tears and Dylan's Hard Rain, home wrote—Maria gave me this small new Chinese book—and eyes closing tired I must turn off light lay back on my pillow & softly relax and lay in my body tired & sleep.

In dark with shorts off lay in bed masturbating fantasy after fantasy beginning with Castro, but really got hot & began moving around when young Che Guevara's fine face come to mind's eye, then to boys in NY— Couldn't even remember their names as they were phantasy fucking me, my legs raised & then to old Mr. Ugly here Feo, & that acceptable, Maria Rosa too & some girls then rose on idea, & still hot phallus stuck out my closed palm throttling up and down from head to tight balls, I began try dancing in Santaria 1, 2, 3, 4 pelvic shift rhythm which just fitted in right with the shafting jack off rhythm 1, 2, 3, 4 as my asshole tightened & stept back & forth & cock tauter and tauter hot till I came still dancing holy Cabana in the carpeted darkness, 8 floors up in front of a mirror eyes closed with the sound of seawaves breaking over Maleconwall way below

Tibetan Chakra	=	between eyes
Shahti "	=	Breast
Zen "	=	Between belly and Cock
Santaria "	=	Muladhara
		between Cock & Ass

Cuba

Santaria pelvic motions dance tambor rhythm evoke Chakra opening below the waist as the top of the body stays still only a frikan lower half moves.

Millions of Cubans jacking off, the whorehouses are closed, girls guard their virginity, no real outlet for sexualization of communist relationships. Masturbating guilt, fear of trust body touch other leads to political relations, ambiguity & fear.

Because there is no open door to love—no Anchor body to body bliss to dissolve the social tension—it all goes up to the head into Marxist/dogmatic *theory* about group social endeavor and Communist purity of motive & act, etc.

[…]

Feb.1—Total collapse today—Woke was totally isolated, didn't know who to talk to who confide in, skulked to breakfast afraid to open up to Nadaists and Whale Roofrers—Entering Orwellian dreamworld—Total suppression of conscious & unconscious fantasy everywhere. Force in all directions suppressing communication except on verbal chessgame level. Got to find the language they talk on this Island, Aesopian. Can't trust anyone. Like having a nervous breakdown, "I got the fear."

Lunch out of town Guanahamo with civil engineer Guturrez who told me what's going on a lot X—had showed me his poems was called in to police & held several hours after coming to hotel to see me on date we had. "Bet he not see you now." Also he'll be in trouble, may be kicked out of school to cut sugarcane. Half the school marvelous, they may all be shifted out to fields to clean up. Several professors dropped for students.

Group that invited me were cancelled out by rector, reading of my poems Cancelled. Later in week, students advised not to have private meeting. That's why they never showed up. Everything closing down around me, I felt as he explained. He himself had story of his ultimatum.

At this point, Ginsberg was beginning to believe his fears. He felt totally isolated and unable to speak without drawing unnecessary attention. As we will see from the following entry, he was so afraid of bringing harm to those around him that he even resorted to using initials in his journal. His fears, as he will learn, were justified.

Analysis of Govt policy, sex repression for training of obedience. Castro a great Charmer but Absolute law. Preparing emergency military state buildup like Russia–China, no change possible but increasing control & rigidification for 20 years or until U.S. threat abates—advised me not to sleep with anyone—they'll get into trouble.

By this time I've given up all ideas of scoring for some pot. Too much humorless threat everywhere. with M. R. explaining the parties of Naked Lunch. Waiting to see Haydee. Later M. came out & said she was angry, M. very upset. Had I said Raul C.[38] was a fairy & I wanted to sleep with him? I don't remember to *whom* I said that. Couldn't see Haydee—M. made date for later tonite to explain. They got me a nice white pair of sneakers/my desert boots had a hole.

To Writers Union Guillen charged the boy there. Said they'd been

38. Raúl Castro, Fidel's brother.

Cuba

taken accused of hanging around foreigners hotels & looking as if "effeminate appearance."—Act of Accusation. Have to go to trial unless it squashed by the Writer's Union. Guillen no time for records, no time—ran away. Said he'd talk to Haydee—I said let's soften things. Ask her exactly what the limits of speech are here. I'm getting too many contradictory suggestions. He said, oh, & call him at 6 tomorrow.

Rushed to M R's & long discussion there. Everything I say reported 5 times over changed by gossip, go with group to see Dorticos by Marc.

What I do threatens Casa. I have to shut up & stop blabbing. Close down.

Afraid to write in book. That's why style so short.

Boys came & long discussion ambivalent Roy Cohn attitudes by elders, as well as lots of understanding. But nobody trusts anybody & I could no longer speak freely. Left at 2 AM fatigued. All varieties of force/brainwash all done in rationalizations. Afraid to write details lest book be read. Paranoia & reality identical at last.

The Lazy Policeman

Morning. I had been pleaded with by M. not to go to Dorticos official meeting with rest of delegation. All afraid I'd flip, embarrass everybody. Ada Santamaria & Maria Ross came to hotel to cheer me up & watch over me, took me to beautiful open nursery school nearby with dozens of little 5 year old boys naked on my lap, touching my beard—I said I was from the moon, they wanted to see the wings I flew down on. I said they were only visible in moonlight. Everything real neat, dozens of little red tricycles in an alcove, all the toys dusted & shiny lined up precise military formation on wall shelves. Many women tending the children quite friendly & efficient.

They want me to see the nice things about Cuba & not be an obsessed brutal homosexual dopefiend individual capitalist-society-produced neurotic.

Suddenly wondered where my old notebook was, panicked & couldn't find where I left it. Found it on bed after a minute.

At lunch met young photographer & his wife who wanted to take me to their studio in Cathedral Square—leaving met man from Radio Havana who asked me to make program- commentary on "achievements of revolution"—I explained that I could not at present as I was preoccupied with arrest of friend for seeing me & preferred not to go into politics without complete sense of freedom. I suggested I might read poetry, but, on the other hand, that too might be too strong with the word cocksucker. Left at impasse, he left me alone, said he was sorry.

Home in room relaxing after late afternoon with the photographer in studio in Casa de los Condes De Bayona on Cathedral Square Columbus—old place with the lone palmtree under reconstruction as museum, the room was filled with plaster dust with colored sunlight blue green red filtering thru a high arched mosaic window—I sat on floor & rang Jap cymbals & sang for an hour while he took intelligent photographs— lively cat Chinese-Jap-Spanish face.

At supper with Elmo Valente explained arrest scenes to him. Apparently Cela heard the boys were arrested leaving my room at 5 AM. Also phonecall from Ugly asking about my health—My absence at Dorticos meeting was explained as temporary illness. I told him Casa had requested that I stay away. Then evening Conferenica with Nadist, Mufadaist (Argentinean wild poets) & Techo de Baillena (Roof of the Whale) group. They were all excessively politic in congratulating the Cubans for their Revolution & apologizing for their own psychological & artistic lost-ness in not having revolution in Colombia Venezuela Argentina & then presented picture of their own struggles with Bourgeois,

Cuba

police, govt. repression—actually interesting material but too boringly presented. I gave slow deliberate explanation in Spanish—beginning with explanation of Poetry art as exploration & expansion of consciousness, explained technical means adapted for the purpose i.e. dreams, waking, fantasies, marijuana-mushrooms, peyote, spontaneous composition, meditation & yoga singing compared to Chango-Santaria dancing ecstasy, explained how all this led to embarrassment when communication actually began as result, & then went into long Aesopen description of anti-brainwash techniques for combatting universal sloganism, dogmatism, mass media hypnosis etc. concentrating on cut-ups. I don't know how many got the point of what I was saying, which is a measure of the extent to which my communication has been limited by pressure to protect Casa & the boys from destructive embarrassment caused by my presence & style of thinking & being—on the other hand previous direct communication while it stirred up vast clouds of anxiety & finally police action & perturbation in Casa, did not succeed to changing anything tho perhaps the chessgame over the unjust arrests might be helpful. However since P. & E. say that actual policy of the 23 ruling members of the Party is really organized & regimented to production & defense, courteous rational discourse is not likely to communicate much of the peril to anyone or serve, by shock, as an object lesson on the basic hypocrisy here & suppression of un-Conscious information by showing the difference between relatively free private human fantasy and what little bit of that phantasy is allowed to be communicated in quasi-public manner, even art works much less newspaper interviews.

The key is in the control words "Revolutionary" & "Antirevolutionary." Who determines the application—even arbitrary—of those words controls all public & a lot of private communication.

To suggest a cut up of those words, or an exclusion of them in discussions of structure of state or policy (to avoid semantic confusion &

stereotype/control thought) is unacceptable & might be considered an antirevolutionary proposal.

I would probably have been completely safe to say anything here had I announced myself a faithful North American rather than independent sympathizer. They don't mind so much what a Gusano (Worm!) says as it's considered outside the realm of applicability. Mario the guide, trying to show me there was really free speech, said "Look, there was a reporter here who interviewed gusanos & reported their views & *they* weren't arrested.

[...] Walked home with Nicanor Parra & Elmo, & Nicanor described the meeting with Dorticos, some tension as V tried to define limits of state control of Art. N said Art freedom had to be absolute. Dorticos said everything was allowed except anti-revolutionary. N asked who says what's revolutionary. Dorticos said, the Writer's Union. N asked *Who* is the Writer's Union. D said, anyway, the people will reject anti-revolutionary Art. Anyway, our problems for the moment are not these: they are industrial/economic military. N said how do you know the same thing won't happen here as in Russia? Dorticos said "I promise it won't." N said, oh well, if you promise, I feel much better. But there had been considerable tension. N also defended Ferlinghetti's Dinner to Impeach Eisenhower. Dorticos fumed, it's only a mask to deceive people. N insisted on the validity of that aspect of U.S.A. Nobody much came to his aid on any of this. We drank refrescos and talked, across from the hotel. He thought of the idea of the Lazy Policeman & we sat & giggled an hour fantasizing situations & movies—No bien, yawns the Lazy Policeman as the maricon walks by, flipping his fairy wrist.

Wed. Feb. 3—Woke phonecall from Prof. at University School of Letters cancelling my Whitman lecture with very complicated long excuse about examination coming up. I told her to read Melville's poetry. We talked a little while double entendre. "Perhaps we can make another date when things are more relaxed."

Ran into Jaime Saruski & Cela downstairs Lobby, explained briefly to Jaime what had passed, he was relatively silent & said nothing more than question "Are they released now?" and we left the subject fast. A few minute later I asked Cela alone where he'd heard they were detained leaving my room at 5 AM—He said just vague gossip, not an official story. I told him they were taken leaving the theater. He said, "Best not talk too much about it to the people here, it only confuses matters." Yet it was he who'd told Elmo they were arrested on our floor in the Hotel.

Cela muy digro, that is to say a portly aristocratic Spaniard with Burroughs-bureaucrat eyes, looks like a diplomatico & wears silk suits—apparently been out in the night streets secretly on his own "having his time" as Parra remarked at supper. Cohen dislikes him, thinks his an empty aloof hostile entity—I associate him with the summer of Burroughs—he carried notebook around as I do and scribbles small neat notes paragraph by paragraph.

Parra's notebook consists of paragraphs very short, or apothegms, almost a Witgustinien pithy fragmentary style. "Lazy Policeman."

We all got in cars to lunch a vast lunch in old country club, for the Cultural Council, now the place is big Architect Porro's school of plastic arts vast system of constructions. Huge mansion we were at last week, this time many assembled guest, all the invitados to the literary concourse, as well as Guillen who passed by short & squat & white haired & dark faced embracing people in fat arms, looking around in the middle of conversations to see who he could spy behind him to do business with or have secret politics or poetry or old drink friends converse with—Haydee repeated he thought it best for me to keep away from the youngsters in trouble (as he has a strictly pessimistic faith in the Revolutionary Policies he thinks it's against the grain for me to persist defending them, it'll only make things worse). Said Reglo Guerrero was still in trouble, but he thought Reglo was the best poet of all the young & would because of such suffering added to his early whore mother fuck living room drunk beatings childhood be perhaps the greatest of the young—asked me to take some of Reglo's poems back & perhaps have them published in the States—"It means a great deal here somewhere some reputation from abroad, it would help him here thru his difficulties perhaps."

Then Haydee came up shook hands & immediately launched like a Yenta into a big speech style of public speech speaking very rapidly I had difficulty understanding & had to keep nodding in agreement trying to concentrate at times trying to calm myself saying mantra inwardly to steady any clarity of senses om om om/Sa ra wa/bu da da kidli yeh/Zenza Wani yeh/benzo Bero/Tsa ni yeh/Hum Hum Hum/Phat phat phat So-Ha. I had difficulty concentrating & finally got thru it twice inwardly. She was again telling me the economic needs/facts of the revolution—"We have established 20,000 schools"—"20,000," I said, agreeably surprised—"and we need more cement—work & cement is our need, afterward will come other matters."—After a while I moved the subject over,

"There's one thing I wanted to clear up—perhaps you misunderstood. You see when I left you last time I was quite happy & relieved at the rapport we had and felt so good I slapped you sort of exuberant & affectionate—I hope you didn't misunderstand . . . in my country"—I had difficulty saying this in Spanish & had already 3 iced tea lemon drink waiters were serving—the only drinking occasion I've been to formally, yet—I asked if she had cleared up matters with the boys & I couldn't get a clear answer from her, apparently yes, she began another long more pointed explanation—paraphrased thus, "You see, you have ideas of a

Cuba

rare type & they're yours from another country & you don't understand that they don't fit here. For instance—the marijuana problem is solved here now—it's always been a crime & it's a definite crime and that's how it must be for the time being, that's the policy we've adopted."

I tried to be as scientifically sensible as diplomatically possible & commented "Well yes accept that, all I was trying to do was bring in other legitimate information useful to any discussion of marijuana as a supposed social problem . . . that is, as you may know, there are a number of scientific documents, medical reports of long standing in England & America saying it is not really a dangerous or unsociable thing"—

She replied leaning now against the piano & apparently willing to talk to me for a while—which surprised and excited me & I began to re-lax—getting into it—huge room full of artists & functionaries all dressed up & she the chief personage & here I was all involved alone talking to her—a kind of egoistic amazement at the position I found my-self in, being such a serious/embarrassing problem for her to handle— "Yes but we have work to do and cannot afford these extra luxuries which impeded the senses" (I'm paraphrasing half understood & mis-translated Spanish)—

"So then look what about Alcohol? That's much deeper drunkenness & more unsteadying"—

"Well we don't drink much here but there are times and places we do go to & once for Instance I went with friends and family & we were celebrating & drinking & then I got a call from Fidel to join him im-mediately and I had to leave—I immediately was sober—When Fidel calls I must go and do my work with him & the drunkenness had passed from my body"—She swept her arm down her small corpulent blonde frame—she looks sort of Dutch Jewish matronly—"and by the time I got in the car to leave I was clear"—

"Oh excellent & amazing," I said. "All I mean to say is that marijuana

Cuba

is much less deep Drunkenness than alcohol—But my point is not to convince you necessarily but to be able to talk about it as social issue—free discussion—and information—I'll send you from England some medical books on the subject"—

"Well perhaps they have had certain investigations in North America but we haven't had time for that here, we have other matters more urgent, they may come to their conclusions, we have different ones . . . In any case, you realize, we have to raise the young children here with revolutionary ideals . . . the revolution is for them the life, the reason for being, the Ideal, the future, all of our energy—We must give them that Force to survive, that Esperanga that Why For to live, that por que vivir, our united revolutionary cause . . . and yes though you may discuss such matters with people on a high level or mature officials you understand we can not have you spreading such ideas which are against the Laws of our Country & our policy among the young people. They are too young, too impressionable, you come as a foreigner and invited here by us, as a great poet of fame & we cannot support that you spread ideas to the young against our own policies we have arrived at . . ."

"Well I mostly talked to journalists about this problem . . ."

"We cannot have these remarks published where the young people read & misunderstand them not having mature enough judgment. Certainly among older mature people to discuss when there is occasion, but public statements of conferences or among the young, that is not right for our country & our ideals."

Tom Maschler came by, I introduced him & he began suddenly inspired into a discourse on The Beatles to Cuba as a great gesture to World Harmony & incidentally as a fine propaganda gesture. I seconded him, interrupting a moment to explain how well loved they were by the youth in the U.S. & then stopped talking & let Tom carry the ball. He back from Oriente Sierra Maestra looking tanned. She still leaned

Cuba

against the piano, looking at him, waiting to speak, hardly letting him really explain his idea—he being John Lennon's editor, he knew what he was talking about too—that if Cuba invited the Beatles it would be a great popular triumph—

"Very few people know about the Beatles here."

"You *know* who they are?" I asked.

"Yes, but they have no ideology."

"Yes," said Tom, "but they're like Frank Sinatra— the young girls swoon over them & weep if you want to attract the young invite the Beatles"—

"But you see like Frank Sinatra 3 years pass & he is forgotten, while we want to build Something permanent here, a life, a hope, an ideology"—she pointed to her head "for without a true ideology, a true understanding of life here can be no Future for the young ... The Beatles will, come it will be like our Fiesta, everybody will be excited for a few days & then that will be the end of it, we want to give our people here something *more*, some truth & work & food."

Tom & I tried then to explain that it would make Time magazine fall & change State Dept. policy & end the Cold War if Cuba & the Beatles accepted each other joyfully—that the brainwashed children of U.S. would see Cuba in another friendly light & it would influence policy—

"No we must make ourselves strong & defend ourselves ... What the Americans & the State Department think is none of our business, it's their problem not ours, it doesn't relate to us. We can't be doing un-ideological things just to please U.S.A. our Revolution is stronger & purer than that"—

Then Cohen came over also & began to talk about freedom for the young—mentioning Ana Marie Limo—but she'd had enough, was distracted & went away.

Cuba

Later he said she was always making public speeches like a loud-speaker system as far as he could see.

Lunch, I sat next to Maria Rosa, who seems depressed & fond of me & worried about all our rules, even offered to get me some tea if it would make me feel better—I said no it was a matter of principle to be free to talk. She seemed a little surprised that I did not *need* it, as some sort of mental addiction. I said I was more addicted to talking & she laughed.

Parra all thru the huge banquet table drama in the huge airy room with window half the wall opened on sunny tropic garden tall palms framed outside so close as if growing interior in the room—later he said had same conversation with her on Freedom of Arts. She began lecturing him & he firmly quietly calmed her & explained she should wait to learn, to listen, to talk more directly to him person to person & not as if addressing a meeting, "You must realize I am sitting here as your *friend* not as an enemy."

"If you were enemy I would not sit beside you," she replied.

"If I were your enemy I would sit beside you ... remember how Kennedy and Khrushchev sat beside each other."

He said he spoke very softly, calming her, rebuking her for her insistency loudness, & when he returned with the K. & K. but she hung her head as if stopped. My guess was that she was furious & that Cuban attitude on K & K confrontation is not ours—they wanted more say & were bugged when K & K overlooked Cuban pride & calmed the storm. Parra however opined that she seemed ashamed. He's a calm schoolteacher. She sat with him & conversed apparently because the argument he had with Dorticos had reverberations & she wanted to put Parra in his place or explain the Revolutionary position to him, still.

There seems actually to be a basic division on this point of freedom of expression—as if the Revolutionaries like Guevara took a firm Communist position of complete military/psychological Necessity dictating

Cuba

uniformity of ideal in revolution, & secretly plan a totally conformist state, while the liberals & Haydee & say Dorticos & others still assume that the revolution includes free flourishing art.

After lunch spoke to Guillen briefly, he still had not spoken to Haydee, said he would later today—He avoids complete discussion on the arrests now, & people keep telling me he first wants to enjoy himself, big house, big wheel, big position—or maybe he's annoyed with me I didn't make a big business how great a poet he was—When I first came, so said Ugly or someone I forgot.

Then at hotel we settled prize at 6 PM—I had slept & gone to Parra's room where he told me of Haydee Lunch Conversation—& later at Writer's Union met Ugly & Manolo all sitting together.

Ugly said the big worry of everybody was naturally sorry that the incidents had happened . . . I complained I still felt paranoiac & afraid to see people, especially after Haydee had said I couldn't spread my ideas to the young. I felt fear for what happen later to Manolo & Jose Mario—He said, as if he'd deliberated his thought, that I should understand & sympathize with problems of the Revolution & not mistake mistakes of petty police bureaucracy for the Revolution itself. I reassured him that I agreed but was just worried, & further worried what I could write—really I couldn't publish anything that wouldn't be *used* say by Time if they picked up on it, abused.

"Of course the real worry or disturbance here in the bureaucracy is whether what you'll write when you leave will do damage to the revolution . . . discourage people abroad from helping"—

"What can I do? I can't write anything at all now until I get some kind of real assurance that the boys will not be molested on account of my problems, my ideas, my loudmouth."

He told me he'd speak to Haydee & have her call me for that tomorrow. Settled the whole thing amicably.

Cuba

Couple of stranger kids took me out on huge walk then to old Havana, they were queer they said & read "America"[39] poem & wanted to know what I had to teach. I sat with them on Malecon wall explained all I knew about body-consciousness, Flaming Creatures, Warhol movies —Genet movie—sex freedom, human contact—& they took me on a walk of Calles "Pelligrosos" i.e. "dangerous fairy streets"—all around Prado —they said that there was a huge growth of homosexuality—partly because of the issue raised, partly the turbulence of the years, but mainly a thing "very mysterious." They made it sound like a huge social event among all the young. How mad!

The only way for govt. to curb homosexuality is to encourage heterosexuality.

But they don't want to encourage any kind of sexuality, it's decadent, they want the energy to go to work building the country. Sitting cross-legged at night on the Malecon wall with curve of bay around us and animal white waves flowing up against the rocks, sat & talked, talked an hour, lighting cigarettes against the wind. One boy a big delicate negro, the other thin faced with wounded smile & hornrim eyeglasses—

Said Lunes de Revolution was stopped because Infante's brother made a movie *P.M.* all about Havana night life, the editors contributed their money, the Movie was too scandalous & Luney tendencies were closed down on at that time—Never heard this gossip before.

(Besides as M R said, Castro is not such a good dancer, & isn't very sexy.)

While new atmosphere of totally unofficial secret youth life with these kids, they all 20 yrs old one nice masculine looking—walked till 1 AM talking, they said practically whole Dramatic Arts school was queer

39. See "America," *CP*, 154.

Cuba

now, & girls too all Lesbians. Mainly the youth wants to escape from the paranoia/counter paranoia of the War with the U.S.A. & wants a free life of creativity and pleasure, and that's inimical Government plans for total revolutionary control over everything for purpose of giant panamerican Marxist reforms. Taxi home after explaining plot of 8 ½, 400 blows, and Vita Dolce, and several other Italian picture shown here, very controversial, had left great catalytic impression. I described New York orgies.

Walking on streets downtown with them near Pizza joints like Rikers by the Prado marble promenade and up around old Gomez corner at Marte y Bella saw many sweatered youths with tight pants and thin bodies, a few gangs of young strange girls and boys camping like on 8th street Saturday night. The same as always everywhere, red sweaters, white sweaters, delicate haircuts, neurotic bony arms waving in surprise gestures—as we four passed by one group of seven, one let out a high pitched Ohlla! and the others replied with shrieks of affront and joy, astounding! And everywhere by huge doors of glass buildings the serious olive green clad millcinianos sitting rifles on their knees on guard with mustaches, and sober Spanish types old ladies waddling and weary family men passing by late at night as we marched forward on the narrow sidewalks under the old stone buildings in street darkness—

An open huge venetian window—Juan commenting dryly—There's a typical bourgeois interior—I looked in quickly big old television set against the wall turned on with blank blue light buzzing in the tube—high walled room and tile floor, brown and clean polished—the old folk sitting in wooden armchairs at the other end of the room bored and silent and content, an ancient huge grey photograph of 1920 parents hung from the center wall—like a Cuban pop art stage set—it all sprang into place thru the quality and quickness of Juan's laugh, glowing inside.

Cuba

Feb. 4.—went to movies early morn saw some average documentaries except cyclone wanton Waving palmtrees floods dead bloated cows Fidel with eyeglasses near helicopter children's bodies stuck on barbed wire fence and animated maps showing the Chakra path of hurricane Fiora thru the long Cuban Isle. They obviously do have such a tough struggle to survive that their defiance and resentment of U.S. obnoxious intrusion and blockade is understandable completely and even their blank dumb miscomprehension of my own queer rare literary extravaganza and they do suffer too much to take it easy.

Lunch and received a copy of God issue of Fuck You[40] by airmail via Mexico which I'll pass around and deposit at Casa de Las Americas Library. Later in day long conference everybody at Casa round table discussing whether future prizes should be Spanish or first Latin American, and nobody knew an answer that wouldn't exactly exclude Brazilian Portuguese.

Then I hitched ride in *Revolucion* newspaper Volkswagen to Writers Union, sat around reading and translating Creeley's[41] *For Love* (one of the few books of US poetry they have) to Manuel Ballagas and Jose Mario and a few kids who were listening—I got enthusiastic and the atmosphere today was lighter—the paranoia probably disappearing and the scandal slowly dissipating and everybody getting used to me, All feeling sort of guilty too guilty about the arrests to be anything but serious and sympathetic to my presence. Jose Mario found a copy of W. C. Williams' selected poem which nobody knows here, so I'll begin teach-

40. *Fuck You: A Magazine of the Arts,* edited by Ed Sanders.

41. Robert Creeley (1926–2005), poet associated with Black Mountain poets, prolific author of poetry books.

Cuba

ing out of that text. Ballagas very fast and enthusiastic about idea of concrete imagery (a la Pound) and trying to figure that in relation to Creeley—Creeley's consciousness, despite the generalization of his diction, lied in his dramatic use of specific hesitant rhythm personal style, and his dramatic use of personal conversational generalization—"to buy a thing like that!" for instance, the turn of phrase, tho common is used in context so naturally and aptly expressively, that it is a satisfactory dramatic correction, tho not as in Fenelossa idea, a *visual* concrete image. It's a stylistic concretion.

Met Feo and he hadn't been able to see Haydee yet, but seemed satisfied that everything be alright. In two weeks I'll be babbling away again freely and nobody yet shocked.

Met Nati Frere the lady journalist who probably helped fink me out last week and told *her* about the arrests, she acted as if she didn't know. Every time I tell someone they act innocent but always counter with, "But they are at liberty now? Are they not?"

She laughed "Well a little experience like that won't do them harm." I said "If it happens to you I'd like to hear *you* screaming."

Later party with Amigos de Cuba in gang of American living/working here and like Camp Nicht-Gedeigat[42] old labor folks or young ex-bohemian girls all sort of humane and serious, eccentric babies or normal kids with the basic simplicity of high school teachers, and gave run down on Film Maker Coop, legal fights, Supreme Court decisions on literature free, MFY, Marc Cahielffer's beret, new Coleman—Cecil Taylor jazz, Lower East Side Cock Conspiracy and slow shift of U.S. psyche to same realization and relaxation. One elderly comrade lady shocked— "pseudo artists" she spoke of—and we played *Drown in My Own Tears*

---

42. A communist-run summer camp that Ginsberg attended with his family in his youth.

Cuba

and *Blowing in the Wind.* Home 2 AM. Nicer day, feeling better, in fact
would like to say and spread some kind of relax gospel and teach poesy
a month to whoever hath ear.

The rays of the palm trees waving behind
    iron grillwork—
The old lady's wrinkled face on the couch,
    she leans in her print dress
    against the arm rest,
immobile face, nose, eyes small and black, her
    mouth has no expression,
Like in an old scratchy movie, like a
    dead woman staring fixedly—
She has no place else to go to start eating fresh—
& huge black limousine turns the corner
    and the shiny hood fills the eye screen.

Feb. 5. The key structural question here is if someone doesn't like a spe-
cific policy of the party or wishes to criticize a specific policy, what av-
enue has he got to do so publicly? Or, if he feels that one of the leaders
is foolish or silly or neurotic, how does he go about expressing this in
public?

       * * *

    How many people are in jail for what?

       * * *

    Dream 4:20 PM—a huge theater like Hotel Havana Riviera—I get
out of tourist bus and am taken inside nightclub so vast it's got balconies
and pillars—all modern and carpeted—I see a show and among the cho-

Cuba

rus girls a gang of nuns who make obscene remarks and dance religious dances in the balcony and in the audience—however there isn't much of an audience only themselves the Cubans the theater participants that most of the seats in the house are empty.

The show is over like a World's Fair advertising show in a Motorama theater, and I wander in lobby and get lost. I see next busload of actors arriving and have to get out of their way—they file thru the big carpeted ante-chamber wherein the nuns all stand on top of their seats and jiggle up and down dancing to jazz—even a few up way high in the balcony amazingly—oooh! There's one way up there climbed up on the balcony guard rail and swinging on that—Wow! Watch out! She's getting too frantic losing her grip with her legs wrapped around the railing—She's falling—a sinking feeling in my stomach, I'm going to see someone die!—she falls all the way down from the balcony but midway flips over, as if she's an agile youngster, it's happened here before, she's nosediving—I move in closer!—Nosediving like a performer in pink tights with lights spotting her as she descends becoming more and more miniature into the aisle of seats down front empty—*Ooh* I scream—as she falls in— and bounces back like a little puppet—Wait!—she *is* a puppet—I look up, the puppeteer is jiggling with ropes and she's rising, tiny, above the seats again—

I somehow am sitting next to where she fell, only it's in the balcony and I want to move out of the way of attention, as they are making a movie of this scene—I move a few seats away—the cameras are rolling and they are folding up the [?] the puppets in the balcony—I don't understand the whole scene.

Earlier in the dream we had been in a boat as in Venice or on a yacht traveling thru a bay or outside a city in water toward mountains and I suddenly recognized the gorgeous primeval scenery—Oh! It's like Walt Disney here!—it's just like the magic landscape of blue seas and weird

Cuba

peaks and purple sunsets in Wizard of Oz or Snow White—that's what Disney's big secret is, he photographed it and retouched it a la cartoon—What a mystery nobody knows—I was awed in the dream to be in on this Big Secret—He'd been here before, before the Cold War shut off travel and communication, and had seen and cinephoto'd this marvelous lunar bay and then finished it for this Children's Marvel Show, unknown to millions. A very awesome spectacle, almost religious, the Southern Tropic bay aflame with cosmic sunset.

Anxiety again increasing today as I begin realizing how limited my freedom of speech/communication/expression is.

How many people really in jail? What really is policy of Govt on Fairies sex freedom speech publishing—Could Regio publish his cock against revolution poem here or abroad?

Parra warned me against straightening out Regio's arrest—just leave situation alone.

The more involved I am with Casa and the boys the more difficult it is to speak instinctively openly giving vent to insults or questions or fantasies or serious arguments.

Robt Williams on phone said heard Cuban radio talking how friendly and happy Famous Beatnik Poet is with friendly Cuban citizens literary scene. Castrated propaganda not news.

To what extent was similar stupid sadistic puritanism and dogmatic idealism responsible for categorization and creation of gusanos anti-revolutionary mentality and classification, to refugees? How many people so unjustly offended by highhanded police govt or communal Orwellian pressures they just flipped and got themselves denounced as "anti-revolutionary!" How much lying and hypocrisy is there in relation to Yankee plans and CIA monster propaganda?

The more I probe this last Question the more dangerous here my position might become for the friendly people that talk to me.

Cuba

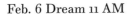

Feb. 6 Dream 11 AM

With a child walking down stairs out of a house at night, the child is holding on to the back fur of a cat, the cat I can't see too well seems to have a kitten or mouse in its mouth—I try to stop the child from disturbing the cat, it is awkward the way the kid's arm is stuck out descending step by step with the cat also paying no attention to the child but suffering its limitations almost unconsciously putting all attention on the mouse—When we reach the bottom of the stairs I look close to see exactly what the cat's got and it seems—why it's a red big squirrel half the size of the cat—I push the cat away and stroke the head fur of the squirrel which is lying there stiff, glazed eye immobile—after a few seconds the squirrel comes out of shock and the nervous system begins operating again, eyes move and ears move and a shudder runs thru the back of the small creature—I'm a little terrified and don't know what to do—I want the child to grab the cat now, so I can try and save the squirrel—one ear is chewed off, I think, but maybe not mortal damage—but the kid has run away and I'm left alone and don't know how to keep off the cat and at the same time heal the squirrel with my two hands.

Drunk last night so didn't write.

Went at 8 PM to Cocktail Party in Writer's Union—yakking and gossiping and shaking hands and talking to actresses and the boys there too and Haydee Santamaria and Guillen—I began drinking and wound up talking to Santamaria but by this time found myself calculating new approaches—Feo not having reported in with any reassuring news, and Guillen apparently by now tired of the whole affair—I brought Manuel and Jose Mario over to meet her—She immediately launched into another speech—"I want to introduce you to these 2 young monsters of the Puente group."

"Oh, Groups," she began, and talked five minutes about how there were all sorts of "special" groups and what the people wanted and what they needed was art they could understand, maybe not groups—actually I couldn't hear her well and left the boys to carry the ball—they were smiling—I kept pushing Manolo to *talk talk*, just don't stand there with eyes on the ceiling—and they did talk finally—apparently she reassured them it ws all a mistake and they could go see me at the hotel any time they wanted. But if any of them had gotten sharp with her, or if I had, I don't know what the consequences—sort of a psychic cat and mouse game with the Power of the state in her lungs—Later I said I felt left out of it, I couldn't hear, and she laughed and said they were talking low especially so I couldn't hear—She brought up "marijuana" again and they reassured her I hadn't "corrupted" them and turned them on.

Afterward I went out back to the kitchen to get some more lush and Manolo tagging around with me got me worried—Guillen passed by and said Haydee again and saw us together. I began to feel they'd think we were in some special isolated cabal so told Manolo better we circulate separately for an hour to avoid the Police Eye mentality—my own paranoia, or the situation—He worried, said laughing he'd better give back the $10 I gave him to score with. Mario introduced me to intelligent Santero folklorist poet expert and he had better brains sense (look at his dark bearded happy face) than most anyone mature there—went into cafeteria as party was breaking up and drank beer. Met redbearded young hipcat painter who told me I'd made a mistake coming on too strong at beginning so now people be afraid to turn me on and associate with me too openly. We discussed whether that was true or not, I was by now a little irritated—meanwhile all night people came up to me

Cuba

and said they all loved me and "Everyone in Havana" is feeling sorry for you—

"I'm going to make everybody feel as guilty as I can till they all start crying," I said, giggling.

By that time midnight drunk a gang of bohemian girls and boys older than the Puente group was singing a funny rhythmic Cuban lyric song about Marijuana around a table full of beer bottles—Amazing!

We all went out and a group of negro painters took me thru the streets. I pulled out my little Jap finger cymbals and began chanting which they joined after a few minutes, walking past lights and night-clubs downtown—Hari om Nam Shiva—Went downstairs to a jazz spot—a cave with modern plastic sophisticated bar and bandstand and little tables huddled in *total* darkness—it took ten minutes before I could see the fellow next to me who was telling me that this was the real great jazz spot in Havana—The darkness is for people to have some privacy for necking if they want. The spade cat from the Writers Union friend of Manolo and others scored for a little pot and we went out again to an expensive looking old building nearby sophisticated streets went and found big room—U.S. spade cat with white cap sitting in rocking chair, the host, a thin middle aged agile fellow—another half a dozen Cuban spades there also—big hi fi set and huge collection of records— a music pad, with a bed and bureau and high ceiling as if a vast antique invasion with [?] over fireplace and everywhere the walls decorated with pictures of Marx, Castro, Fidel, Cienfuegos, Che, Lenin, Mao—on the wooden clothes bureau little funny anti-Yankee cartoons—across the room, in a chair, [?] rolling joints in little pieces of soft pink wrapping paper or towel paper—Mario De La Garde, the host, been here several years and runs a pad and stays cool, is "arranger, composer, and copyist" as his card says. Left and walked down to China monument with tall round shiny marble pillars and sat there smoking a joint—after a while, subtle change overtakes all the liquor and I began singing again with clearer rhythm—Walked uphill, one bearded cat and I, with cymbals really chanting aloud to the windows and skies Hare om—and suddenly as we finished a verse a cab stopped, so I ran and got it to the Hotel—

Walked in and found Nicanor in the bar tipsy with Ada Maria Simo and Joe Mario and Umberto Norman and black cat from that group— We tried to call Maschler, who took phone off hook—finally drinking and singing I told Parra "I love you" and he said, "We've loved each other for 5 years"—as I went out the bar door drunk the waiter asked me if he could have my ballpoint pen—after a flash of hesitation I gave it to him and that's the last I'll see of the beautiful golden pen that has filled up these two notebooks.

February 6, 1965

[...]

2 A.M. This afternoon after getting up late from drunk and woken by cat and mouse dream estimate of Authority Police state, went with Tom Maschler and Miguel Barnet to the museum in the vast *Capitoleo* building downtown Havana—blocks of colored marble deluxe passageways, where ancient Senators must've portly tread with white suits and fine cigars doing business in the rum and tourist and sugar markets and discussing its laws & bribes & police payoffs—now a big empty museum— Saw a giant prehistoric owl skeleton, the owl as big as Haydee Santamaria—and then into the Folklore room statues of Chango and Elequa —Chango a red phallic Shiva—Coyote War Sex God (supposedly my divinity here) and Elequa the god of Destiny Ways and Crossroads who's worshipped at beginning and end of Santeria ceremonies.

Cuba

[...]

We took car to Guonabocoa to see same Santero Mr. Arcadir whom we'd visited with last week—his huge house filled with people singing softly to soft drums—the back room a Palo altar and tonight Sat. a palo ceremony—Palo a branch of Congo as Santeria a branch of Niger religion. The room hung with herbs, branches of trees, an array of specific leaves and bush pickings dried and hanging from the ceiling like bundles of oregano in Italian groceries—an altar with many fruits and rocks—some black stumpy wax-bead stones—Elequa's with seashell eyes and mouth, lined on a shelf, general disarray of stuffed Cocks and Vultures, high perched over door—an open window in the night air—everybody seated around the wall on chairs, facing the altar and a sacrificial stump adorned with years of feathers beads a black treestump mainly for worship of elements vegetable and natural universe.

As we arrived at this house we found a police car and Arcado's lady out front arguing with a policeman—seems they wanted to take Arcado down for questioning, for having a ceremonial meeting without a license. Much confusion, we went inside continued the ceremony but the olivegrey militia in NY policecars came back—The company was split between following the ritual in the back room or wandering forward to front rooms and kitchen to listen eavesdrop on the controversy. Presence of foreigners so many black limousines had brought down the law.

Feb. 7, 1965 On the treestump altar with its head down very silent and stunned red rooster. Had they cut out its heart and liver and left it standing there?

Arcadio the priest a robust lithe man of 60 with a white wife that looked like Myrna Loy—barefoot in his house temple making magic signs on the floor in chalk, leading singing with gestures of hand severity to roof, to altar, to the guests—almost like an opera—But more

Cuba

attention and commotion in the front rooms—messengers, assistant priests came in to whisper in Arcadio's ear, "The Chief Cop's here, want to talk to you."

Different groups in different rooms were discussing what's up—Barral was there and his wife, and a Colombian painter, and Miguel Grinberg, standing by tall and thin like a cynical question mark needing a shave, Rogelio Fure, friend of the Puente group also there, a big sensitive, bearded intellectual mulatto, handsome regular face and big expert in folklore—He and Miguel Barnet, who's brought us and one other man I hadn't met are the 3 chief Santeria folklorists in Havana working with museums and departments of ethnology. Charlie Barnet at museum had said he didn't want to have anything to do with the Party and so far the party left him alone—after all, anybody who wanted to intrude on his field would have to come prepared with experience, work, learned papers, etc. and that is impossible for a square dogmatist. So he felt secure in his position.

In the front room by telephone Maria Rosa was talking with a short hard-voiced militia man. "We are here with strangers-foreigners invited from the Casa de Las Americas, we often come here as a matter of folklorists, patronized by the Museum and the Conjuncto Folklorist and the Casa ..."

Cop looking at her gravely and determined in his role: "May I see your identification papers?" She pulled out all her cards from bag, Member of Militia, Casa, Writers Union, etc., which he examined objectively, asking questions a little insulting sardonic tone of voice: "You claim then that this is a folkloric exhibition and not a fiesta?"

"Yes," she explained again. Meanwhile, Mario from ICEP service & many other of the guides had arrived and looked worried, all gossiping among themselves and talked Maria Rosa aside.

"I'm afraid that we are not able to accept your word on this. Must go

Cuba

Nicanor Parra, Miguel Grinberg, Ginsberg, and
Casa de las Américas director María Rosa Almendre

into the room and see for ourselves"—So three cops in olive green (there were now 2 copcars in front) went thru the two houses-chapels & glared into the chicken-bloodied black magic Palo room with everybody sitting around, looking like Baptist parishioners waiting for the priest to continue service—

Arcadio gave a little speech of protest to the cops "I've been practicing Senteria for 40 years in this house—I've lived here all my life, 62 years—that Cuba tree is 62 years old—This is my house and my earth and these are my gods and these are my friends—My house is open to whomever in peace and tranquility wishes to learn of our religion—on every Saturday night all these years I've conducted this ceremony—If there is a fiesta with much singing and dancing I take out a permit but this is a small family ceremony and some invitados are visiting—I cannot shut them out of my house and wait your word to continue the service."

The cop was dubious. "I'll have to call my superiors." We all stood around him, his position was difficult. "Hello ,.. let me speak to Georgio ... Yes ... this is officer Campleanos." He stood there with gun at belt, mouth to telephone, and mufti cap on, a short man with dead Marxist face and dead eyes, trying to be efficient—aware we were all listening. "Well, the situation here is complicated ... There are many people in the house ... a service is being conducted, there are various foreigners here including representatives from Casa de las Americas ... Yes, this is the place you know of ... yes, I have asked them to come to office to explain ... but the lady from the Casa claims it is in the area of Folklore activities ... Yes, Folklore activities not witchcraft"—Long pause. "Yes, I will do that then ... take the names."

He put down the phone and spoke to Arcadio. "We are sorry to have intruded but my orders were to investigate a fiesta here and as you know the rules are that any group of more than 5 people is a fiesta and therefore this gathering is as it were a fiesta, and without a permit. However,

Cuba

in view of the complications of the situation we regret we have disturbed you, and invite you to continue, but must warn you that a decision has not yet been made as to the status of this meeting. Therefore, I have orders to leave you in place, however, I am ordered to take down the name of everyone present in the house at the service."

Maria Rosa talked with him some more, explaining and being very courteous and severe. One of the other cops, a very young kid, meanwhile had been looking over the Santeria altar alone with Arcadio and explaining, "I'm one of you, I'm a Santero myself, just that there are these many foreigners and Cars and you *are* having a fiesta which requires a permit, I don't know how this situation rose, I'm just following orders."

"Do I take down their names *and* addresses?" a young officer circulating in the hall with a piece of paper.

"In this case I think I will end the ceremony," Arcadio, standing in the hall, looking at the short chief cop.

"You may do as you wish, we have no wish now to interfere with the service, and I am sorry for the difficulty, but formally we have no objection to the service continuing and it is at your own choice to continue or not,"

Maria Rosa talking aside with Arcadio, encouraging him to continue. In another room an officer at desk sat taking names. I thought, "There's a man going round taking names." We foreigners all came in, Maschler and I first and wrote our own names down after the initial dozen colored Santeros who'd presented themselves. There was stuffed condor on the wall, various evil eyes painted on the wall to ward off interferences and small statues of gods, feathers, symbolic toys, etc. Arcadio was showing Maria Rosa his licenses to practice, his books, his lists of clients, his registers all stamped and sealed 30 years back by City Hall. He was in baggy pants, white undershirt, barefoot. little white strings of his underwear hung out of his pants over the belt in the back. He has a big Buddhic pranayama belly from which he sings, and 1 tooth missing, but otherwise strong and handsome face. I had got along well with him last week singing Shiva Mantras and comparing them to Chango songs—He decided I was Chango's boy—all thru tonite we'd been looking in each other eye and touching hands to belly.

The cop taking down names was polite but saw the hopelessness of the situation and left off with only half the names registered and the cops returned.

Meanwhile Arcadio had gone back to the main Palo room to continue the ancient ceremony.

He took chalk and marked a great design on the floor, on which he danced—design of 4 directions with arrows and bows and notations like a long mandala. Then he cast dice of cut potatoes and bananas on it, singing all the while, then began dancing on it.

Miguel explained this was a spiritual ceremony to ward off the evil that had come to the house. Suddenly one colored man seated against the wall stiffened, rose, and began trembling, making jerking motions with his hands and stomping his foot to the earth.

"He's Chango . . .Chango is very angry . . . Chango is speaking thru him now."

He went around the room for five minutes flicking arms in air, stamping his foot angrily, his eyes almost fixed, spastic motions. One of the big priests talked him trying to calm him down & thought perhaps they were trying to tone down the hysteria in view of the guests—but he continued in trauma outrage till another priest came over and began singing to him smiling.

The Santeria possession traumas are very good—an expression of unconscious which takes over, in given social place and form, and created with calm. An outlet for basic phantasy.

Cuba

Arcadio meanwhile getting more excited, singing to the crowd, drinking aquardante, dancing beautiful Greek-like whirls and jumps on the beat of the Palo drums—Eggs were brought in, a coconut, all placed on the magic sign on the floor, then a plate, then 5 eggs picked up by different priests and touched to their eyeballs one by one and put in the plate, and the plate wrapped in white pure cotton and passed around to touch the forehead of everyone watching. Then a chicken, a white chicken, was brought in, held over the altar, and tongue pulled out. I was behind someone standing in back so didn't see properly. I think it was pulled out. Then Arcadio carried the chicken, legs tied, to one end of room and began throwing it like a football to the other priests. Threw across the room with hard motion of arm, much force, and they caught it with an off—The chicken must've gone unconscious I hope—Tossed back and forth in a ring, sometimes missing the chicken which thumped against a chair or feathers came out, little white feathers scattered all over the room—fell on the floor—kept tossing it around with increasingly brutal strength till they were all free of inhibition—Then put the chicken down on the plate—by this time the white bird was senseless—or still, in any case, few movements of any kind, limp—and suddenly poured white petrol over the place and magic sign, lit a fire, and the whole center of the floor burst with flames—plate full of eggs and potatoes and coconut like a head in the ashy fires of the burning ground black and the live chicken now woke a little and struggling for half a minute as it—gasoline-soaked while feathers were haloed with blue flame—then fell limp again—the breathing then stopped breathing—Arcadio meanwhile began dancing over the flames singing in Congo language, "Now the evil spirit is burned"— and chorus "Now the evil is burned," running back and forth increasingly excited and powerful dancing over the flames barefoot, the other priests following him and the audience in a pitch of tension—I looked at Maria Rosa, her face dark, her eyes narrowed, her cheeks hard, her teeth

Cuba

clenched, staring—and took her hand—The dancing and singing continuing and getting louder—Arcadio filled a goat horn full of Aquardante and brought it thru the circle of watchers for me to drink. I drank and passed it on to Maria Rosa, to Mario of ICAP, who was also watching with the rest of the chauffeurs and guides who'd assembled—Barral and Tom Maschler, all the European editors fascinated like hip tourists —then the priests spread out, five negros singing each in turn, as one of them dragged a machete and began chopping savagely and awkwardly at the body of the chicken—One by one they bent down with machete and chopped down, iron-ringing dully on the concrete floor littered with ashes and chicken feathers and aquardante sprew—till the chicken body was maxturated and split up and finally the head severed by Arcadio with half a dozen dull blows—the smell vaguely like the smell in Manekarmika Ghat, the pounding of the chandals with long bamboo poles on the human bodies turned black in flames—

Then a long series more of songs, "Now we take the bird to the graveyard"—Now the evil gods down to Hell"—

Arcadio came over to me and took my hand and led me thru the group to the altar—I'd been swaying and dancing to the Congo rhythm and singing the choruses repeated as if they were Mantras like Om Sri Maitrya—He led me by hand to the altar, looked at me and picked up aquardiente bottle, pointed to his each eye ("Watch how I do it," I understood the message) and gulped and spewed out a fine spray all over the great shit black featherstuck and blood soaked treestump power center—I did the same, no trouble, spray of alcohol over the altar, and he offered me a seat at the side near the altar next to his chief disciple, and began another series of chants and response. I picked up on the responsive choruses with the rest, old white haired friendly disciple pronouncing the words clearly into my ear for me to be able to repeat at chorus time, each chorus repeated over 20 or 30 times before the verse changed—

Cuba

Arcadio more and more open, more self-assured, more powerful like a great blues singer summoning his soul freak feeling by now began a great improvised epic chant in Bantu Congolese language with fine danced steps—one minute one knee down, arms spread like Al Jolson, eyes to heaven, calling on the powers and spirits to hear him in his sincerity, another passage standing up arms folded in victory on his chest, another verse one hand chopping the air in rhythm as he invoked his tribal history and survival of his family and Gods from pre-history thru Africa thru colored days thru slavery thru XX Century to now, another minute despairing gestures back on his knees, chanting that he didn't know the names of his god only knew that they were inside him and inside all men, another chorus arm sweeping around the room to follow worshippers recalling all times they had danced and sung for the living and dead together, another chorus pointing to the foreigners and ICEP guides with fierce eyes welcoming them to share in the human spirit circle they were creating tonite as centuries ago, another soft-voiced Demons and all Stupidity and all those Men Souls untouched by the excitement of the Drum, Dancing and Song to the Soul given Congolese god names, finally an excellent series of verses with his hand cutting his throat, his hands and in dance steps making noose for his own hanging, that there was no death, no death he was afraid of, only the glory of his knowledge of his life and the beauty of his own body which only bullets could stop, as he pounded on his breast where past bullets had entered in other centuries, that nothing could stop the Congo drum inside the body, that nothing could stop his religion his gods, his heartbeat, nothing human, no law, no police, no slavery because that was eternal in all human body and that if he forgot ever that he body was BLACK—he spat on the floor—life would not be worth a spit on the floor.

Long sublime improvisation which I think everyone understood. I'm improvising my own version from the gestures and fragmentary trans-

Cuba

lators I got later tho the awesome incarnation of confidence and power was apparent thru dumb show and the changes of tenderness and exultancy in his voice and the opening of his eyes to all in room and toward the ceiling as he manifested the total emotion of his body (physiology McClure)[43] to the open ears of his own soul—

Then one by one a sense of joy in room the police episode surpassed no paranoia left—but confidence—the priests danced a little, Arcadio motioned me up to drums and I danced a little nervously got the beat but not the simplified shuffle-snaky India dance steps till suddenly I fell into simple 1 2 3 4 step to complex beat and he said "That's it, you got it" in Congolese—and the ceremony petered off after a while—we all taken into next room—huge table spread with fricassee liver and bread and beer and aquardiente enough for all the guests and the secret police too and the chauffeurs and ICEP people and folklorists—we all ate slowly, they put me at head of table—I was sweating and exhausted and happy too, the other guests had all seen my little show of Hecho or power or rapport with the primitive—old experiences from jazz, poetry, pot, gurus, Amazon—the confidence and trust in communication in the Secret—selfconsciousness inhibition hand touch and love tho only illusion—just being in your own skin and feelings as Maximus[44] experiencing the blare of his Being on a street in Gloucester—"I compel Gloucester"—one hand raised in Abbya Mudra I imagine that huge bulking poet—

Evening ended, Arcadio gave another big speech passing into song and more speech, I didn't understand. I think inviting us all and for-

43. California poet/playwright/novelist Michael McClure (born 1932) used animal sounds and physicality in some of his experimental poems.

44. Postmodernist poet Charles Olson (1910–1970) was the author of *The Maximus Poems*.

Cuba

eigners *and* the Ministers of Culture, too?—to his house in a month during the carnival for a 3 day feast and the release or sacrifice of a dozen white doves—all the world open to my table, he said—and singing songs one by one to the different guests. "Our religion has always been a family gathering," he leaned over and told me—a few of the women served the food joking with Miguel Barnet and banging on the table exchanging songs with him; Tom Maschler had yemaya blue beads he'd got today and so Arcadio improvised a ceremony to bless Tom's beads—Tom kneeling on the floor and beads soaked in rice water it looked like—Then crosses made over his skull on back of neck, on his palms, on his knees, on his knees—Evening ended with everyone seated and standing around table improvising and exchanging Yoruba songs to different gods as to different guests, attention paid according to their special god—I sat cross-legged on floor at Arcadio's invitation and chanted some Hymns to Shiva (Hari om Namo Shiva) which they compared to a song for Chango—Met son of disciple who is leader of regional orchestra bands and discussed the Brandenburg Concertos—later he was tapping on a beer-bottle with a spoon while the women of the house banged on the table smiling and shook their hips teaching big secret Yemaya songs— Yemay's ocean to rock, to cover, to owe and protect him—and then late at night back home in limousine to La Rampa to meet big literary crowd, Tom's last night and Vargas Ilyos too—I am drinking big orange-rum drinks in the Mocambo restaurant at foot of Hotel Havana Libre— Drove home began to write—saw Parra in lobby and decided not to go on boat trip tomorrow—began to write but fell asleep.

Feb 7. Work at 11, went down to lunch with Nicanor, talked politics and decided to translate some of his poems, and were going to go for walk but I fell asleep in afternoon and dreamt:

I was in a room in a friend's house here in Cuba, finally a little free and Manuel Ballagas was with me. I looked in his eyes and he looked back tenderly, I took his hand and he gave it to me and squeezed my hand, we were lying on a couch in front of the other people, some young, some old, and we held each other closely, then he put his face next to mine and began to kiss me on the mouth, opening his mouth to mine, we melted together tenderly, only there was someone in the way, the room was full of people, there was no privacy, in fact we were in bed with a third person, a big, fat person, maybe a girl, well, I thought, can't be exclusive, accept her, too, the three, we held each other, then I rolled over to get near Manuel again because the bliss of this meeting was the key sense feel of the whole trip to Cuba, but it was another male, big poet in between us, one I'd met drunk at party the other day—woke— called down to find time and brushed teeth and phone rang.

It was Manuel, calling to see if I'd be free later, we made date for tonight at 8, he'll call again—but what to do and where to go?—and phone rang again, Arch Jovio calling to invite me to supper tomorrow night—Had he seen photo in paper El Mundo—odd strange prophetic photo "Recepcion a Jurados en la UNEAC" showing Haydee Santamaria with fingers together at breast and purse over arm, looking at me, talking piercingly, my back and long hair in camera but eyeglasses and beard visible. I'm holding a glass of rum, listening courteously, and on other side of Haydee, with backs to the camera, Manuel in striped shirt and youthful fuzzy beard on left cheek, and profile of long black hair of Jose Mario—in the background, other folk ladies and gents in suits at cocktail party with faces and hairdos, intent in conversation.

Almost like a secret plan, that photo, by some sympathetic editor who knew the drama of the situation and wanted it recorded in public.

Cuba

Went out at dusk and sat on Malecon wall by the sea—young kids
fishing and an old man standing on the wall with his line strung out in-
visible into the boiling ocean—Sun setting, I had planted four hemp
seeds in the empty lot in front of the hotel, in a bare spot prepared for
a tree which had not flowered—The bare aspect of the city with vast
modern U-shaped hotel standing out in the sky by the oceanside, & des-
olation with towers of cold architecture guarded by guides and chauf-
feurs—dreamy flesh contact impossible in this landscape—I'm preju-
diced by dreams—

Walked over to Maria Rosa's house, they had napped all afternoon
as she had seen Tom off on plane to Spain at dawn—Sat and had tea
with her and Eddie, I gave him copy of *The Change*[45] and explained it,
he asked about Burroughs, sitting then at round tea table in afternoon
pajamas—I demonstrated cut-ups with *The Change*—"O negro beaten
in the old bed of my skin home."

[...]

Feb. 8. Last night with Jose Mario and Manolo walking Malecon from
crowded La Rampa, along the dark ocean talking—Sat in bars by the
port—no beer so drank rum and ginger ale—felt a little bad—wanted to
be alone with Manolo but no place to go to bed and lie together like in
dream—The dream on tip of my tongue but all night talked politics—
They described the joy and massy crowds of Cienfuegos and Fidel Cas-
tro's entrance into Havana, a genuine delight as Jose Mario waved his
feminine hands—That previously young kids were killed in park by
Batista cops so we would not be safe walking as tonight—Retemar poet

45. See "The Change: *Kyoto-Tokyo Express*," *CP*, 332.

their protector, a nice guy, you can get drunk and scream in his house—the old group Retemar Enfonte and Fernandez of Sunes—How Sunes had been stopped as result of art controversy over *P.M.* movie with sectarians (P.M. a review of photomontage of Havana mad nite life?) a huge assembly of artists, writers, intellectuals, and Castro's concluding speech, "Everything allowed, anything goes within the Revolution"—and Sunes then stopped all the poets editors kicked upstairs to Cultural Attache posts—Anyway, they concluded police trouble now was minor compared to before Revolution—didn't even hardly publish zany books here before, now all writers mostly have jobs or get place of dignity—

Wound up in Sloppy Joe's, I began feeling sick—told my dream to Manolo who said, "There's time"—We were embarrassed and kept pursuing conversation about revolution—They wondered how I would write about it, could I like Arnold Wesker make some Socialist declaration? I began getting paranoid that they were afraid they'd influenced my gossip negative like all the old Haydees said and were now trying to be optimistic and adjust my thoughts more positive—got anxious and then told Manolo my dream of him and said the only life I trusted was what I felt and not generalizations and anyway such manifestos did not much good—that I'd better run home someday and complain they were persecuting fairies and teachers just like in N.Y. would be more pro-Cuban propaganda than any square Socialist declaration.

Walked down beautiful moonlit marble tree arched Prado but I was feeling uneasy with them and in my stomach uneasy and waves of abdominal pain—

Home in cab, lonesome and in bed all night, cramps and watery brown drip out of my ass the style of Old Mexican dysentery—took Enteroviaform, no help then hours later by dawn took Sulfa-Guanadine for Bacterial Dysentery that stopped the pain but I was weak and slept sweating a little till noon.

Cuba

American girl came to bring me monthly review with more surreal talk about local splinter groups, promised to explain another day, when I came back from Oriente.

That night huge reception and prizes announced for Casa Americas contest—I didn't eat or drink except ginger ale, circulated among psychologists and journalists and editors and poets, being charming and intelligent and subdued and lively but I looked ratty with torn jacket and dirty white sneakers—avoided the young kids most of night so as not to attract too much attention and isolate myself from the older folks, everybody sort of testing me, "Are you afraid?"—"Do you have any marijuana on you?"—"I enjoyed your speech other night"—ran into several poets who'd translated my poetry—everybody really very friendly. Walked home with Manolo—we had no place we could go to be together—and loaned him records to hold while I went away.

Wed. Feb. 9. *[sic]* Losing grasp on continuity of transcription—all the different [?] gossip and dreams—Last night early in sleep a long consecutive movie dream about Fidel Castro—conversations with him, travelling with him in houses, trailers, movies, parties, sex, and affections—couldn't awaken to write it down and by the morning mostly disappeared from consciousness. Otherwise unknown or forgot—Out the Riviera window the great blue ocean with a few big white sailboats— Last night saw Haydee S. but nothing much more we got to say to each other—shook hands with Guillen who asked me my plans but not much conversation with him—he'd told the Puente boys to watch out for me, I was a faggot dopefiend irresponsible and unpleasant person. That was the day after I met him re-Manuel's arrest.

Cuba

Today in El Mundo—Reactions to U.S. attack on Northvietnam—Essay on Artaud on editorial page of El Mundo by Lolo de La Torriente.

Visitor this afternoon left me with drawn book of cartoons (a la psychic Steinberg) by Chafo. Long conversation, he member subud, a few others here too—depressed he wanted to leave Cuba for States "for a shake-up" or change. "They want to get your soul here" with the word Marxism—Castro a sort of "Antichrist"—Said Lacra Social was only gone more subtly underground and would arrest everybody queer maybe after Zafia harvest. Castro will get on the air and say the island is full of queers, and suddenly everyone will be conscious of that—just like he suddenly said there were too many officeworkers—next day everybody will be thinking the same thing—The Lacra Social made lists of persons active or suspected to be homosexual. "Well, we'll see what happens, there may be a change of policy before the harvest is over."

No copies of the movie P.M. exist in Cuba, there are only 2 copies in N.Y. with the cameraman.

Described a friend of his who got up at Writers Union and began beefing about Castro statement, "There were no intellectuals around during hurricane Flora"—Like attacking a totem, everybody scandalized, now he's writing a science fiction mystic cosmoconscious experimental form—given no more work and all prerogatives taken away, isolated, and reading St. Thomas in the library.

Said he'd heard I went into doctor here and said I wanted "something big and stiff and *that* long in my mouth as remedy for my illness." Also Chisines, that I'd scandalized nurses by picking ladillas (crabs) out of my hair and showing them. Heard that from friends at newspaper.

One problem here is that everything I do since officially unreported gets gossiped about to ridiculous lengths and becomes monstrous.

Cuba

A measure of the insanity of this society.

Also heard I'd threatened Haydee I'd leave the country over the arrests. More gossip.

He looked around room and was worried there were microphones. Said he could be arrested and sent to local jail in harbor for saying as little as he said just now.

He's employed as journalist, sort of down in the mouth, obviously mystic temperament, misfit anywhere but here, no latitude for his eccentricity and no creative channel except private and socially dangerous for him to express himself openly. As he also described his friend he wants me to meet.

All the time my paranoia that he's an agent.

Said the reason for wave of homosexuality among young primarily among the scholarship students of "Beardos" because first, revolution had freed manners somewhat, second all the boys thrown together in dormitories and on trips in nature mountains brought out freer play secretly among themselves. And no girls?

Fidel passive in bed supposedly by gossip and no strong sex scenes except when he has time. Che Guevara more sexualized, Raul supposed by gossip to be sort of queer—accounting for his feline sadistic temperament—tho he's married—and Dorticos, well, he's a strange case you'll understand when you see his wife.

Done much of this note taking following my own interests as to what's significant, leaving out many noble socialist moments and praises for Revolution by all concerned and this mostly preoccupied with police state paranoid ambiguities—I suppose plunging into the economic physical Zafia construction wholeheartedly would be experience of another kindly universe—all existential the various universes yet.

[...]

Evening supper with Ardch P. Purge of homosexuals *and* those who don't have proper revolutionary mentality—Two distinct classes—with Union Joven Communistas as main accusers and finks—continuing in dramatic arts school and may spread to University. Regio G.'s trouble was, aside from the fact that he quit the U.J.C., he also disputed with the Dean of his school—so may be kicked out—By disputed, means he got into verbal arguments about matters of aesthetics, morals and politics. Nobody sure whether purge will spread to university or not. P. says its ordered by Castro.

Italian journalist for *Unita* said he thought trouble in Cuba was they hadn't sufficient philosophic culture in Marxism, were experimenting without consulting previous history in order to make their own existential scene.

Clearer story of P.M. movie and Lunes De Revolution suppression—Lunes the most advanced international literary sheet, everybody waited for it to see the latest, including my own poetry. Carlos Franqui editor of Revolution was confidante of Castro but no member of Com Party. He defended P.M. ("a rotten mover anyway") from "dogmatic" communist criticism. Communists complained to Castro—they were preparing a drive to Stalinize art at the time and seized on P.M. as a fine example of decadent art—"With all the achievements of revolution, why now this sinister review of Havana nite life putas pimps and Maricons?"—big convocation of intellectuals battling it out. Rodrigues the head of ICAIC (Cinema) and others now liberal also attacked the movie. Castro declared "all art inside revolution OK" and that was a supposed victory for free art. However, new proposition emerged: close Lunes de Revo-

Cuba

lution and open UNEAC (Union of Artists and Writers) with a jazzy sheet open to all. So that's how UNEAC was born. Lunes editors all kicked upstairs, New UNEAC paper didn't emerge—later on UNEAC Gazette came on, but it was a lot tamer than Lunes. The liberals thought they had won but in effect they lost what they had in Lunes.

What Schleiffer and others told me was only that Lunes was dropped because of oversize circulation. Not the real reason. "I been lied to."

The Stalinist art rollback continued with an attack on Abstract Art later by wife of a Communist guy now in jail or dead for betraying Castroite students and Bastista Ordochi or someone, I never got this story straight.

However the fall of Escaloate[46] the head of Communists is, for infiltrating bureaucracy with Communists presumably for a takeover, ended the pressure on the arts.

Everyone seems to agree the newspapers here stink, are mediocre and don't criticize and have no independence, which was my experience. Anything controversial is considered "political" in the light of the "Revolution" and has to be passed by upper board, CORE or something.

More gossip chismiss reported in. I'm supposed to have had orgies with all the Puente boys and girls.

Since the papers don't report anything serious, all discussion is done by gossip privately which creates chaos. Political and economic planning by word of mouth O.K.

[...]

46. Aníbal Escalante, head of the Stalinist PSP (Popular Socialist Party). It originally opposed Castro's seizure of power.

[Feb. 10]

In plane, explaining Reich's theory of orgasm to Maria Rosa. Now flight over Sierra Maestra Mountains in Southern ocean shore and Santiago—big hotel on hill overlooking city—we went into town in limousines and walked along narrow main street—saw place where Frank Pais, an aid to Castro, organized supplies from town, was killed on sidewalk police blood—supper in hotel with talkative rubicund Portiondo a dullard I remembered no lively anyway in consequential except interesting description of his fear writing friends in U.S. or sending books because police labels it Communist propaganda and if they sign a form they get in academic trouble maybe?—

Around swimming pool all South Americans mellow two bottles rum singing Bral singing different half moonlight soft stars songs.

Feb. 11 Dream: Wandering around grand hotel, old city establishment, looking for a queer bar or basement Turkish bath—I walk in several street bars a la Modern Havana, they're empty and even the toilets are closed and some of the toilet cubicles don't have any urinals or seats or faucets in them, just empty Egyptian tombs, like, finally I go thru one restaurant by a labyrinthine backroom—the young pudgy waiter follows me into the lobby of the hotel like Bellevue NYC to show me the way, friendly, to the john. I ask him if there's a queer bar and he says no but there's a big men's club-bar upstairs, we go thru floors on escalators and elevators into a huge ballroom carpeted and club like filled with tables at which men sit, their Sentaria necklaces gleaming like jewels, clinking glasses, doing business, singing, theatrical, like the basement of the London Sewer visited by Prince Hebert in Harry Smith's movie. It is

Cuba

not what I'm look for, I want a straight, dirty underground Turkish bath, like in Seattle.

"Well, I'm in hotel training so I have to know about these things," he explains to me like an ICAP guide. And in more subdued but scrappy voice, "Of course, Pot is another matter and I know all about that." He's an old head, too.

Feb. 12, 1965

Yesterday woke early and went on red open air bus with benches in back, starting off for a place called "Grande Pidra," second highest mountain in Cuba. Everybody cheerful and singing like summer camp. Wheels on bus spraying oil, went to bus station, dozens of red truck-busses with 1930's snub-noes made in Russia—suddenly realize the vast involvement Russia has here—and how vast the U. penetration has been. Will all the U.S. autos grow old and die without spare parts?

Had cheap 5 peseta refrescos lemon and gas water sweet and then with Parra on main street looking for straw hats.

I bought a little evil eye prevention card with a funny motto "May your conscience stub you for putting bad eyes on me." Thought of sending it to Nate Gorz-Frere journalist lady who'd probably been cause of a lot of gossip about me.

Since public communication so faulty, maybe half the public policy is run by gossip. So, natural development of evil-eye psychic systems. You can't defend yourself any other way but by magic, or counter-gossip systems. Had almost choked her last time I saw her at the big reception for us jurors.

Long ride up and down hills and on mountain roads outside of Santiago, passing valleys and memories of other valleys in Bolivia in Sikkim in Peru—thatchroof cottages down on knolls below overlooking banana

Cuba

tree clusters streams and hillside farms—beautiful Southern Carib shore in distance and vast stretch of sea-singing—arrived about 1000 meters where clusters of workmen and machinery were building road— Stopped in tourist café for beer and sandwiches, they're building vacation hotel on peak tops very nice—Then visit to 1830's tea plantation— rusted slave chains in the downstairs barns—Climbed up to top of rock on mountain nearby 1300 meters and overlooked vast low valleys in Central Cuba—distant whiteness of Guantanamo Bay shimmering in distance—odd that the U.S. should still be here in a foreign place—Fidel C.'s Sierra Maestra in other direction and the great sad Carib waters spread out toward Haiti invisible. Descended, rode back to hotel, everyone tired and a little bored, passed Moncalpa Army barracks once site of first attack on Battista—now a school—

No advertisements anywhere on highways or in cities but many Revolucion signs, giant paintings of martyrs, slogans painted along walls of factories—"Win the Battle of the 6th Grade"—"Patra o Muerte Vencerems"—"Who Sabotages the Revolution Sabotages Christ"—Back to hotel, passed early revolution housing projects kinda crumbly but better than Peru's El Monton of garbage I'd been describing at lunch—We'd eaten at a workers' club where hundreds of little kids were bathing in swimming pool and getting Phys. Ed. exercises, lots of childish flesh happy—

At hotel I went swimming and coming out of pool Mario the guide and Nicanor Parra and others talking—Radio had announced raid 145 U.S. planes on N. Vietnam—huge headlines about attacks the day before, Russian Minister had been in Hanoi—Everybody talking serious as if it were 1939 beginning of World War II—Mario very angry like a U.S. anti-red newspaper reader—"Russia and China will not be able to accept this—it's completely an affront—completely insane." "The Capitalist countries can't get away with this"—"Yes it's a confrontation be-

Cuba

tween Socialist and Capitalist nations"—Standing around in groups of five in the tourist hotel courtyard near the ICEP cars. I felt left out and said nothing, suspecting the whole panic was explainable some *other* way—apparently a head of the Russian Govt. was in Hanoi when the U.S. strikes occurred. Probably the U.S. version was that attacks were "provoked" by N. Vietnamese attacks on U.S. bases. Who knows? Read thru all 4 Cuban newspapers to see how they "handled" the story. Feb. 11 *Revolucion* Banner Headline "Triumphal Offensive of the Patriots: 600 Dead Yankees and Their Puppets." *Hoy*: smaller headline USSR–Vietnam Accord to Fortify Defenses of RDW—Imperialists suffer 600 Casualties. *El Mondo*: New Yankee Aggression on North Vietnam. France Asks Geneva Meeting: Demolishing Actions by South Vietnamese.

Everybody discussed the new radio news as another stage in escalation of conflict to global war level. By the morning it all calmed down except in my head. The local Sierra Maestra paper main headline today the 12th is "Declaration by Fidel: First Million Tons of Sugar Produced." Side story on the U.S. 148 planes attacking with quote from Geo. Reedy affirming that said aggressions were destined "to respond to new provocations directly from the Hanoi Regime."

I went back bathing and then sat around swimming pool with others and tired went in, took shower—jerked off in hot shower bath pressing my cock and belly against the tile wall as I came, thinking of being screwed by 17 year old red-sweatered Cuban guide from ICAP hector, formerly a member of Analfabazation Brigade.

Up late reading Sheer Jeitlan "Cuba, An American Tragedy." Got up to description of Matos trial—Matos resigned as a provincial governor charging communist takeover and was tried as anti-revolutionary. Earlier in book was worked up into froth of irritation at U.S., at that point began resenting Castro.

Cuba

Woke after mosquito sleep. Beginning to formulate what's awry here. Later—last few days pattern of sympathy and community with revolution alteration with withdrawal and disgust for the whole communal scene.

Feb. 13, 1965. On way in limousine caravan to visit Carmillo Confiengos school. That's a big new school. Camp for 10–18 yr. olds from Sierras. Stay 3 years, 4 years.

In car,
more news of Vietnam, protests, imperialists, etc. Stopped for drink of green sugarcane sweet-milk.

Tour of
school—boys all looking at TV in modern open building dormitories—Mickey Mouse with comic music.

Thru the dormitories, bunks piled 3 high and the smell of lockers and boys—Classroom, the schoolbooks of University History from Slavery to Socialism in five epochs including feudalism and capitalism, like giant comics with illustrations.

Lady guide wife of Director. "Sex is not a problem. We don't tell them it's bad. We simply tell them it's against the rules here, there's no provision, we don't want to have any problem. Homosexuality? No cases of that—we supervise them closely, we do keep careful watch. They have dances, they hold hands, Platonic relationships, but we have work and study activities from 5 A.M. scheduled down to cover every minute of day to bedtime." We were sitting around in her office, and Elmo Valente and Parra led off with questions. She said there simply was no sex, and it was against rules *here*.

That's how homosexuality has spread. Everybody thrown together & faute de mieux no place to go except the fields nearby (or the dorms late at night, the longing under bedsheets and the stealthy kisses).

Cuba

Back top cars and Manzanillo old hotel to supper and I took walk around square and talked to kids. Faces looking up, innocent and gawky, wanting to know about the outside Panama New York India and Peru and Columbia.

Feb. 14, 1965. Saturday. *[sic]* Up early in hotel in Manzanillo, rode back to Confuegos School and then by truck up into Sierra Maestra—fantastic road dusty and steepest gradient I ever been on Himalaya or Bolivia both, thus ascended straight up and special Russian trucks churned up slowly like in a dream—the landscape thatchroof huts, bahias, Royal Palms and valleys, everybody standing up in back of truck bumping and singing along, I played my finger cymbals at dangerous passes, then the ascent to an eyrie alongside the mountain by dust track single lone truck path so steep a footman'd have to step sideways to ascend lest he slip— Arrived at beehive shangri-la in valley at mountaintop with Pico Turquino 2005 meters high in cloudy distance except here sky clear blue and looking down outside could see vast central valley of Oriente that leads to Guantanamo, see in fact all the way across the island to the N. Coat dime blue horizon distance, and looking in to the valley—Charlie Chaplin goldrush out heap—dinosaur trucks and earthmoving machines from Russia slowly ascending red roads on the other side of the valley, thus bowl enclosure surrounded by treestumps hills and green peaks picked clear of large forest growth, cavities eaten away by lumbering and dredging and scooping a huge red field in the order of the Minas de Frio bowl, and on levels and platforms all around long dormitory buildings, small ironworks for coffee roasting with smoke thickening up smelling to the distance, ant files of kid Cubans walking on steep paths, playing fields, barren campsite—

A huge like summer camp way up in heaven filled with 13 year old children—

Cuba

We went down, met sub-director Negro beautiful youth, iron faced tho soft decisive camp coach—stubble beard growth and white eyes and square jaw and lovely brown skin and short hair solid chest and thighs—later talking to him his kind courtesy eyes but couldn't dare dream place face to his breast as I would—tho he smiled when asked a Marxist question—

Thousands of children in fact 5000 children learning to be teachers in the mountains, they come here after 6th grade those who want to be Maestros in the scattered faraway Sierra Maestra thatchroof wilderness—or Maestros anywhere in cities—all sent here first year of teacher training botany history Spanish thru high school years in other places later other mount schools or down in Santiago or Havana, but here first roughing it in vast Boyscout community with blackboards filled with diagrams of Law of Production and Surplus Value, basic history orientation—We walked over to the classes—beautiful in hillside forest dumps where they had dozens of little Howlas or wood forms made of tree poles they put together themselves each term to learn how to do it alone in villages later—the gangs of children in olive green dress with [?] individual undershirts, all sloppy and suntanned and unified and serious & gazing at us foreign visitors and looking at blackboards as in jungle very respective really learning what they were taught by young forthright teachers the girl teachers in pants that zipped up the buttocks crack, the girl students in army tightlegged olive green pants all—beautiful to see vast schools of children in the forest under bark learning—a girl teacher sort of fat with hard voice loud mouth explaining strictly the Law of Capitalist accommodation, I took colorphoto of her blackboard—all makes as much sense as any civics only more radically interesting to me—Imagine teaching teenagers big courses universal on Marx and inside secrets of private property leads to theft and selfishness

Cuba

and egotism and monopoly and war on Cuba and Vietnam—they orient the day's news first half hour before breakfast, too—

We took walk up hilltop to survey camp after seeing classes and here it seemed even more vast and plutonian other planet children's universe, all the directors in their twenties too—

"[?] and self supervision so they form committees and correct anti-social behavior"—"Here they experience the Sierra Maestra and encounter and conquer the conditions they will later meet alone without fear as they form part of vast army of teachers founding schools throughout Oriente mountains province learn qualities of socialist co-operation and work for the Revolution to bring education to hundreds of thousands living in primitive conditions in small farms in the unde-veloped part of Cuba—here they learn the true Revolution and become integrated with the real work of Fidel—Far from here, where Che held his camp—in that small mud hut thatch roof in the center of the valley 1957–59—also they can visit, we organize groups 300 five days trip to Pico Turquino, it is a mystical experience the highest point of our Cuba when they graduate after 8 months here they make this vast exploration of the highest natural grandeur of the Island, they have reached the most difficult earth in Cuba to possess and they own their own country without fear or mystery—Also can go in groups studying the history of the Revolution to the different camp sites and historic outposts—There is X mountain village where Fidel signed the agrarian reform"—The beautiful teacher almost mystical in his determination and eulogy of the experiment of which he is leader for several years with all his beauty—married and has wife teaching here and child—I saw nobody fat—

Then we had lunch served by little Negro girls in a uniform I learned later were professors here, staff of 250 who stay permanently, live in dor-mitories with students and excited by the Kibbutz-like Revolution (that

Cuba

magic word truly magic now—) talked with short little girl who told me which texts they read to teach simplified Marxism—monthly Russian histories and synopses and Communist Manifesto tho not at this age Kapital—Histories of Cuba from that angle then assembled and taught to kids—

Then to visit kitchens—meanwhile long lines of boys around main cooking building with hundreds of trays full of rice and meat, sitting outdoors on tree stumps and walls and bridges, eating while the prehistoric water trucks coming down with huge earthenware giant stupes full of water raised dust on the nearby roadpaths thru the barren red earth all around—gangs of kids in the central sport field overlooked by rickety wooden stadium—seats playing high jump and beisbol—Vast sign on the cookhouse pavilion "Ser Culto es a ser libre"—Jose Marte— or some similar apothegm—painted so every child can see—

Went to visit dormitories led by little brown teacher with lovely eyes and delicate hands and big kissing lips very sexy but so sure of self as teacher revolutionary camp captain girl lady you wouldn't think of molesting her besides when I asked her later she said sex was banned here. The professors married or had boyfriends down in the cities—

Approaching dormitories met by groups of solid young teenagers in all stages of hairdo and roughness pubescent breasted short all colors of skin Chinese blue-eyed black black yellow haired Spanish white big eyes Confidence of masses of them all together confronting visitors—a few schoolbooks pushed forward for autographs and real curiosity but in such large gangs together no chance for individual mental intercourse—I went inside one girls' dorm—huge long barn like a long house 300 girls sleeping 16 hammocks to a small section strung so close one on another—absolutely no privacy and total social closeness, their wooden personal valises and cardboard cartons piled up under the windows—sweeping floors, climbing on rafters, a dollie with yellow hair sit-

Cuba

ting rigid on windowsill. The teacher has a large permanent space to herself and can hang a sheet or towels over a rope for privacy, own coffee burner, pictures on wall.

The girls all dressed high gathered round and we talked a little I excited and terrified by such a demonic mass. They began singing, a hundred voices in one tone piercing all universes

"Oh Fidel Oh Fidel"—

Distinct clear myriad girlvoices all in one note call like an army of birds at dusk in a tree. Clouded plaza downtown any tropic city—myriad girl voices all together, deliberately singing to the time of Spanish revolution. Folksong Los quarto Muleros or Los quarto Generalos 6 songs for Democracy. "We're here to learn and to be teachers, any cowards pack your knapsack and go home, country or death, we will win, into the mountains we will go and teach everybody culture and Cuba will be famous forever"—or some like words—I was astounded their insect unity and high confident treble voices and exact song call at me—like huge surge of a new unconscious—that was the wildest thing I saw in Cuba.

[...]

We got on truck and slid down mountain road all amazed and in a sort of ecstasy seeing 5000 teenagers all at once so curious and unified and Marxist and Cuban Revolutionary loving Fidel all at once in a vast camp high in a peak top. Long ride home.

Talking hours with Maria Rosa. She says there was a period 1962 when "Sectarians" that is party line communists all over Cuban Bureaucracy were taking over, power structure headed by Amibal Escalante—everybody getting nervous and complaining—they put a Paraguayan political commissar in the Casa de Las Americas who tried to set them old liberals all one against another paranoid—but he stole and drank and gossiped and drove in limousines too much and finally on all levels of govt. nervousness spread.

Cuba

Finally Fidel got mad at university because they left out of big dedi-
cation to an early martyr a sentence that he believed in God too. And
later took to radio and denounced or explained Escalante and then in
one nite the whole crisis was over and everybody relaxed.

So she feels secure now the "old ones" will die off and the revolution
never became Stalinist but stay pure to July 26 humanist basis, experi-
menting forever as it goes along.

"We were all complaining to each other till we realized he was a *bad*
man trying to make us quit the Casa. Once we realized that, it was all
OK. We decided to stay even if we died—they'd have to take us out as
corpses. That was the revolution. I stayed up whole nights long talking
to Eddie, trying to figure out what was happening. Later I found out
Haydee was up all night talking too to her husband and *her* friends."

"Who was Fidel talking to?

"They must have been talking to each other on their level, every-
where, till they finally realized what was happening. Everybody was
complaining.

"The sectarians were trying to substitute Gagarine and international
and May Day for July 26 and weren't even mentioning Monteceda and
Haydee as heroes. So we knew they weren't right."

* * *

Earlier in day had met the Director of Camila Cienfuegas school
again. Quoting Parra, I said, "Y se entender de conversacion de ayer
que aqui tiena una politica de masturbacion."

Her reply a laugh but later seriously, "We're just beginning here set-
ting up the physical school under circumstances of need and organiza-
tion and nervousness, we simply have no solution to that problem, not
yet, maybe later."

E. V. says, "They're training a whole generation with rigid minds.

Cuba

The artist is sort of free now but in 15 years all these thousands of kids will take over and be just what they're taught, dogmatic and efficient. Yes, Cuba will be the industrial marvel of Latin America and artists will sell lots of books but the art will be social realist and very narrow."

N. P. on the city of children in the clouds—"It's a crank university—Costs much to maintain—just because Che Guevara lived there?—Costing all that water—Could've built it closer to ground—where there are forests and trees"—

Uruguans says, "Still they have to do what they can. Revolution has its changes and adaptations. It's still open . . . Cost more to build road than cost whole camp."

Jaime S. asks me what I think. I quote Parra on roads. [?] annoyed, says he thinks it's Byzantine argument. I explain more carefully, referring to Parra. Paranoia. Am I being too abstractly critical? Am I brainwashed one way or the other, Capitalist or Communist? Brainwashed *all* ways. I'm an idiot. He's mad at me again! I get high in my room & write. We all finished supper and sat round the swimming pool then by the bar. I leave group to write home.

[. . .]

At last, alone in Cuba midst a lonely society—

        high chorus

groups of pure girls—What do they think of in their

    Hammocks to themselves—

What hump the hammock?

What Bee the ring?

Do they dream of Fidel, Raul, Che, Canillo? Dream

\of each others brown thighs? Dark softness! Approach

the tender young! To the toughness of the hot woods, or

palm tree solitude—To what Farewell? Sweet Comedy Life

searching the Earth thousand Acclaims? Language mixture,
if anyone cries they send them home—
I am thy crying Child sent
　　home
　　　　—To Die
As beloved Castro must die
　　As beloved Kennedy died—
Old Age of earth, young age of
　　　　Man & Child—
New Age of Revolution, come with
　　Delight, come with care,
　　Come with Dark Softness and
　　　　Ascent—
Come with sweet flesh to the old,
Come with sweet flesh boy and
　　　　girl to each other's hair
　　　　　　and gentle
　　Intimate mouth to mouth and
　　　　arm chest and nipple
　　　　　　and thigh—

Come to the young with heart in
　　hand—offering Rule &
　　　　Discipline and Work
and the sciences of this own
　　　　My body these many eyes
　　　　　　faces and new shapes—
A deep black girl walking in your
　　Line of forest Lore—
A picture of Fidel as a red head of

Cuba

Change—with all that
    need for Father Hope—
Hail to thee Castro, faithful to
    your first tenderness—
To thee Che thy beauty & mind &
    knowledge—
other Images, I know not
    older Dorticos or true Raul—
the fear to be a hypocrite! My
    mind changes, the dragons
    of anxiety, or War, the Bomb
    the fearful U.S.A. what is
    the Governments going to do,
    What is the People's own Say?
What questions, for no one is
    God but Man & Man's power
    to a Greek & Roman God have
      also gone—
But I know no history but now &
    no feelings but my trembling
    hand and body fearful
      To be always Born.
or what cough over the page!—
or what crickets speaking in the
    darkness behind my back—

I'll go out naked, or
    with trousers, under the stars
    & meeting eyes, will sing,
      or sing alone.

Cuba

Out under the moonlight full sky
    where four sat at a glass
        cracked table talking,
The gossip of Now Yevtushenko
        anti-Sectarian,
Now am I making you mad at me,
    another Cigarette Hope,
the crickets, the car exhaust rappp,
the titillating nerve words of
    lights stretched over the
        black sleep of Santiago,
the calling of dogs, the broken cry
    of rooster answer to roostercock
& chain over the city, the hum
    now of machinery in my room,
    are you still mad at me?—
The wrath of a single God! What
        Horror for any Cuba or me—
Unlax Honey, drape your coat over
        a chair and think of me, my mink
your furs over my chair.
I feel sleepy, with my changobeads
    & red shirt and my fingers
    familiar moving in the book
    which is the continuity of my life,
    for lack of Man touch
        Revolution
I have nothing to hide but my
    loneliness—
I am too Righteous, often my

Cuba

Language afflicts—
I am a homosexual & my ass longs for
   a Cock (another explanation)
I am a realist, I am a Choochoo
      train with black skeleton
         Cars full of sugarcane poles—
         packed like toothbrush
      To the smokestack black whirling
      factory down from the strange
         place schoolred city—
I cough, & close my eyes on the
      speeding black car on the
         dark evening roads—
To Santiago alight in its place &
      Soft angry paranoid.

Feb. 15, 1965 Sunday— *[sic]*

On plane returning to Havana—Sunset now, very tranquil, the vibration of motor roar in soft seat, orange light over the mountains of clouds right below the plane, can't see earth, a full moon, alpine yellow mist peaks, great valley distances and furls & billows of God-smoke, white sand castles, giant cotton fluff off in the distance—the magic modern airplane riding above the silent cities of grey cloudiness, anonymous forgettable phantom shapes home above earth alone to themselves.

Feb. 17—Yesterday met M in the afternoon, we walked to UNIAC talking, got key to Jose's house to go there, make love and work, hung around Union an hour reading & translating newspaper interview questionnaire that a Mr. Julio Castello gave me for paper *La Tarde* and also poems by R. Gueneo kind of Futurist style for 18 yr. old.

Cuba

R. G. still in trouble at school, may get kicked out—U.J.C. finked on him, he had one homo experience it seems, according to Porteus, so he's "accused." May lose his scholarship in scenic design in Theater Arts School. Jose came by, read his poems & wants to print one.

"Shall I ask Jose for his key?"

They walked off together. "Yes, if you want to . . ." Later M came back & said he had it. We took cab to Marianso section—in cab M looked out back window, "I feel paranoid—they may be still following"—After all these weeks finally we were alone together in the cab going toward rendezvous—both silent, a little worried. Like sneaking out on the whole society, & besides would it work out? I hummed mantras to myself & realized I was dying. He sat quietly, not much to say, small thin kid with lively eyes & earnest manner, face covered with old acne scars, very thin delicate hands & manly courteous manner, but kid-frankness & humor,

M fitted key in lock & gave me his books & papers to hold while he fumbled trying to open, at last we got in.

Jose's apartment empty of furniture, he'd sold it all for 5,000 pesos to go to Mexico & then didn't go—lived at Havana Libre Hotel & held orgies for 3 months—& then moved back to his empty apartment ground floor with tile floors four rooms. Last time I was there the lights were turned off for no payment—$15 in arrears—water's free. He inherited apt. from a married sister, it's a little way out of center of town.

We went into back room where there's a big soft bed & typewriter on a table & a radio & closet full of Bridge books. I made the bed—rumpled—"Jose says he's a big whore—sleeps with everybody so they won't gossip about him"—

I looked at my big naked serious bearded face in writing table mirror & laughed.

We lay down on bed & talked a little—M eating hard green squares of Cuban mint drops—had a little white paper bag full, I ate one to

Cuba

sweeten my breath—Cubans always complaining that some foreigners smell very strong—Mr. Cohen especially, said Maria Rosa—mouth exudations apparently.

I lay back on pillow, M read, translated me a short story of his about block rectangle symbolic ceiling he's always fighting with. Also a poem beatnik style too long 2 pages, we cut it down to essential 5 lines. I put my hand on his small back while reading, & after a silence smoking I pulled his face down on my breast, he came willingly, we both relaxed & lay together, awkwardly, then shifted position & nestled close fully clothed, hot, I began to sigh, held my hands around his waist and on small of his back. We pressed loins close, I had a hardon & he too I think felt that way, couldn't tell, worried I was taking him over without his own desire. But we began moving together closer finding more complete ways to put bodies together belly to belly face to face—I tickled his ear & he pulled away, ticklish, stroked his short black hair, put my hand on his naked back under his shirt. We lay together changing positions & sometimes kissing—he began kissing me on the mouth, his lips together, tasting of green mint sweetness—

Just like the dream several day ago—I felt down between his legs thru rough jeans he had a hard on along his pelvis—put my hand on his buttock, felt like the narrow small kid's ass of my dream—Sweating too, finally began unbuttoning his shirt & he unbuttoning mine—We sat up to take off shirts—& lay down again half naked caressing & holding each other close, silent, I very happy the whole weight of fear of politics & physical doubt relaxed, my body light, sighing with relief & pleasure at last in complete rapport & physical tenderness with M who I'd longed to hold close like this for several weeks without any leisure chance—police, gossip, papers, brainwash state, authority paranoias, tourist organizations, ICAP, no place to go, no one to trust —at last in bed with a happy sigh in my solar plexus. But I couldn't exactly tell what he felt except friendly & acquiescent—"I slept here with Jose too." "Wow Jose surely *does* corrupt everyone like they say." "Once we slept there four in bed—but just slept tired"—We smoked cigarette, & then I leaned over & began kissing his breast & belly & touching my fingers along his thin arms. Amazing same bliss delight of corporeal tenderness which my face-cock breast longing comes forward & I'm myself as I feel with someone I'm softhearted for. "Desire gratified"—We lay there an hour, & then took off pants too—I began by wanting to put my hand under his belt hold his ass, & so tried to unbuckle belt, couldn't figure how to unlock it, he reached down & undid it, then I unbuttoned his pants fly & his white underwear front & leafed back his clothes & put my hand behind him & pulled him in close, his naked cock with hard on against my breast, then pulled his pants to knees, & moved my mouth down to his small prick in a mound of soft black fur—his belly & breast thin & hairless very smooth skin—blew him awhile, he almost came, moving my mouth up & down shaft of his prick & pushing aside his foreskin with my tongue so as to touch the tender part of the prick head—After a while quit & took off my own pants & we lay together face to face kissing—the more active I became, lying on top of him, the more responsive he was I discovered feeling his hardon against my belly—then we rolled over naked, him on top of me, my hand covering his small head, his mouth in my neck, his cock between my legs hard, my own stiffer hardon bent against his pelvic bone, changing face positions & kissing a lot—I asked him to stick out his tongue & he did, surprised, I tickled it with mine. Got sweaty, blew him again, he was near coming, it was hours already—Suddenly voices at the door—ah only Jose—asking did we want to go out for supper—friends with a car!—We hesitated, I said no, let's stay more, I like this better—Jose went off without coming in room—I got up sweating & took shower, wiped myself with bedspread, no towels—"Come on in, & take a shower." He did, trembling, cold wa-

Cuba

ter—I handed him the cover to wipe off with, & we went back into bed-room—Lay a long time, smoking, listening to radio, talking a little, not knowing what to say—I told him I thought he was beautiful sexy & manly. He said in grammar school people thought him effeminate. He isn't tho he's serious. I really felt warmth love for him in breast but couldn't say so, received better to show it more direct with physical breast softness together. Lay my head down on his loins & lay there re-laxed, sighing a little, then we began stretched out belly to belly again, kissing, & I rolled over on him & began wetting my cock with saliva & put it beneath his balls between his legs & began moving up & down losing myself in the pleasure & excitement of his acceptance—till I came, sharp jolts of hot joy rushing into my cock & thru to the bed-spread, I kept coming & saying, "May I come—is it alright, M?" he was silent but stroked my back & kissed me while I sighed over & over again—& then lay there quiet & tired—& worried he hadn't come—I fig-ured it was alright, I'd blown him a lot & not rushed into the scene & come—next time he come—I be sure—anyway the less anxiety I have the less he have—rolled over holding him, sighing, & after five minutes si-lence began humming om om om aa raw a Dy Da Daki ni Yeh Benza Wa nee Yeh Benzo Beri Tza neeyeh Hum Hum Hum Phat Phat Phat So—Hum—Over & over in deep voice from breast vibration like sigh—he laughed & unclasped from me—We sat up, I went & got paper from bathroom to wipe cover. "Leave it there for Jose, a souvenir"—"No, I'll clean up, there'll be a stain anyway"—The paper was a leaf of proof from one of J's books—The closet full of Bridge books—then we sat naked awhile, translating interview questionnaire exactly, so I could under-stand what I was being asked. Put on clothes, finally, a little relieved no police followed us—"Well, now, if they break in they got no proof," I said. "Yes, all they can do is arrest us on suspicion."

Earlier in the day Jose at UNIAC had shown us a trial notice he'd

Cuba

received—from the arrest after the Feeling Theater night—supposed to report to court March 22. Said he'd get Writer's Union lawyer & find out the charge. Told me not to tell gossip about it, this time he'd settle it quietly. Act of accusations had set "Bothering foreigners in hotels & effeminate appearance"—"It's a ridiculous charge, the judge will throw it out if I have a lawyer." "Can't you accuse the police of false arrest?"—"suppose so"—"What'll happen?" "The judge'll probably give him a lecture."

M & I went out to eat & work on M translation—I was tired & wanted to go home but held up an hour on La Rampa, eating pizza & going over phrase "Ray Charles blues shout blind on the phonograph,"[47] trying to find exact Cuban equivalent—then on wet wall by ocean in dark, talked some more, & then walked up La Rampa to catch bus—M left me a block from the Hotel—didn't want to come near. As we'd left the hotel early that afternoon, he'd pointed out the plainclothes pink shirted man sitting in lobby reading book—"He's the one who took me in from ICAP car the first time." I had walked back to desk to get closer look but embarrassed to stare direct, didn't get good fix on his face—As I went out—like in a dream, lacking the evidence—M said, "He's reading Sherlock Holmes in Spanish." He really was. "He's taking his job too seriously." M giggled.

Got home fatigued & fell in bed asleep.

Woke in morning depressed, didn't know what to do today—feeling uncanny not know what—tired of the Revolution, the hysterics, the fear, the hard mindedness, the U.S. threat underneath it all—boiling down to economics as the Sheer–Zeitlin book points out—threat to giant U.S. investments directly tied in growth of hostility to revolution, & that hostility & armed attack & economic strangulation directly tied to Cuban

47. From a line in "Kaddish."

Cuba

paranoia & hard-minded revolution—spreading Marxist dogma doctrine—everybody crazy & hopeless big history breakdown impossible to escape on any side—sad & tired & no place to go not even home, & poor M caught here. He reports to Militia henceforth every Saturday. "Can't publish a story with homosexual theme/action"—"I published one about beggar knifed naked in a bed, it was all [?] and symbolic. I didn't know what it meant ... everybody gossiped & thought it was about a homosexual experience. It was just a beggar knifed naked in bed."

Next morning woke, dressed & ate—then came upstairs, didn't want to write, face description of day before—went clothed back on bed looking out at room, and slept fitfully. Telephone call, M at 11 A.M., "Listen, Allen, I wanted to warn you ... you know that questionnaire?—Well, be careful with your answer—don't fill it till you see me—I'll call tonite at 7 p.m."—& woke again for lunch, troubled—ate & then saw Jose—he'd come to see me also—"Listen, Maria Belkis & her husband & some other journalists seem to be planning something—remember L? the little girl—she was in Santiago last week & R there's a friend of hers & told her to be careful, sort of testing her—They'll send you that questionnaire & you'll write things & sign your name & they'll use it against you, the group of them together & denounced you accuse you of making wild exaggerated statements against Cuba. Better not fill in the answers. L came back from [?] last night & told us."

I went over to Casa, saw Maria Rosa, gave her addresses of US mags & Pub Co's & composed letter for Casa to send asking for free avant-garde books and texts, couldn't afford to buy because of dollar shortage, used my name to request they send books to Casa Library for young Cuban intellectuals to read.

Asked her about questionnaire, without mentioning names. Then walked her home & looked at huge bound vols. Of Lunes de Revolucion. Heard more of that story. 200,000 copies—Too much! And the lowbrow,

Cuba

"Snobs" & middlebrow bourgeois intellectuals also were perplexed and angry—"What kind of mixed up typography is this—letters upside down! What's this mean? Who's Geult? This doesn't make sense"—They were experimenting in those days—actually had begun far left with reprint of Comm. Manifesto & Mayakovsky Politics action poems, then went loco with all sorts beatnik & cine issues & articles on marijuana—& the Sectarians led attack on Carlos Franqui thru P.M. Lunes—he was getting too powerful, almost master of Mass Media—had a wild TV show & on radio—but it was too upsetting for everyone—the last issue was all Picasso. Toward the end they tried to save the Lunes by putting in Vietnam & Bulgarian politics issues, but too late. The intellectuals were up till 3 a.m. debating before Fidel cast the dice. When *Lunes* was dropped, a new supplement literaria for all papers was to be formed—but never came off. Just the "official" *gazette* of the Writer's Union, very tame.

Supper at Hotel with Uruguayan who filled in more gossip from theater world. H. L., former head of Dramatic Arts school, told him Carlos Lechuga, pres. of the Arts council, called him in some months back & asked to fire five queer professors. But be quiet about reason. H. L. told one of the professors, who went to govt. for help. Lechuga called H. L. in again, complained he'd talked too much, & last month H. L. was dropped as head of school Now working with roving troupe of Union Amateurs—Spent all day yesterday interrogating two of them on accusation of cocksucking. Turned out they were innocent. Uruguayan says new head of Theater School is a board of five, including one slightly sectarian lady but very intelligent, a friend of his who estimated that H. L. was fired because "he wasn't hard enough" on the fairies.

Seems last year lots of Locas (screaming queens) were making an awful noise on La Rampa. That's what scandalized everyone. Arnold

Cuba

Wesker went down purposely 3 nites in a row, camping on a famous streetcorner in Old Havana, hoping to be taken in by Lacra Social, as a protest—they didn't. He also made speech criticizing Lacra on his farewell night here. Have to get text of that, see how far he went.

Meanwhile, a week after Xmas vacation, the whole Dramatic Arts school was shut down—boys sent to country to cut sugar, girls sent home. Last week girls were called back—the boys be back in a month. Meanwhile a board of psychiatrists is interviewing all the girls.

H. L. had translated Siesta in Xbalba from Evergreen some years ago.

Young kids in Prague laugh at Socialism, they say.

Parra & Vignes of Argentina at lunch talking about Mines of del Frio—"It's medieval—this conception that loss of semen means loss of vital energy—These Marxists are absolutely stupid—Just the same old Catholic superstitions."

Parra "Una politics de masturbation." He's tired of Cuba & wants to go home, instead of staying on as invited teaching a poetry workshop for 3 months. "I have my Lolita waiting for me at La Reina"—his house in foothills of Andes suburb of Santiago in Chile, where I stayed for a month in 1960. "From now on my mouth is closed I'm not a politician."

"I can't keep my mouth shut"—I say—"I'm too hysterical to be quiet more than a week." He told me some Casanova-esque stories of early sex adventures when he ws 14. I didn't realize he was so picaresque. Now so laconic & a lovely a man. Never talk sex to a woman you want to sleep with—strike directly to an unconscious level & touch her pussy. "Especially in the dark, it always works." I remembered his insight yesterday with M.

Cuba

Cuban military, American military, Vietnam military—the world is a mountain of dogs!

Yesterday 17th Wednesday ate early and 10:30 went to meeting at Cas de Las Americas, judges together deciding contents of next issue of Casa Magazine—Review of this Concourso—selections from the prize works, the cranky Argentinean poet who was anonymous—Would anyone write a chronicle of the days and events? I smiled thinking to offer my notebooks—or maybe parts—but decided wiser not to mention these writings anymore. Grekaberg going to write a Brown Chronicle—furry anecdotes and stories—"Ginsberg with his 2 banners Marijuana and homosexuality" Parra suggested—I hadn't heard the joke section thought he was serious—"I beg your pardon. Consciousness & Sexuality"—I stared at him, paranoid. "Oh, it's only the funny section, Senor Allen" Parra told me. I thought, anyway, shit, people kicked out of school & no civil liberties they'll still make jokes. Lotsa hypocrisy. We're all caught in the situation—I was doodling while they were deciding serious contents in Spanish—tried finish translation Parra's little poem [...]

Back at hotel ate with him and Argentinean David Vignes whom I hadn't seen much of before—we talked about education here—seems chief advisor on Pedagogy another invitado living at the hotel a Uruguary Mr. Jesualido—had written a book in the 30's about county schools, a bestseller?—and done much Marxist service in his land—Was sitting at table by window. A sort of grim greyhaired man with livid face —I kept staring at his hornrim glasses fascinated—was he the main Cat responsible for Cuborussian Minas Del Frio masturbation Politics of Pedagogy?

"I keep staring at him like a rat fascinated by a snake," I laughed— "I noticed," Parra said. "You should go over and introduce yourself." Vi-

Cuba

gnes had, before, avoided sitting at table next to the Pedagogue's party. "He's a big bore"—that's how conversation had started and thus I knew who the man was.

Had date with Manolo at 2:30 outside the hotel by the Malecon Concrete wall embankment overlooking blue ocean—he didn't want to come inside again since Mario received trial notice. I waited, he was late. I afraid he was picked up again? or got the directions mixed up, maybe he meant not near the hotel but Malecon by Havana Libre La Rampa area?—Waited there with my bag—guy in striped shirt had come out of hotel and was waiting a block away on the sea wall, I thought maybe he's the same Sherlock Holmes? He was watching some kids swim. I walked over, they were diving for pennies in a little concrete pool below the wall, as waves flowed over the abutments eroded years back—No Fuzz I guess just leisure—"Senor throw us a kilo"—"Huh?"—"Throw us some coins!"—"I don't have any money," I lied—"Are you Russian"—"No"—"American?"—"Si"—"Hey, mister." They were swimming in bathing suits, one in skin clinging white underwear pants—I hesitated to look too long, someone might notice I was really interested in those bodies, slim brown thin kids of the World's Carib.

Finally Manolo came, hastily late. We shook hands, he was same friend eye—had a paper to report to Court *also*, like Tore Mario—What to do now? Well, let's see, it's go over to Casa Ge & talk to Maria Rosa—"Jose doesn't want to do anything, he wasn't sure what the charge was, now that I've got a notice it means it's a hangover from that arrest at Amerdeo Roldon—for making 'public scandal.' I don't like the idea of a trial, I guess I'm getting paranoid. I went to talk to Haydee."

We walked along sea wall and took sad photographs, the Havana Riviera Hotel in background—he took me—I took him—sitting on the wall looking into the camera

At Casa Maria was getting Venezuelan poets address from Edmundo

Grey—working on file cards as I had done the day before. I felt a little estranged interrupting them for more paranoia police problems. "Haydee isn't here, Maria will be back soon, I'll tell her yes we should take care of this before the court. Probably it's just more bureaucratism."

Then walked up long hill to Writer's Union, met Jose and Weechee the spade Associo & Herberto and played ping pong, sweating, and sat around translating some short Kaddish poems—The End & Message—and took some color photos of the little group at the orange table on the porch under palmtrees—read Sunday's William Booth aloud to them to get the live rhythm—Compared court summonses and photo'd them, too—in color—written in green at top of Jose's "public scandal"—I'll be here for the trial probably—Mar 22—anyway get the other invitado to write a letter with one explaining that we'd invited them to the Roldo Feeling Theater Night.

Jose wanted to keep it all quiet, settle it bureaucratically as a legal matter—Manolo had scary premonitions. "I don't like the idea of being sent away to a reeducation camp"—"you think that's possible with a lawyer?"—"You never can tell—maybe this judge will just give us a lecture."—Jose said, "I didn't tell anyone at the Union here"—"Why? Wouldn't they help you?"—"They're just waiting for a scandal to get rid of us—They think we're a nuisance"—

"Would it do any good if I spoke to Guillen again?"

"No, I'd rather not involve him. He's just a bureaucrat, he has a nice house and a job and airconditioned office and he doesn't want any trouble. When a big crisis comes he'll act, but with us he'll just tell us to go to Court, it's nothing, anyway he told us to keep away from you that day after we first met him."

Couple weeks ago the kids reported Guillen told them I was "unpleasant" and a fairy and dopefiend and nothing but trouble, stay away. We

Cuba

no appeal to him now. Jose had said, "Probably the trouble was when you arrived and were interviewed you didn't make a big fuss about Guillen's poetry and wanting to meet the greatest Cuban Writer Guillen, in the airport." Kind of catty, Mario's intelligent and sly catty but very pleasant, actually sincere courage queen.

Manolo and I went out down steps to eat, he was hungry—and there was Miguel Barent by the leafy Writer's Union stone entrance gate—stopped and gossiped with him—"Any more news about Arcadio?"

Barent myopic and sturdy in sport shirt. "No, I haven't seen him yet, I have to go out this weekend to Guanabacoa and find out, have a talk with him. I'm afraid he'll have more trouble. Once the police start they'll just keep bothering him to get a permisso every time he has a Bembe (Palo woodspirit & meeting)—and maybe he won't be able to get a permit every week—Or they'll require him to have smaller ones, or for shorter hours"—

"Well, as big expert folklorists can you fight that—get all the folklorists together and advise the govt?"

"We've already had meetings to figure it out. I've written a letter, if he has trouble I'll send it."

"A letter?"

"A letter to the parties. We had trouble before in Oriente and in Las Villas Provinces—the local priests, police bothered them when we went to investigate and do research, so we wrote a letter to the party and straightened it out in those places. But it's the lowbrow bureaucracy—the higher government policy is friendly—first that trouble keeps coming up in different places one year Santiago, the year near Havana"—

"Well, keep fighting."

"I'm tired—or just, like, in Kafka, I'm not courageous. You have a

Cuba

different culture you're used to—I was more courageous till 2 years ago—now I don't feel like changing the world still—too many love troubles"—

"Well, the main thing in this kind of scene is not to internalize the fright—don't let the police anxiety make you feel guilty inside."

"Well, that's what I feel, I'm not a romantic like you." We poked each other in the stomach and shook hands, Manolo & I went off Pizza Dolce Vita place near Rampa—"Via Veneto," in fact—I drank a *son* coke and he had round melted cheese and ham pie—I wasn't hungry & he kept urging me to order—he had some extra money, I was broke, "I can eat huge free meals at the hotel"—

And he talked. More depressed than before and more secretly openly wise for a 17 year old, I guess since we'd made love he felt more free to reveal his thought. "I expected they coming 2 years ago and wanted to get out from under—go to the States maybe. But the missile crisis came and flights to Miami were stopped, with the blockade. I think Castro's fucking up the revolution. They don't know how to deal with the United States, they just get mad and insult each other. He could have found a way to ease the tension. It was supposed to be a humanist Revolution, now it's Marxist-Leninist."

"Did he plan that or don't you think the existential circumstances battle with the U.S. monopolies forced him to his position. After all, as far as I can tell, the real trouble came with Nationalization and diversification of trade to Russia and the regular Marxian analysis of the U.S. reaction does seem to make sense."

We talked whether it did or it didn't, Monolo, "Aw, I think he could have found a way out, paid off expropriations or not got so mad. Anyway he should see that exporting Revolution to Venezuela is getting us into trouble with US."

Cuba

"But how can he refuse help to same movement in Venezuela? He'd be a fink"—I was trying out regular arguments.

"We had our revolution, we didn't have a Cuba to help from outside, let them have their own revolutions, we give them moral support, but not make their revolution for them at the expense of Cuba. This way Cuba's getting all messed up."

"You think people here are tired of the Revolution?"

"Probably most people secretly don't like all that Marxist dogmatist propaganda—Fidel didn't himself at first. Then later he said he was always a Marxist-Leninist and would be till he died. That's silly. He probably wasn't, but just the same, there's lots about Fidel's early life—he was student assassin, too, once, I once read in an old newspaper—Anyway it's a little strange—I don't know.

"But I don't think Cubans like to hear all that narrow minded talk. At the beginning everybody was enthusiastic, we all volunteered for the alphabetization campaign, all the month, I went myself into the country and taught, now I don't think everybody would volunteer. They've changed the spirit and made it too bureaucratic and rigid and Marxist. I don't know if it'll get worse. I feel depressed."

It was dark night now and we walked down Rampa thru a little green park near the sea to the Malecon wall, and decided to walk all the way to the hotel. We were trying to figure out exactly what was wrong with the Revolution.

"I'd like to make some kind of declaration before I go, say the worst I've got to say here in Cuba, so I don't have to go abroad and feel like a hypocrite and be *used* by Time Magazine."

"Yes, you ought to try that. It might shake them up if you make a scandal—They won't publish it but you could get up at a meeting and start shouting."

Cuba

"What good would that do?"

"Castro would hear about it, he might get worried, Haydee might get worried. If everyone who visited told the what they thought, well, it might not change much, but at least it would make them think."

But exactly *what* do I have to complain about? Lacra Social? Persecution of Homosexuals? Controlled newspapers? Bureaucracy?"

"Well, you could talk about it in general terms like Bureaucracy, that would fit in with Dorticos's latest speech's emphasis."

"Sense of fear-guilt, no legal protection for civil rights, dogmatic Marxist oversimplified pedagogy, Masturbation politics?"

I had said at table earlier, "You ought to read all Marx and then be in a position to criticize fro*m inside* the Revolution." "Oh I did that already, read all those books—but—well, the party determines what's inside and what's outside."

"If you wrote a Marxist essay on Cuban politics analyzing criticizing the government structure, that would help," I figured.

"Yes, but I wouldn't be able to publish it. Only party members really can publish in 'Cuba Socialista' magazine—like Che Guevara publishes essays—or it would have to be in the newspapers, and the Party would have to pass on it."

Well, why don't you all join the Party? And work from within?"

"They don't accept everybody. You have to belong to this and that organization, or do that and that work for the Revolution—only real revolutionaries can get in. Or else stupid people, that's easy, people who read a few essays on Marx and repeat a few dumb ideas they don't understand and shout a lot about how they believe in the revolution."

"Why don't you fake it?"

"They probably wouldn't ... I'd have to join Joven Rebeldes or UJC ... I figured that was coming 2 years ago."

Cuba

"Well, you got to figure some Zen way of getting the Revolution straight. Maybe if all the young kids made love to the Party members"—

We gossiped about old political scandals—Matos? "See what he did was warn the Revolution was getting too Communist. He's still in jail."

"The young kid who betrayed the students?" "He wore sandals, they made him out a sort of emblemo. Ordoqui who protected him was a CIA agent, after the revolution. At least that's the secret story that's going around now. Makes it look bad for the Communists."

Ordoqui's wife had attacked the abstract painters—she's in jail now. She used to be married to Annibal Escalante or someone. And the time Castro got mad because the Communists left out that the student hero believed in god—some martyr betrayed by Ordoqui's beatnik disciple—it's all one bit gossip small town scandal sheet involvement—brothers in laws and Communists married by CIA agents all forming a big chain of simple big town links, all tied in with *P.M.* and Carlos Franqui and Fidel's enthusiasms and state police educational masturbation politics.

"Actually you'd have to read all the books and know all the secret diplomatic dealings and economic structures and counter stresses and day by day history for the last 6 years to be able to tell who's at fault or if it's both faults US and Cuba, or if there was ever another way out than what we got—revolutionary military state in real panic with dogma and rigidity closing down and dictatorship of proletariat which is getting cranky. And we'll never know *all* that. I followed in the papers but never could tell, and nobody really could know, it's all gone into memory like abstract—so I guess we have to begin right here where we are now." That felt right to say.

We kept walking around the sea-slippery sidewalk blocks of the Malecon, stepping down into the huge avenue, and crack long wall, not hardly paying attention to the ocean. When we'd got near the hotel—

Cuba

"I'll bring you my extra typewriter tomorrow," he said—We had a few weeks left to work on translation of whole Kaddish to put in Conconeso issue of Casa Magazine. But tomorrow no good, I got date with Nicanor to translate with him, some long poem of his—for New Directions and Cape book—"Parra's leaving in a few days so I got to spend all the time with him I can—call me tomorrow"—we shook hands and looked in each other's eyes, nice—"Goodnight, honey," I said, he laughed awkward—turned and head bent went off along the dark empty lot in front of the vast hotel.

Upstairs, call from Marcia Overton—I came down to lobby and gave her back her Guillen book she'd lent me—ate with her sitting drinking my free beer, showed her Scheer Cuba book[48] and asked her opinion of criticisms of Cuba in that book, which is otherwise friendly, sympathetic.

"More or less," she said—"It was worse 2 years ago—now it's better." I was kind of sharp with her, repeating ideas from afternoon conversation with Manolo, in hard voice. But after softer—she gave me her address—had been afraid to before, fear or scandal, or threat to her position here, my making so much noise. "The worst things of revolution," she thought, "are hangovers from old Catholic bourgeoisie Cuba."

Sitting in lobby, talking—Marcia and Sesaiden there too, I chatted with them—the rest of the invitados going to Ada Santamaria's house—Ada younger sister of Haydee, works in Casa editorial board—kind of a sentimental sharp almost Jewish wifely type—I'd seen a lot of her, too—at huge official lunch weeks ago she'd passed me a note, "I admire your courage"—and later when I was depressed had come to room to take me to see the school for naked babies.

48. Robert Scheer's *Cuba: An American Tragedy* (1964).

Cuba

Sisandro looking sly—"Nobody told me about Ada party," I said—
"I'm going over to Yves Espin's house"—

"Oh, my, you do get around, how did you contact him?"

"It's a secret," I said—Maria Rosa had arranged this meeting. Espin,
an architect, is Raul Castro's brother in law or something—she said he'd
read my poetry and liked it.

"He's very intelligent, he went to MIT, he'll like you—a bit of a snob,
maybe—Oh, I can see the circle now, Porteins and all"—

"No, not Porteins, as far as I know," I said. Afraid of seeming too
cabal.

Maria Rosa phoned. "I found the right word—I didn't mean Espin
would recognize you in the lobby because you look awkward, but I meant
you look conspicuous . . . If you leave there early, come over to my house
and tell me what happened." I said I guess I could talk freely with them?
or at least freely discreetly, and would come over if I came home before
midnight—

Espin came, slacks and friendly faced, young MIT look with sleeve-
less shirt and odd hairdo like dandy from children of Paradise, tho not
so long or slick. David Biegelmn with him—all architect friends. Drove
in their Volkswagen to open latticed excellent apartment in Vedado.

Group of friends, most chic looking, sitting around , . . [. . .], I talked
a lot as they asked me questions mostly first India, then description Mi-
nas de Fria and what I thought about revolution. I was summarizing
most of the general ideas of last few days, without being too extremist
sounding, and anyway they were all young intelligent Dolce Vita looking
friendly—got a little drunk—"A politics of masturbation," I quoted
Parra—None of them had been to Minas and the literary situation? My
opinion? "Too much suppression of communication of unconscious con-
tent dreams fantasies intuitions jokes here—actually too much fear—
everybody in Cuba secretly thinks they're antirevolutionary in *one* part

of their soul—so everyone's afraid—actually the words revolutionary and counterrevolutionary have lost meaning and are just fear stereotype now. How could an artist sit down and write blind poesy and know in advance if it would be categorized as pro or anti? If he thought about that he'd be paralyzed—A big Dostoyevsky with no sense of guilt and huge brown humor if he wrote a novel here about Lacra Social with terrible lesbian chief and art school and everybody's sex lives and Marx dogma and gossip, could it be published here? Nobody wants that kind of genius art."

Espin laughed and agreed, witty, "They'd never publish it here."

I wandered around apartment and in bedroom—they have huge foamrubber mattress on floor—also big collection Santaria Collares—I showed them my little red and white chango beads under my shirt—sat on floor and talked about mushrooms and Leary and Hitler's psychoanalytic character as figured out [...] by means of analysis of written Hitler data— Hitler liked to be shat on by Eva Braun—got his kicks that way—big historic fact—or maybe not fact, a likely story, and I did hear it as a fact—I sang Shiva Mantra and clinked my little finger cymbals feeling friendly—They offered to exchange collares with me—told me about Che—an ascetic, like flagellates himself mentally—yes, has wife, kids (almost as if by accident) they laughed. But fortunately Raul and Fidel are sexy. That keeps things human.

In kitchen, drinking, intimate, said I liked Fidel but he took on too much responsibility—everyone depending on him—maybe an egotism not good for state—Described Haydee's reaction to idea of inviting Beatles—

Espin's wife—her fingers red with mehiolate she'd burnt her hand at supper stove—pretty zany girl 24 with slightly modern classy hollow cheeked but sporty beauty—"If you meet Fidel, talk to him about this." They were slaves? Maybe so, they seemed sort of solid and alive.

Cuba

Drove me home—"I like you," I said as we came to huge curved drive-way of hotel. "I really did know you were Raul's relative"—wanted to get that off my conscious—Waved goodbye—but felt slightly bad, as if the remark came out insulting instead of frank—or came out too obsessed with my own machinations. I had wanted to be charming.

Upstairs too tired to write and 2 A.M. Drank a little settled sleep. Bring Bring phone from Room 1820 down the hall—

"Ginsberg, we're all here having a party come join"—Carballeo's voice, but he's a thin mustached big eyed Mex dramatist been here 3 months had a TV play on weeks ago—leaving next week for S.F.—I got up excited, put on Indian white pajamas, both sets of chango beads, big red plaster bone, one I'd bought with Miguel Barnet last week—put finger cymbals and cigarettes in pajama side pockets and went thru the green carpeted hall barefoot.

Opened door—everyone there for the first time all the invitados in one small room happy late at night drinking and all shouting greetings and applause at my late arrival, drest in costume, ready for delight! What a really allegre roomful all sprawled on bed, against wall—Camelo Jose Cela in his distinguished pajamas barefoot—Stubbed his foot and he raised his eyebrows campy and rubbed his foot over and over—Edmundo Arey whom I'd come to dig, and his wife—she sang Venezuelan communist and sexy and Spanish songs with lilt and sureness and care—He economics professor and looks maybe not plump, but when he gets drunk gets truthful and moody and sings and laughs like a sadly kind Venezuelan poet should—Miguel Grinberg grinning—Carlos Barral in dandy beard and his Spanish international woman wife sitting in corner—later they sang again great song I'd first heard from this old baritone Catalan voice in Santiago—

Quardo Venterano
Crescen los Venduras

Cuba

Maduran los Frutas
Y los ichos de putas
   turu luru lu
   tu ru ru ru tu ru

When it comes to springtime
Vegetables are born over
All the fruits get riper
And all the sons of whores too
   Tu ru ru ru tur u

And she stayed later alone and sang Edith Piaf pariez mais in perfect tone and accent—We rang up Parra and sent delegation to bang on his door, he came in pajamas sleepy, we all applauded and cheered, he rushed with alacrity into the bed pulled sheets over himself and settled watching with hands clasped on breast—I began singing his Guera Larga but he wouldn't raise voice song—

Grinberg later lone song some old Jao Gullbert long oriental Jewish Brazilian complex worded song very sad—Cela in almost toneless voice with big bleary eyeglasses big belly hair pushed out of his pajamas did too sing in toneless friendly shy voice with hint of tune some Castillan dirty peasant limericks—

Big nosed Mex poet Jaime Serrano chanted drunkenly some Jalesco Concion, and told me he just today read my Palante letter and finally understood me—"First impression of you is horrible but you're an admirable man." "It's a part of my Mabusin," I giggled, actually embarrassed. "Anyway we didn't actually pay attention to each other till three days ago"—Big mustached Vigres was sitting next to him and I suddenly realized I thought he was Vignes and had them confused in my mind—they both laughed at me and waved hands—Everybody started singing "I'm a ship with 6 sails and 15 cannons," and "Show me the way to the

Cuba

next whiskey bar"—and a Uruguayan actor dramatist lay on the floor and sang in campy pseudo-professional Brecht–Lenya accent—everybody so smart and funny last night—and the Mexican lady poet with tortoise shell eyeglasses and thin pencil brows and Chinese makeup came in with a Chinese nightgown embroidered all blue and sat against the wall and joined Mexican songs—hours, a little moo rum, big Uruguayan poet white haired lay back on bed and relaxed, listening—we all sang some more tu ru ru ru ru.

Parra suddenly sprinted to door and disappeared—others drifted—Greenberg Carballo and Arey and wife and I were left last collecting $10 for one to score for some pot for a party next Saturday night—Greenberg left and Arey and Carbello drank got into heated argument over Marxism and who the Cubans should invite—Mondragon Corno? —Carballo saying they were unimportant and had no fixed ideology and Arey saying they were good people—which led at the 5 AM hour into a sudden bitter polemic—Carbello suddenly coming on like a Time Magazine Marxist. "Unfortunately poets in the first place are not so important to the revolution and *unfortunately* these poets even Ginsberg here have no real real place . . ." I kept out of it, Carbello went to piss, Arey's wife Sophia wound her finger around her ear to her drunk husband to warn him Carbello was low tonite.

We were left alone, the three of us, I took a copy of Arey's White Roof magazine—liked him, finally, among all the Invitados, almost the most, he had good open sentiments and kind reactions and funny poet pride so he could beat his breast drunk with fist and smile and say to Carbello, "There is a whole new consciousness coming into the world and poets are the forebodings of this youth."

Went back into my room then and slept, leaving message with operator not to ring my phone till noon—no calls—deep sleep.

Feb. 18–19, 1965

Woke with sudden knock on the door—Who?—I cried—"ICAP"—I
got up and put on—"one minute"—Indian pajamas—I was naked and
had jacked off before sleeping, thinking of being screwed by Manolo or
Jose—supposed to be early visit to Sugar Central Factory today but I'd
told Mario Gonzalez of ICAP w/his little nice mustache that I'd stay
home this morn and work with Nicanor—

Opened the door—the ICAP face familiar but not one of the boys as-
signed to me—with three soldiers in olive green neat pressed uniforms
beside him—"What's up"—they come in "If you please get dressed and
come with us"—"Where?"—"Please pack all your belongings also"—
"But what's happening"—"We will accompany you to the Immigration
Department this morning"—"What for"—"The officer there wants to
speak with you"—I realized the jig was up and got chill thru my back—
adrenalin panic—more like a cold fear thrill—everything sharp and
clear as in a dream but I was still too sleepy—"What time is it"—"8:25"—
"Dios, it's too early for this, I went to bed at 5 in the morning"—"Please
get your clothes on." They were looking around the room. What did I
have on me—The $10 for pot—that's ok—I was moving around sort of
blurrily looking for my underwear thinking—"My notebook! Libreta de
Technicos black notebook on the bed table—yesterday's description of
love scene with M.—Thank God I used his initials—but there's still
enough in there for them to get me on something political or amoral?—
Will they search?—Can they read my scribbled English?"—"Right
now?"—I meant, Naked? "Here."—I dropped my pajamas and sat in
chair putting on undershorts—kind of funny fearful modesty—still wor-
ried about the little black notebook—What were they going to do?—
Fear of jail, kidnapping—"Have you called the Casa de Las Americas"
"No, it is not usual in this procedure." "I think you should call Haydee
Santamaria and the Casa and check out if this procedure is regular"—

Cuba

"This is the regular procedure"—"Who wants to see me?"—"Capt. Varona"—"Who is that"—"Head of Immigration"—Well that sounded not bad, maybe technical, it's not Lacra Social or Dept. of Interior or G-police. Still total uneasiness in my body, and worry about Manolo and Jose—have they been picked up again? —Find out later—I dressed, awkwardly, and went into bathroom brushed teeth—

"Electric toothbrush?" one of the soldiers in green cap.

"Si electricidad, muy utile & sano"—I said by this time regain some composure tho still cold-thrilled. I should have known it was serious and not been so loose with my talk—last night the Espins complained? Who finked?—But my notebook full of secrets and thrills!

I started emptying drawers wondering if I should protest—"I want to call the Casa"—"Not allowed to make calls"—So I sat knapsack on bed and put in pants and a few odd bed table books and odd empty notebooks, picked up the black full sexy one and put it under jeans in bottom of sack—then filled in—put Feezoo's crazy coffeecup in a sock, and Santa Barbara statue that Manakosa'd given me 2 days ago—chango syncretistic substitute—in a sock—put on both beads and then took off the big one and put that in little carryall bag—emptied drawers and envelopes into big envelopes and put in sack—"To hurry the process"—a soldier had brought my sweater and torn skin jacket in from the closet, all still over hangars, on the bed—managed to get everything packed except big pile of books—soldiers sat around, I kept asking "Are you sure you know what you're doing and have the authority for this?"—Icap man sent for a fresh elevator to be waiting—I didn't know what to do with all the Cuban books and newspapers—they piled them all around on a hand cart and I was ready. Thru hall wanting to shout next door to Elmo, but they'd all be sleeping—and embarrassing to shout, as if being kidnapped by Nazis?—or just being bothered for a few questions—but they'd made me completely clean out my room of possessions—to disappear?—down elevator into the lobby—stept out and ah! Mr. Lundquist and his wife with eyeglasses—"Ah, Mr. Lundquist—Mira, yovoy—" I began in Spanish confused—and continued in English. "I seem to be arrested—" "Ah" said he jovially stupid almost "That's alright, same thing happened to the Danish journalist I told you about, they'll hold you in jail till there's a plane and send you out of Cuba"—I was still worried about my notebook on the bottom of my knapsack on the hand truck—oddly they stopped—soldiers around me Icap guide—to let me converse—"Listen, tell Parra what happened,"—"It will be all right, they'll put you on a plane"—"I mean, call the Casa de Las Americas." His wife interrupted more urgently "Arthur, he's saying you should call"—"Yes call the Casa and tell them what's happening—fast"—He finally got the message and assured me he would, immediately.

I went out front hotel, saluted the cab boys, blue uniformed door keepers—everybody staring but with old kindly Kafkian smiles—scared and sympathetic or just dumbed?—got in car with the three green attendants and waited—nothing yet. They put my bag in the truck. I saw Mario Gonzales coming up the walk to work—As he came near the car and called him: "Oh Mario?"—He leaned in surprised and tentative—"What's happening?"—identifying himself as hotel Icap chief—They explained "Detenado por Immigration"—

He looked at me—"Did anything happen last nite?"—"No I said, everything as usual, no special scene,—call the Casa—Call Haydee or Marcia or Maria Rosa"—"I'll do that now he said"—keeping his diplomatic aplomb—tho surprised he accepted the scene without temper or question—"adios Mario"—

We rode off—along Malecon to old Havana sidestreet white ancient edifice Immigration Service and they put me in huge hall-door, waiting. "The officer will come soon." Then I picked out my finger cymbals and began chanting very slowly and low so as not disturb much. After awhile

Cuba

they led me in to barred window locker room on one side—offered me chair, bed, went to buy me cigarettes—came back with Hoy—I sit and sang a little and glared nervously thru paper—"1,332,056 children vaccinated as of yesterday"—"Cuban Soviet business 440 Million"—"USSR Rockets with 100 Million tons of TNT"—"Mexico won't break Relations with Cuba"—"Employ Yankee and Gusano pilots in Uganda Bombings"—a photo of Vilma Espin inauguration some Plan Bureau—an Editorial on new Soviet declaration Isvestia says they're mistaken "those who think they can promote good relations with USSR and same time maintain aggressive line against other Socialist countries." Great sugar harvest. Statement by Chilean Communist Octopus. The world is a mountain of dogs. If they kick me out it's an unthinkable scene. That rigidity both sides a vision of war. Caught between lines.

A huge window with high bars looking out on the small street—suddenly an anonymous other soldier appeared sat on bed and said "We've arranged your departure this morning at 10:30-plane to Prague London and N.Y.—You have your passport?"—"No, they took it when I came in at the airport"—"Oh, Icap has it, it'll be waiting at airport. We'll leave now."

"Fine but if I may ask, what's this all about, why, and have you not made a mistake? Have you consulted the Casa de Las Americas?"

"No, we will call them. I have an appointment with Haydee S. at noon."

"And your name?"

"Carlos Varona"

"Your position?"

"Chief of Immigration"—"For all Cuba"—"Yes."

We got in car and went off along Malecon—passing the ships in harbor—suddenly on prow of a [...] cargo boat the name "MANTRIC"—I pulled out my cymbals and began singing very low OOOM OOM OOM

Cuba

SARAWA BUDA DAKINI VEH BENZA WANI YEH BENZA BERO TSA NI YEH HUM HUM HUM PHAT PHAT PHAT SO Hum. And then Hari Krishna Hari Hari Krishna Krishna Hari Hari Hari Rama Hari Rama Rama Rama Rama Hari Hari, singing easily and low for some time. It cleaned my senses a bit, very useful and felt good steadying influence as we drove out thru city. Varona reached for the car radio so I put my cymbals away.

"But exactly, can you tell me what is the purpose or reason? & why so suddenly?"

"We called for you last night but you weren't in."

"I was in Espin's house." Hoping that would surprise him—He didn't register.

"Well," I continued, "what about Czech visa—I want to stop over there and have business a book coming out work with translator have you arranged a visa"

"You can do it easily in Prague"

"Are you sure you're not making a mistake acting so rapidly without consulting the Casa?"

"We know what we're doing, as this is a Revolution we must do things quickly, we do lots of things rapidly." He smiled.

"Yes but on what exact basis are you kicking me out—it's an embarrassing situation for me *and* you—I admire your revolution and have sympathy basically and so am embarrassed to be"—He leaned back—"What's that?"

"I say I basically sympathize—basically—with your Revolution but a situation like this makes it difficult for both of us—In any case have you anything specific in my activities you are acting on, or what?"

"Respect for our Laws, compliance with our laws."

"But *what* laws"

"Cuban Laws"

"No I mean which specific laws"—

Cuba

"Oh just basic immigration policy . . . also a question of your private life . . . your personal attitudes"—

"What private life I haven't had much of that since I've been here" I laughed, so did he. "Too much public life."

I figured I still might talk him out of it by some inspired yak but—at this point they weren't going to look thru my papers apparently so—almost—glad excited to be going on—this too much nightmare here—and didn't want to beg, hypocritical—what truth to say?

"Especially are you sure you're not making a mistaken judgment on the basis of chismei (gossip)—I have heard much gossip exaggerated about myself"

"In that case it's not gossip because gossip is behind your back," he replied.

"I mean, Havana is a small town and full of exaggerated gossip"—

"Havana has more work to do than gossip. Havana is a serious place I'll have you understand. Do you understand?"

"Yes certainly but are you sure you're not mistaking rumor for real acts and kicking me out for nothing serious."

"We may be making a mistake."

"Well then why not take your time and discuss it with Haydee S."

"I called her—I am sure she will accept our decision. I have appointment with her at noon."

"What time plane leaves"

"10:30"

I sat back. Relieved really, it was only the airport, for Prague, not a jail or interrogation about the boys or pot or gossip or Che Guevara's narcissism from Argentina.

Arrived at airport filed thru to a waiting room office on the side—several soldiers guarding, going in out office, I sat in chair and opened my knapsack to pick out Ferlinghetti letter with Czech addresses and my address book—hoping they wouldn't get new ideas when I pulled thru papers and books. But it was already 10:15—

Passport arrived, a guard examined it and filled out a form—"Renodita?" "No—Poeta" I replied and he filled that in.

Outside waiting to go toward huge silver jetplane with CZECHOSLO-VAKIA painted along it liked the backbone of a fish—great gang of Czech visitors being greeted farewell—

Changed that pot 10 pesos for $ at air bank—saw cute eye-glass lawyer Icap fellow I'd given Whitman lecture to in Veradero. I waved goodbye—he was at entrance waiting for another delegation to arrive, the neurophysiologists?—coming next week?—"Looks like I'm being expulsado"—"Oh" he said?—"Goodbye"—"Ho!" I said back—

The milicanos standing waiting—to each other "I'm going to report you for this kidding," picking at an empty buttonhole on the uniform and then examining each other's relaxed uniforms for signs of sloppiness, an ill-tied shoelace here, a loose belt buckle there—and my knapsack with interest—same color as their uniform—"Aluminum," I said pointing the frame—"Too narrow" they criticized—"No good for a gordo or if you have wide hips"—I'd noticed that when I bought it.

Shook hands with them goodbye—walked out, silent and lone to the crowd of Czechoslovakians and got on plane—before entering turned around and waived at the Cuban soldiers waiting across the airfield. They waved back.

----

9 p.m.—Gander, Newfoundland—

Black Horizon dim cloud light uncanny is it Boreal aura?—Stretching out of the wingtip of the giant Czechoslovakian plane—a thin far display of city lights past the blinking airfield strange signals and red tower warnings—the boat rocking in the 90 [degree] snow waiting to

Cuba

run—Ah, move on, we're off to leave America again—over the ocean at last—to busy brown Prague—all of a sudden! To Prague? How? And here in Newfoundland today? What Hap, what laconic, what arrest, what jump, what hemispheres crisscross of a sudden like a Shakespearean dream? What new roar is this? O Bard, continue the tale of today! Blink! Blink! Blink! On the spot—jet power moving slowly to position to zoom speedy onward, a vast aereal donkey waiting to do.

I spoke to Peter on the phone an hour ago, my house is moved 5 streets away.[49]

There is no God but man see now hears now knows.

Cuban military, American military, Vietnam military—the world is a mountain of dogs!

Midnight on plane—had slept thru 6 hours Cuba–Newfoundland, delaying last chapter of this daily narrative—slight shock state left over—Vision of world of socialism and capitalism as a mountain of dogs—and what will happen to the poor boys, and all the poor souls of Cuba, or America-Vietnam—wherever there's military force or duress or poverty? Maria Rosa will she cry? And Manolo, will he cry and translate Kaddish this month? And what can I say to help the world?

49. Ginsberg's apartment building had been condemned by the city and Peter Orlovsky had moved their possessions to a new building a few blocks away.

Cuba

Red Square, Moscow, March 1965

Czechoslovakia

AND THE

Soviet Union

MARCH—APRIL 1965

Ginsberg flew to Czechoslovakia with the hope of finding a country less oppressive than he'd found in Cuba. In letters home, he admitted that he might have spoken too freely. "I committed about every 'infraction of totalitarian laws' I could think of, verbally, and they finally flipped out & gave me the bum's rush," he wrote his father. "It was half Kafkian & half funny."[1]

He promised himself to maintain a much lower profile in Czechoslovakia. As in Cuba, he was a guest of the country—he would be given excellent lodging and an honorarium that afforded him good walking cash—and in exchange, he told himself, he would shy away from interviews with the press and avoid making the kind of public pronouncements that had caused such trouble in Cuba. Early during his stay in Czechoslovakia, he learned that the Cuban press had announced that he had been expelled for smoking pot, and he'd been accused of bringing it into the country, supposedly to corrupt its youth. The false accusations angered Ginsberg, but he chose to remain silent, largely because he worried about the welfare of the young people with whom he'd been associating while in Cuba. As he'd learned, the government officials and police needed little reason to arrest youths they considered to be problematic.

Ginsberg enjoyed the time he spent in Prague. He discovered that he had celebrity status among the city's young people, and that the Beat Generation writers were highly regarded in the literary community. One particular café, the Viola, was especially receptive, and he was able to arrange a couple of readings that paid him enough, along with due royalty and performance fees, to realize his dream of a side trip to the Soviet Union. While arrangements for the trip were being made, he toured Prague, sightseeing and visiting museums, immersing himself in what he deemed to be a wonderful

1. Letter, Allen Ginsberg to Louis Ginsberg, n.d., circa March 1965.

old European culture. ("Prague lovelier in miniature than Paris almost," he wrote to his friend and publisher Lawrence Ferlinghetti.)[2] He made a point of visiting Kafka's home and grave site, and he found himself ruminating on the idea of the free spirit trapped in a totalitarian society. He inquired about day-to-day life, but he was cautious about the way he approached the subject until, in time, he felt confident enough to loosen up his talk and actions.

He kept up with his journal, recording his thoughts and new poetry, but, unfortunately, only fragments remain. As we will see later, he ran into trouble with the authorities once again, with similar results as in Cuba, and his journals were either stolen or confiscated and would never be returned. For the sake of continuity in the biographical narration of Ginsberg's trip, two letters, one written during the first leg of Ginsberg's stay in Czechoslovakia, the other written well after his departure, are being included, along with the brief extant writings, Ginsberg's interrupted attempt to record the events in his journal after the fact, and his later musings, including the first draft of "Kral Majales," one of his classics, an account of his expulsion from Czechoslovakia.

CZECHOSLOVAKIA

Nearly a month passed between Ginsberg's journal notation written while he was traveling to Czechoslovakia and the surviving fragments from his journal in the European country. The following is a portion of an undated letter that Ginsberg sent his father, Louis Ginsberg, sometime in March, packed with the generalizations and hyperbole typical of Allen's letters to his father.

2. Letter, Allen Ginsberg to Lawrence Ferlinghetti, n.d., circa March 1965.

Czechoslovakia

. . . Prague is absolutely beautiful. Old Medieval town, the Golem synagogue, weird castles and cathedrals, Kafka's homes—Kafka just published here this past few years after 15 years blackout—by that you can measure the winds of political change—I wrote Gene—Everyone here official & non-official complaints about the Horror of the '50s as if it were a nightmare. They're slowly working out of it. My visit seems to have done some good. Everybody here adores the Beatniks, & there's a whole generation of Prague teenagers who listen to jazz & wear long hair & say shit on communism & read *Howl*. I gave a reading at Charles Univ. (on the banks of Die Moddau river with big audience & answered all sorts of sex and brainwash questions. Food good middleeuropean soups & pork & knaedlich—I live in expensive Ambassador hotel at Writer's Union with expense & my picture's in all the literary supplements with long strange explanations about marijuana & LSD and Hari Om Namo Shiva Indian mantras—and I run around with teenage gangs and have orgies & then rush up to Writer's Union & give lectures on the glories of U.S. pornography Henry Miller etc. All very happy— Love to you—

I'll send you card from Moscow.

Love
Allen

Mon. 15th—All afternoon in café with Jan Zabrana correcting images in his Czech head from text of Kaddish—

At 5 p.m. w/Peter Shelphi & gang young girls & boys to cellar on outskirts of Prague, we all read poems in room hung with fencing masks, a coal stove, old sofa, huge burlesque bass fiddle box filled with vodka bottles & aluminum foil—the upstairs neighbors come down to complain, only 4 were allowed to use the Mimeo Mag office—threatened to call police—But all 20 of us stayed & took photos & then read then to

Czechoslovakia

At the window of Hotel Ambassador,
overlooking Wenceslas Square in Prague

tramcar walking, again misty smog grime cobble streets—red tram
came took us downtown Prague, a girl's house, vodka & wine & we
played truth game ala Dostoyevsky—a dozen of us, I was horny so pro-
posed, "Who each will tell who how many he she would embrace with
orgazim in this drunk room"—and we went round the table—everybody
loved 2 or 3, I loved almost all—

Drunk we walked out & sneaked into family apartment of 1880's
fuzzy bearded blond Johnine friend of Pauline, & all our clothes off in
small singlebed room with 3 am door locked away from family which
had to wake to go tailor shop at dawn—Pauline I saw a real naked pink
well formed Ganymede boy with baby skin on thighs & fair belly—three
of us naked in the bed all night made love & slept & woke & made love—
I blow Paul & this time he sighed & came—his cock a rough even under
the neck of head—but so overwhelmed by his open heart a youth wrig-
gling I was happy old beard—

Morn woke & embraced some more, it was noon, time to go, I
climbed on top of him & moistened my cock with saliva & screwed him
came fast between thighs had waited all nite—then we looked for clothes
and snaked out all misty eyed, without being seen & into snowy down-
town street, & walked thru vast grey Wenceyas filled with tramcars &
stores & noontime crowds kissing & saying, "ahoy!" on the fine black
street saliva—grime—to hotel, all three of us washed, & they went off,
they said, to hitchhike thru Slovakia & Moravia—we cried "ahoy"—in
the sad youthful tone of voice of a dancehall movie. Yesterday.

March 16—All morn in & Cedok arranging perfectly Visas & tickets &
dollars & Intourist coupons. At hotel, boy from Korlov baths was wait-
ing, and soon Peter S—I had made too many love dates—so said goodbye
to both, I had Arbeit work, upstairs wrote letters, then worked with

Iabrana translating—then to night party & talked & danced till 2 am—
publisher's cocktail, buy your own liquor from the bar—a roundup of all
the mature types I met—Eva K. & ———, and new poets & novelists—

Mar. 17—Well it's all mixed up I also went to Semaphore Club & met
sophisticated nite club types one night, at their house, we gossiped
about Dali—then went to Alpha Café & saw Amateur Contest, & one
cheery Peter Black. Peter kid sd/ "May I be your son?"—Says all youth
admires America Freedom, Cowboys, Jazz, Movies—Believe in Social-
ism?—This is a political question—No!—nobody does—"I work morn
sleep in afternoon, dance at nite, and that's my life—I don't think about
future—"

All youth here in Czech wants to travel—Czech's too small to be an
education. No can travel so feels hopeless closed in.

They were dancing a delicate hully-gully—hands up & hands clasped
& pelvis moved by magic, eyes in the distance—one tall boy looked
straight at the girl and hissed gentle intelligent directions, how she
should whirl.

Then I go to Viola, & drank a very little drew pix signed autographs,
a boy tried to take me to an old artist poet's apartment to sleep "We all
love you"—but I went to hotel & slept instead.

No dreams remembered late.

Czechoslovakia

SOVIET UNION

Ginsberg's interest in Russia dated back to his boyhood, when his mother, Naomi Ginsberg, told Allen and Eugene harrowing tales of the persecution of Jews in rural Russia, the events including stories of the pogroms and Cossacks charging on horses through terrified villages. Naomi had come to the United States as a young girl, so naive that she was afraid to eat tomatoes for fear they might be poisonous. Both she and her husband, Louis, had grown up to be schoolteachers, and while Louis also had a deep Russian background, he and Naomi would quarrel bitterly over politics: Louis was an avowed socialist, Naomi a communist. As Allen would recall in his poem "America," he accompanied his mother to Communist Party meetings in New Jersey, and every other summer the family would vacation at a communist camp in upstate New York. Allen inherited his interests in radical politics from his mother.

As it turned out, Allen had relatives still living in the Soviet Union, including a cousin, Joe Levy, on Naomi's side of the family. Louis mailed Allen Joe and Anne Levy's home address, and Allen designated a visit as one of the most important stops on his trip.

But this was only the beginning. Allen had a strong appreciation of Russian literature, particularly for novelist Fyodor Dostoyevsky, poet Vladimir Mayakovsky, and Ginsberg contemporaries Yevgeny Yevtushenko and Andrei Voznesensky. Not surprisingly, he held a keen interest in dissident voices. He hoped that a trip to the Soviet Union would give him occasion to meet some of these figures. He also figured to fill his hours with visits to art museums, the Kremlin (and Lenin's open mausoleum), and, if time permitted, a side trip to Leningrad. He regretted that Peter Orlovsky, who had come from a strong Russian background, was not with him to take in so much of his cultural heritage.

The trip required every bit of Ginsberg's prodigious energy and ability to live on the cheap. He would be traveling with his leftover Czech money and would have to move more quickly than he preferred. Fortunately, when his time in the country was running

Soviet Union

out, Soviet officials decided to take him in as a cultural guest, which meant additional lodging and money, and he was able to extend his visit

He knew none of this, of course, when he caught a train and headed eastward, his attention captivated by the sight of the rural countryside speeding by.

March 18, 1965—3:58 p.m. on train Prague–Moscow—late afternoon in compartment with Czech military attaches, travelling rocking thru sunlight by the river Elbe—Hares in the fields, a warm day, the snow of black Prague streets melted in green winter fields, many stands of tall disciplined trees; a brown landscape thru which Elbe flows to empty into N Sea? at Hamburg—

9 p.m. March 18—
Night, I am approaching the house.
The 4 czars, Stalin are in hidden tombs—
A full orange moon, the snowy fields
        of Moravia, the Carpathian
        mountains ahead at 12 o'clock—
At dawn, the Russian border. In the
        compartment of a train
one hundred years ago Prince Myshkin
        stared at the black hair and white
                eyeballs of Rogoyin—
At the end of the book, in the funereal
        apartment, by candlelight,
the corpse of Rogoyin and Myshkin
        sobbing like a baby—

Soviet Union

"Nikolay, Nikolay, how can we
      forget you?"
My Slavic Soul, we are coming home again—
once more on Red Square by Kremlin wall
      in the snow to sit and write Prophesy—
Prince-Comrades of Russia, I have
      come from America to lay my beard
      at your beautiful feet!
                          Trembling
in the Railway Station, amazed at the
      great red train Moscova–Prague—
The train doors open to the corridor—
      A Sealed train—Lenin was a trained
            Seal—
I'll trade you one diamond Sutra
      for 2 Communist Manifestos—
      I am approaching the throne.

March 19
      Carpathian villages, snow patches—pink mist, later thatch cottages—
Cop (chop) bordertown at dawn—I walked around an hour till I came
to end of Chagall lane and pissed on an earth bank overlooking icy pool
& trees & fields—ducks in the stream—chicken in the wet road—
      and wouldn't change my state for all the mud in Svov—Jacked off in
R.R. car can before reached Svov—tightening my buttocks muscles,
flashback to Cuba & Manolo, and back 25 years to Haledon Avenue
bending over in dream to be spanked by playmates for telling a lie about
the roof of a chickencoop. Dr. Mahler, my teeth stained, I speak a few
German words, Donald spracht Deutch for Medical school, I never got

Soviet Union

to the circus from my cellar door—Not for all the mud in Svov. Everything turns out to be prophetic 25 years too late, life has a meaning but you don't find that out till it's all over. Elanor & Max,[3] thou shouldst be living at this hour! The train rocks forward thru the snow patches toward Kiev. Mud roads. Black fields. Landscape rolling small flat hills between Svov & Kiev. Horses in distance drawing sleighs thru mud. Isolated houses, figures in black clothes walking up snowy roads thru fields. Women shoveling dirt, in black boots. Police with long 19th century coats & epaulettes Svov cathedral in the distance from the R.R station. A country church, bulb-topped & brown shingled. Dark falling over the trees & snow, in mist. Vast space past Svov. Tea in glasses with lots of sugar, from the lady porter. We went past her room on way to diner to ask her to lock up our cabin—She was lying in bed with hand on thigh of other middleage lady conductor. Fitful sleep all night. Morn.

March 20—Birch mixed with pine, snow flat land, woke tranquil—No more hymn singing. Wooden houses, picket fences. Sleigh carts & men wrapped in ragged thick coats & fur hats. Old green box cars. White sky the color of dirty snow by the railroad tracks. Low grey houses in dead stillness, the mud roads frozen over. Snow everywhere to the horizon. Woodsheds, outhouses.

Shoveling snow into trucks—woodpiles & lumberyards, great blocks of white concrete piled up in the snow. Flocks of black crows. A furry horse—Frozen rivers with footprints trailed upstream. Iron towers for high tension wires, small in the broken fields. Roads of slush leading nowhere visible. Slow sloupy lesbian music lady voices singing on train radio—10: a.m—Men in fur hats in the distance, workmen's padded blue

3. Elanor and Max Frohman, Ginsberg's maternal aunt and uncle.

Soviet Union

coats, walking past morning railroad stations. White smoke out of a brick chimney, rare Brick pine woods on either side of the track. White hill-field beyond that sun thru a road path cut in the woods, a mile away. Train gliding slowly now, uphill, second day out. Yesterday I half slept thru Carpathia Telegraph poles all the way 1765 km from cop (chop) border to Moscow. Moscow—Ulan Bator 6304 km 138 hr 20 min II class 40r. ($50 official exchange)—Moscow Peking 8924 km. II class 70 rubles, 159 hours 58 min. In the wilderness, a huge factory surrounded by village of small orange brick houses, & a railroad spur leading in. Watertowers like in Cezanne. Settlements of Ch. Chaplin Alaska—snow mad streets, picket fences, clusters & rows of peaked houses: more forests of birch 2 ½ hours more to Moscow. Women in shawls, black coats, pants & boots, carrying lunch boxes.

Log cabins in old rows along muddy sleigh paths near provincial railway stations. 2 Man Rocket BOCXOA=2 up yesterday down safe today, voices on the train Muzak system piped into our compartment.

Military-diplomatic attaché in upper berth, speaking Eng Czech & Russ—had also been to China & Pyougyang 7 days by railroad, years ago—"I suppose you are sympathetic to the people's government?"—"I hate all government." He bought me cognac in the dining car, and was vague about China.

A big railroad yard—a long train—wood, tree-poles, autos, coal cars, tractor carrying flatcar, more wood. Big fat women holding flags at R.R. crossing A man standing in the field pissing in the snow, more lumberyards. A house on a hill, a TV antenna, a smokestack nearby. Like the worst of New Jersey on a cold winter white day filed with frost and smog near the Erie, around Garret Mt.

The train compartment mahogany brown & smooth & clean & shiny, perfectly built, a faucet & basin collapsible with the wall panel blue velvet curtains. Great piles of wood, huge pipes, iron trusses, along the way

Soviet Union

Woodsheds. Little square backyards enclosed by wooden picket fences sticking out of the snow. Late this afternoon I'll see Red Squ. Big green passenger cars along the siding A motorcycle with sidecar riding on hard road parallel the train, rider in black fur hat & black coat boots

50 km to Moscow. More wood houses, factories a shell of a church, the orange turret-skull where the dome was bombed out or rotted off. The Germans got this far. Bungalows in the woods, a small fire in the encampment—parasol covered with snow. Everybody looks like a rabbi walking in the white patches of earth. A boxcar marked Roumania. Brown black dirt turned over by bulldozers here & there, & left for the winter?

First smell of Russia at Chop was, surprisingly, the same musty-shit-earth smell as Mexico tropic.

Outskirts of Moscow—many small wood houses like summer bungalows in Belmar, fenced in the snow. Workmen & workwomen padded clothes with huge shovels on shoulders walking along railroad track. Train gliding very slowly. Light music on the piped-in speaker. La La La was this Pasternak's[4] house? Did Voznesensky walk thru the slush by the railroad tracks to get to this fence & in this door? The one with the checkerboard white/black painted wood posts? Like old house on River St. Paterson—the woman waist deep in snow, shoveling.

"I sing the body electric"—said Finkey on the street in Prague. Military girls chorus on intercom.

Oh! There in the white distance the great Oriental 1930's spires of Moscow University—Slavic huge aspiration like ancient fortresses cathedrals spread out in the snow—vast wings with inferior spires, and a

4. Boris Pasternak (1890–1960), Russian poet and novelist, author of *Doctor Zhivago*, winner of 1958 Nobel Prize for Literature.

Soviet Union

central pinnacle topped with tiny emblem—surrounded by huge flat blocks of brown apartment houses—Ukraine Hotel looking like Slavic Woolworth bldg. Time to pack & leave. At rest.

March 20—Nite 7 p.m.—Main Dr.—Popoff-Looe Cure Circus—Moscow —bright ring—Barker—"How our art is loved by the Soviet People"— "right to relaxation after work"—Lesbian girls in blue tights climbing around high wire to oldfashioned Cha Cha Cha jazz—the great red plush box empty—Popoff—check hat cap, black velvet single giant pearl button coat, green vest, white shirt, red tie, yellow striped black pants, red sox, black & white spats shoes, yellow hair, red lips, bulb nose—

Lady acrobat in Ukraine dress almost Tibetan in headdress color style—flowers in crown—

Long hot nite in the amphitheater—comedy jokes so broad as to be archetype—exploding electro encephalographs—giant syringe & needles—sports perfection of young & old like olympics robots—men balancing on each other's heads—very queer rapport all unexpressed except for slow deliberate looks between performers—stolid Russian Uncle Sam pharmacist audience—The lion drinking vodka—Trained baby bears—slavering—rhythmic clap of hands for applause—clap-clap-clap—

After midnight,
    the red brick Kremlin wall, old bells,
    deep red electric stars stop the
    Ruby gate peaks,
    the golden clock moves slowly,
bootsteps echo on the vast black
        lawn of cobblestone,

Soviet Union

Lovers in the giant spotlights
eyeing on Red Square
from Gum's ghostly roof
    cling & laugh & escape
        into the shadow
           of a square red
                Tomb,
    shining marble that will stand
      1000 years—The Bells
of the tower, shouts from the
      end of the square where ant sized
        men cross Asia—
Two guards at the gate of
    Lenin's mausoleum—Stolid
    and robot—
a friend passes, piano Clankin
    on transistor in his pocket—
    The shiver of space, over St. Basil's
      myriad small domes peaked
      with lightning rod
rests at the end of the old
      picture—now I button it,
    afraid, afraid of these
    old dream walls from movies
      newspapers, postcards
    old dream walls of ancient
    celluloid—
This place that thinks it is in the
    center of Eternity—

Soviet Union

Behind my back a red Victorian
    Gothic museum like the hateful
        grammar schools of
          New Jersey—
This is the museum of man!

Red Square, you powerful,
    you robot time machine,
Standing still at the gate
    of Asia, Doorway into
        Siberia,
Flytrap of poets, idiot Bangkok
          wedding cake—
Fuck you, who the fuck are you?

       Boom!
St. Basil's wants to make
    Me groan om om!

Mar. 20—2 a.m.

Met at station by Romanova, looking greyer thinner older & more sinister. She kept looking at me from below tilting head aside—& taxi to Minsk hotel modern glassbrick & small rooms—no rugs here—as at all Intourist provincial offices & Prague Embassy there were threadbare old rugs overlapping each other on the floor.

The Writer's Union—restaurant entrance a huge preWorld War door, solid & worn—into high chub room, giant aristocratic chandelier, old mahogany balconies and alcoves—we took a table behind a carved black wooden pillar—ate Borsht & smoked salmon & caviar & vodka &

Soviet Union

steak and talked—I explained briefly, haltingly, what happened in Cuba, so as to warn them—Frieda Lurie[5] & Ylena Romonova & later K. Simonoff—"you will stay here awhile," said Frieda "but let me advise you that we have an experience—the war—and a different life, so that certain things are best not spoken about—especially to journalists—people don't/won't understand. We hope you'll come to see our point of view, our people . . ."

"I took my job (head of literature of Western Socialist countries) because I believe our system will spread—and being a Romonoff—I wanted to spread my power"—laughed Ylena, heavy humored. I tried to laugh.

"A word of advice" from Simonoff [sic, should be Simonov]. "I guess you've come to Moscow with clean hands—after a month in Prague—best not talk to anyone about homosexuality—"

"We all have a—normal—love life here," said Frieda. "Russians may not appreciate your interests, though possibly you may have some truth or some valuable opinion. . . , still, your proposal to be silent & watch is best . . ."

Stayed late till 5 drinking with Ylena, feeling her out, still a block, no relax, no trust entire, she has opinions, as Frieda—I was describing bad effect of Thaikovsky's put down of Henry Miller's literary quality—& was surprised to hear Frieda say, "Well I could not finish the book . . . it wasn't interesting . . . There are so many books . . . the Russian people would not have interest in such thing"—

Ylena "We have a long history—of happy love—or of deep private affairs—we are all people of some experience—but we don't talk about it in public . . . We find those who talk most are the people least sexually satisfied . . . There's no reason to write about such things."

5. Ginsberg's Soviet escort.

Soviet Union

I explained various reasons & "Well, after all it's part of dramatic novel life" etc. but she merely eyed me in sly maternal way that made me want to scream at her. I didn't want to stay on a month here.

Then walking in thru Kremlin estate—the surprise of the 16th century vastness—the mediaeval fortress still in postatomic operation, offices and central bureaus there with the formal front of the old Feudal shield & wall and turret & clock & gold onion dome and peaked gate keep solid as Bronx Park Zoo right in the middle of Moscow—and the spaciousness—as if all the steppes of a Siberia & Asiatic vague immensities were on display in the Central Powerhouse Castle—Capitol of the Future Spacy Universe Nation—huge walks in thru gate, fields with palaces and old cathedrals, a 16th century iron-embroidered cannon—I felt like a provincial from Pinsk or Magnitogorsk, seeing the Worlds Fair Ancient Center.

Then to hotel, met girl guide with snow-bird hat, dull girl, to the Circus (see previous pages)—to walk past Mayakovsky Statue looking for coffeehouse of young, which was closed—She left & I walked down to National Hotel to eat, lox & sturgeon & milk—and waitress kept 30 tip—and then toward Midnight thru vast Red Square again—by Kremlin walls, by soldiers at gate of Lenin tomb, black & white marble, smaller than I thought, but perfect in size related to the Kremlin wall & centered properly so it'll always be a jewel in the plaza—like Saint Mark's Sq. in Venice the beauty of this whole field of walls, Oniondome Church—Basil is almost as beautiful as Taj Mahal—so *many* domes and cones on it, strange endless gingerbread like a great Fun House at Coney Island—

I walked past laughing roaming couples, who screamed in street & necked near bus stop—to the river, halfway crost bridge & sang om, turned back, hoping to talk—but alone, crossed red square & sat down on a board plank, to write.

Soviet Union

A huge height of crane perched in front of Basil's domes.

Sleepy.

Amazing feeling about Kremlin Tomb Square—each time a space time sense—Monolithic Power, Easter space central station.

Mar. 21, 8 a.m.

Dream—Bloody thrones?

Dragons? Forgot.

And to bring a toothbrush—my gums giving away.

Yesterday on Red Square, approaching Lenin's tomb, the awe of the place at last, walking with Romanova toward the crowd standing around the railing before the closed door—so I asked her "Where's Stalin now?" she said "somewhere in the wall." "Can you visit his tomb?"—"I never visit Stalin!" she laughed. "And what did you think while he was alive?"—"Many, many of my friends disappeared—but I did not know what was happening—we just knew they were gone, and were told that they had committed crimes, but—I believed what I was explained, that perhaps they had done something but I did not know— I was shocked when I found out—"

Earlier at restaurant asked about censorship board—"The Goloyov Board"—same as Czech HSTD—*Who* is it? "It is not well known."

Simonov at table with black turtleneck shirt & handsome silver gray hair, all of them discussing my Cuban experience with familiar slightly hearty cynical smiles of old schoolteachers at Central H.S. Paterson talking about the foibles of the principal—an old story, how to survive.

At tables in the room, groups of middleaged waiters—"Who's she?"— I pointed to a thin faced lady covering her eyes—"She's a critic"—an older looking, short bohemian-Jewish faced chap came up, thin haired

Soviet Union

& a wen on third eye forehead, & kissed Romanova's hand—"That's David Samwelloff"—"You see, he is only 40 years old, but he was in the war—in the war each month counted a year—you can see in his face— That's a difference between you Americans and our experience, you must understand—" said Frieda.

"I hope we will be able to meet soon and I will give you advice how to be here—so that you will understand—certain things here are not the same as America—some things you are interested are not interesting to our people."

10:30 a.m.—In Gum's Vast open hall with balconies, catwalks, arcades, all cream colored, with iron grillwork—crystal palace roof, hundreds of squares of grass, blocks long—I'll meet you after the Cold War by the Fountain at Gum's—under the glass dome—the red marble fountain where fur hatted, black coat Muscovites wait for their families—a gang of young boys in sharp black fur collar jackets, & fur caps standing around—everybody else in caps like Mayakovsky—shopping in little booths crowded so you can't get to the counter easy, & a woman's voice— soft & sepulchral coming over the public address system, lecturing on Gloves?—vast 19th century palace open inside with dozens of stairways and Paranesi light perspectives filled with cosmetic boutiques.

[...]

March 21—Evening

Morn to the Square. Gums (described a bit previous then on tour with a Rabbi from Bronx & a tea merchant from Hong Kong & their wives—tour of Kremlin grounds—all of us amazed to see Shirley Temple in the Kremlin—Great richness of jewelry—all that—Hence to the long line on red square waiting for Lenin's tomb, I scribbled all the way— Kremlin wall not directly on Square as I thought, but separated by small

Soviet Union

garden to tombs—Krupshays I s'pose—then caught bus back to hotel & waited in lobby for cousin J.[6]—He came in hesitated & walked to me, I said "J?"—and we sat down and talked— the history of Naomi's family emigration from Russia, I got straight for the first time. Naomi was from Nevel near Vitebsk, a small town—all the family from nearby there, villages—J now 72 years old—so it seemed, in 1904 the Russ Jap war was the beginning of it all including me—Naomi's father had four children and a weak wife, she was silent and very lovely & physically delicate—"never very strong"—and he was to be drafted to fite the Japs, which he didn't want to do for the Czar—

The news broadcast meanwhile tonite 12 pm continues with Viet-Nam—

So he moved his whole family into J.'s family house—a small 2 room cabin in the town of Vitebsk—living 5 from my mother's family, and any number of his—my Bronx cousins Morris and Max the dentist, and J. and sister Nadia still living in the Bronx today—And the 5 from my mother's family were Sam and Max the pharmacist from California, Sam dead now 5 years, Max lives (whom I saw on my way to San Francisco in '53) in Riverside—and dear Elanor, and Naomi herself and her mother, of whom no picture survives. And they were all cousins—the mother of J. and the mother of Naomi sisters—and also of J's wife, the mother another sister—they were all cousins—and of J's wife alive in Moscow—There were also many sisters and brothers I knew—Elanor's accountant Max, with whom I wept in the Bronx in 1961—and Edie with whom Naomi lived in the same apartment on Rochambeau Avenue—Edie who worked in Gimbels—

The Kremlin bells are tolling on the radio midnite Moscow—and the

6. To protect his cousin Joe's identity in the event of the loss of his journal, Ginsberg used initials for Joe and Anne Levy.

Soviet Union

new Soviet anthem—Da dum da da dum—I light a long cardboard fil-
tered Bebop Kasha cigarette—and now Tchaikovsky violins—I began to
see the dream life of the past flit by—

They were all cousins—and Memele, my maternal grandfather, who
didn't want to fite the Czar, went off to America thru [?] (he bribed his
way out) in company with J's father—And Memele got to Ellis Island,
and was admitted, while J's father was rejected in 1904, he had a bald
spot on his head suspected to be woeful or diseased—so he went to Lon-
don, thence thru friends after a year to Canada, and both boys of 1905
sent ship tickets to the family, so Naomi's mother & sisters and baby
brothers arrived in New York, and the Frohmans arrived in Canada,
and that's why, and in 1920 moved to New York. And some came across
in 1907 because they had been in jail for revolutionary activities—one
of the girls was in a meeting in the woods, they were surrounded &
caught—in jail for a year and out on probation, so came to America—
and I alone will someday know the ghost of this tale—

As we looked at old photograph album—For J & A stayed in Amer-
ica.

[From] 1920 till 1931—He worked for $4 a week in a laundry, then
in a grocery, then studied mechanics or electricity and made $7 a week
—and hid out during World War I, hid out in Newark with Naomi's
family—the Debs socialists opposed the war, till late, then orders were
to carry on organization in the army, so he went to draft bd. & said he'd
been working in another city "In other words I got away with it"—and
in 1920 after he got back from France—"It was there I learned how ter-
rible the war, everyone should experience it can't be talked about"—the
Com Party US was organized and they all joined—

And in 1931 a whole gang of 30 friends went back to visit Russia, "we
had some money"—and J & A stayed, tho A. came back to get the fur-
niture—it's all still there in their room, an apartment they shared with

3 other families the kitchen—they have no children—but the old 1922 Victrola, with Caruso and [?] records is—and the bed they brought over, and the huge Chinese vase they got for getting married, all the brothers & sisters chipped in—40 years later in Sokolniki I saw it all—and the photo album—Beaver Soap Co. Winnipeg the boss & secretaries where A. worked—1917 photos, the whole gang of kids in front of a tent on City Island—they had a tent & boat—and Uncle Max of the Mustache was there, looking like roué, Elanor on the beach with sick smile and funny nose, looking down sideways, and the Max & Morris dentist older brothers, and all N's Canadian girlfriends—and the I L D Bazaar of 1920 with the girls sitting under old purses in America, working for the revolution—

Chopin on the radio piano now—it's all too beautiful, these dolls faded into death—And the old picture of myself as a sexy little four year old in shorts with a thin belly—and Eugene with 10 yr, old glasses looking painful and shy & thin—and Louis & Naomi in the 20's, he with teacher's mustache & she of the 30's I don't remember, perhaps sitting below him in tennis clothes—and early photos of Maxes and Morrises, and Edie of Bronx singing by the ocean "The Nightingale" it was labeled—and another cousin Rose, early, before she had her retarded son that Naomi later lived with—and more photographs, other cousins still alive in Russia, Max from Riverside, Max's daughter, and her husband, and Stella & Eugene Berlen red lipt incompetent who didn't wait to be a watchmaker like his papa—now married with kids, once a friend to my brother Eugene—and later photos in color, all the dentists and their daughters in 1960's dresses for marriage, the grandchildren—till finally the last photos a boy & girl of 1904 or 1917 or my own self & Eugene in Newark in 1933, The expression the sad tragic aloneness never changes in half a century, surviving them the unknown descendants—A. & I were

Soviet Union

sad and tears rolled down our cheeks as we came to the end, the last pictures of the unknown newly grown children in America—

A & J have no kids, on the street I asked him "Should I"—"Everyone should" why "you need someone close to talk to when you grow older—It's not too late for you, you're still young"—

All evening also we talked of Russia, he "Beria was working for Scotland Yard"—"The collective heart is the most important thing about Communism"—A. was more dubious than he about his senile affirmation of Russia—He pointed to Danny [?], who went to Drama School & couldn't succeed as an actor, as example of capitalism's worst—Danny now in Africa teaching drama—

And we rode there on Moscow subway, very beautiful marble solidity station after station—J. proud, when he came here 1931 he worked as electrician on these very subway stops—I'd thought the subway was a myth, only one or 2 splendid stations, but *all* the stations were spacious clean palaces—and really clean—like giant hotel lavatories of marble, real 19th–20th cent. Russian style, lovely.

Old houses in Schoniki, from Dostoyevsky's day, wood-work frills & little gables on one & two story country houses of that day—now being torn down for apartments—all of Moscow still low, like a giant village—He said in 1931 all round Red Sq. neighborhood was village houses with peasants & horse carts selling vegetables "They still had that kind of business then"—the subway 5 kopeks and thru an electric eye no turnstyle except if you don't put in 5 kopeks the bars spring out to stop you—hit you in the balls and A—"I worked on the radio, as a secretary—people were disappearing, in jail, & they said they were committing anti-state crimes—I didn't know what, I believed it"—and J—"Beria came to Stalin & told him & Stalin believed him. Scotland Yard, Khrushchev announced it, everybody knows"—

Soviet Union

A. kept correcting him here & there—about the Jews—Beria did it to discredit communism—"That's what ruined the Party in America."

I sang them Hari Krishna & Hari om Namo Shiva—A. had said she liked Indian music—& he took me home on subway to Prosperi near Red Sq. "That kind of singing doesn't seem to have effect here" he said tentatively. I wondered what they felt. Home, & up to the coffeehouse *Youth* which second nite in row at 10:30 p.m. I couldn't get in—overcrowded with poetry dancers, or just about to close up. So home washed dripdry blue shirt from Harvard Coop & wrote this sad tale.

Monday 5 a.m–7 a.m. March 22

Dream: Big country house with many rooms & beds—we are exploring. It's like a false-front house very well built, room after room—for a Fair (World's) perhaps, like the piece of Moscow Subway at the World's Fair 1939—down through one bedroom after another, into the big kitchen, & that's the end of the exhibit—oh!—another door I open, it's dark with steps down, it looks like it might be unfinished or just a shell, with no floor—in fact bottomless, better not set foot inside—I find a lightswitch by the door and turn it on, it's a room with floor, like a phonograph library room, with door at other end too—my companion goes on ahead of me, we enter and cross over, nice room in this Disney land—out the other side.

Time to go to bed, we've all taken showers, me and several familiar youths—one I'm going to sleep with. Cousin Joel 10 years ago?—the other doesn't like the idea, a tall blond football player, maybe the blond kid from Harvard—and the tall boy from Kerista that I once did lay down with, it's time for everyone to find his bed, in the different rooms. Kerista boy is waiting naked under the covers, I'm supposed to lie down with him, tho the other blond player in shower was joking sort of seri-

Soviet Union

ously to leave *him* alone—and a third boy on another bed, I'm not sure—
I like all of them & feel attracted, want to hold them all—but got to make
choice, easiest, Kerista waiting for me, yet I pass by Harvard blond bed,
he's not in his bed, I go into next room, Lo & behold the two youth boys
are in bed together, laughing, waiting for me—they move aside so I can
lie down in the middle "We'll give you a good time"—a very happy scene,
all laughing—I lay down, Kerista throwing covers aside for me & bend-
ing his legs up athletically, showing his buttocks—actually friendly
scene—

I wake up, it's grey Moscow morn, as per conversation with Siminov,
I will be silent on this subject here in Moscow and see what happens &
who loves, odd to have so strong a dream morning & prophesy—they
were all like big red blond soldiers in the dream Russian soldiers?

Occasionally, walking the street, I get effeminate mocking catcalls
from men passerby, for my long hair & little like the meaner side of
America.

Morning

"Scientists Research Work"—critical &—the whole set—of articles
books studies, in the Dostoyevsky Museum—photocopies of his mss. like
collages, crisscrossed with side notes, marginal additions, a paradigm
of scenes with fragments of conversation—a *kind* of composition. His
desk his inkwell his photos his first editions his furniture from the Poor
Hospital in Moscow his bookcase from Petersburg his last newspaper
his death Mask—sunk in eyes & giant cheekbones and bony forehead
His wife kept records of his memorabilia.

Central restaurant on Gorky St.—old 19th Century Gilt—

Soviet Union

Later drunk, & went to opening of an artist's show, with speeches, describing how the painter was shunted aside in the 30's, died in '39—now finally by the Chief of Club des Artistes M.—given a private exhibition—

Thence downstairs where I met the wife and self of Vladimir——, as well as son of Novelist X—who, Indonesian scholar, spoke English, and we after paint show, sat and vodka & wine, and into restaurant where I jested with Nekrasov and Kayakov—upstairs to pee, and on way downstairs, I met a handsome bright-eyed blond, who said "Yo soy Yevtushenko"[7]—I kneeled to touch his knees and he stopt me, so tall and handsome I was surprised, since I understood he had pneumonia, but this was his first day out of bed—with vertigo—we spoke Spanish—"I love you" I said. He had slight blond hair and tall body, and striped suit & pants—I kept touching him & saluting him, I wanted him to understand that I admired his nose & hair and mouth & self—but he had friends to talk to—I pissed and went back to table, he came too, we agreed to meet tomorrow night, I was pleased how beautiful his face & blond hair brushed over his brow, short. We talked in Cuban-Spanish. I told him I was kicked out "Yo fue botado de Cuba" and explained why. I can't remember the whole evening except Nekrasov saluting his beauty, and myself kneeling at his waist, he lifted me up from his feet I told him I admired his mythology I will try to remember more in the Morn.

He was tall, and despite sickness, on first day, he came out to meet me in the Club, and I thought him perfect for role of blond true prophet man 1965.

7. Yevgeny Yevtushenko (1932–2017), Russian poet, perhaps the most popular in the Soviet Union at the time of Ginsberg's visit.

Soviet Union

23 March Morning

Woke hungover—ate & then long walk thru streets to Writer's Union—

Big talk with Frieda Lurie, same as with Edmondo in Cuba—She warning me not to make a big issue of Brodsky[8] in Leningrad—"There are differences between our countries—your interest will not be understood." A long brainwash talk about what is "good" for life & what is "bad"—"for the people."

They see me as a foreigner.

Then thru crowds and police lines on Gorki St.—huge files of people, mostly smiling but very silent—we joined them, walking in the "demonstration" occasionally a gang with flags running past the buildings decked with flags—showed pass to "Tribunes" to 2 dozen different rows of police lines, finally under the street in metro passageway, now empty except for stray police walking—finally out into the museum streets leading into Red Square—the crowd in warm sunny air—fur hats & hundreds of thousands of Mayokovsky caps—rivers of traffic within the messy block of heads—three vast banners on the front of Gum, red, one of factories & futuristic rockets flying upward from Earth, another huge face of Lenin with brown mustache, that characteristic idealized pose, looking straight at his mausoleum, the last on old and young worker in Firered (Tibetan color, Asiatic red) with yellow sputnik flames travelling over the heads—the bright blue-gold domes of St Basil's at the other end, the central spire almost has eyes like Nepalese temple—

A flagpole with red star in front of the yellow "war house," and many red banners in the crowd.

8. Joseph Brodsky (1940–1996), Russian poet and essayist (and winner of the Nobel Prize for Literature in 1987), ran afoul of Communist authorities for his rebellious, outspoken work and served eighteen months of hard labor in a work camp.

Soviet Union

The file of politicians—walk out on the steps of the mausoleum, led by Astronauts in grey uniform waving a hand listlessly—a shout roar but not from the crowd—out of loud-speakers perched on the Kremlin wall, dozens of them in the gun emplacements, noise of shouting crowds— maybe from near the stand picked up by the mikes—one would not *want* to be there—up on the stand with all that responsibility for the Universe. Children with flowers follow the line ascending Lenin tomb steps.

I stood on the tribune concrete dividing row-steps and watched over the huge crowd—several speeches, both astronauts saluting the central committee of the party—under the huge sky open above Red Square, clouds floating by—thanking them for giving them chance to take part in this great "experiment" first men opening door & walking into space —Bent my head to listen a little Nina girl's translation of speeches—one astronaut in youthful voice saluted everybody. The crowd had been silent, waiting, while the leaders filed up to podium-balcony—crowd of TV cameras and movie trucks pointed up at them right in front of mausoleum—and there was silence, then into the microphone was one Brezhnev said "well, we might as well begin the meeting" and crowd laughed It was conducted in the form of a union meeting "I now declare this meeting open." Much talk about Soviet achievement, Communist achievement, Communist science, realization of Lenin's dreams.

Then to Tretsjahov gallery—room after room of obscene fustian 19th century style painting—some very beautiful time capsules—one self-portrait of beautiful man who'd painted life picture of Pushkin. and display of mystic Ikons.

Home 6:30 & Alexei Caeso (they call him Alyosha) took me by subway to serodrome stop of Yevtushenko's house—an old modern apartment bldg. in area where streets not finished—a few old wooden houses still standing—we sat on steps & talked, "Genia" not yet home—I found

Soviet Union

it hard to explain myself—A silence on the stage, I'd been sounding him down about Lurie's advice to me—did he agree?—No—it's just her opinion that sounds official.

Yevtushenko's door with 5 or six old keyholes for locks, and the outside padded—He arrived on elevator in big fur-smooth coat, very tall—apologizing for being late—He was at Georgian restaurant, his wife was there, and Aksin all of them drunk with theater people—we entered & he took my coat, helping me take it off—went into kitchen & he gave me kitchen soup, we talked—"You were very drunk last night" he said. I hadn't remembered much of our conversation of last nite. Still I'm impressed by how tall & cleanly nice looking he was, tho ill, just had pneumonia, slightly dizzy still with headache. "I saw you were a good man ... heard we hear many bad things about you, that you are [?], you are pederast, scandals ... but I know it is not true." "It's all true," I said. He told me Steinbeck's account—"Ginsberg announced himself to the literary world & many admirers & many enemies & his problem will be to convert his admirers to enemies & his enemies to admirers."

I explained to him in some detail my Blake visions,[9] & said "as for homosexuality, that's my experience & that's the situation I'm in, so the scandal comes from my talking openly about it."

"I know nothing about such matters, it's a private affair of yours. There was a club in Stalin's time, many pederasts came, I was 15 & published poems and had an income of 12,000 rubles a month—I spent it all there—what made me cynical about pederasts was an incident there—the leader of this group proposed a toast—"To women"—and all stood up & toasted "To Women"—So I asked what was the good of this

9. In 1948, while living in Harlem, Ginsberg experienced what he felt were auditory visions of William Blake reciting his poetry.

toast to women? "Because they are necessary to make born more ped-
erasts." Later . . . "If Stalin had shot only pederasts I would be happy . . .
it was just a joke."

I began a long explanation about use & qualities of different drugs—
He left table to get codeine headache pills—listened awhile but seemed
ill or restless—"But why are you interested in such matters?" I contin-
ued explanation, trying to explain finally religious use of Ganja in Shiv-
aite sects in India & LSD psychedelics in Amazon-Mexican-U.S. areas.
I had gotten to point of trying to explain what the unconscious felt like,
when he drifted off definitely & gave me a speech "Please Allen, I like
you, I like you as poet, but these are your personal problems, please don't
speak to me about them, They are not interesting to me, I respect you
as a great man, a great poet, but these two subjects homosexuality and
narcotics are not known to me and I feel they are juvenile pre-occupa-
tions, they have no importance here in Russia to us, it only disturbs my
impression of you—please don't talk to me about these 2 matters."

"I feel rejected," I said, thru interpreter Alyosha, and continued on
to other subject.

"I have problems more important than these"—

"O.K.," I said, "tell me all your problems & all the problems of
Russia."

He told me a story, Steinbeck again, addressing group of young writ-
ers in *Youth* magazine "I will tell you everything I know bad about
America" said S. and he spoke for an hour "Now you young writers,
show me your wolves teeth and tell me everything you think bad about
Russia" provocation. Many people there were not our friends or per-
sonal familiars. They were waiting for us to say something. Steinbeck
finally said to Akhmadulina "You with so young beautiful face, why are
you so sad your little face?" and she said "Because they took my driver's
license away yesterday."

Soviet Union

And how many people were arrested in Stalin's time?—"20,000,000 were taken—nearly every family in Russia has someone—" "How do you know that number?" "That's what the people know—of course you can't tell exactly, there's no public record."

And how many killed or died in prison? "Maybe 15,000,000"—I told him Parra had reported that back to me. "My grandfather & grandmother were both disappeared."

Does it still go on? When stop? After the Khrushchev speech it stopped, a Committee of investigation reviewed all the cases. Not all at once, that would've been too fast too impossible.

"But, after all, we believe in Russia and in our system. What would it mean to be anticommunist? To go back to Monarchy or Capitalism? Nobody, very few people want that in this country. So we have to work our problems out. It's slow, it's terribly slow, but we think we'll win, But if I told you my problems ... You can't expect to get to the bottom of our situation on a visit here, no American could."

"The public readings have stopped. I don't know when they'll start again. Maybe it makes no difference ... Here is new poems—" he showed me proofs "It was finished over a year ago, still not published—you won't believe—I had to keep changing it too many passages were questioned—"

Do you have many unpublishable poems? "Oh yes, he sighed, laughing, quizzical blond strong look.

"Your best?"—"Probably—"

"You don't know all the problems I have, I'll tell you later."

He recited one poem with refrain "Citizens listen to me" & Alyosha translated line by line—very clear simple, definite images—"people playing cards full of grease." That was published, with a few minor changes.

"I am sorry no readings now or you could come & see"—"Don't tell anyone, especially not my wife, she thinks I am a narcissist, but I'll play you record of my reading."

"What's the most number of people you read to"—"14,000—here in Moscow"—

"450 changes—but, imagine, it will be published in a magazine with circulation of 1,000,000—so you see it is worth it, but you have to pay for it, but it is worth it all"—the struggle to reach so huge an audience, with the censor disadvantages of all that.

He played recording of rain girl poem made in "Parisat Palais des Nacion"—deep feeling voice—his face changing expression as he followed the poem on record with his lips, silent, speaking about the cues, very moved. "This is a part of my early days, another Yevtushenko"—standing up, he hugged & kissed me. I was embarrassed.

We went out to Georgian restaurant, met his wife drunk "You don't like women I know . . . I have waited for you a long time" said wife [?]—I drank not much—explained spontaneous Kerouac style writing to him & Akienov—Yev listened and said "Mentiros" not accepting my theory. Lily Brik[10]?—"Una mirsdova."

Later driving home I asked him about Brodsky & Yessenin-Volpin[11]—

"Volpin good for his hatred but we have much poetry like that in our tradition" Lermontov—but Yessenin-Volpin badly written.

Brodsky not justified his faith yet by a great poem, Talented. "Don't ask about Brodsky, we all already know the case—March 17 he was to go to new trial—he's still in a reeducation camp—so not free—but any day now, we are all working—but if you talk it'll only make things

10. Lilya Brik (1891–1978), Mayakovsky muse and lover.

11. Alexander Yessenin-Volpin (1924–2016), Russian poet, mathematician, and human-rights dissident, held in a psychiatric prison for his views.

Soviet Union

worse— like me coming to US & giving speeches about Negroes in Al-
abama"—"That wd/be best thing you could do"—he laughed & shook
my hand.

Wed. 24 March—

Woke morning depressed—no real communication. Old sympathetic
European tradition absent?

With Nina the guide to Pushkin Museum—beautiful many Gauguin
and at last Cezanne's sneering narcissist harlequin—I saw reproduction
years ago in Cannastra's[12] loft 1950?—This original the red & black di-
amonds on the harlequins suit more rich than in photocopy—and the
sad white masochistic clown following him seemed more philosophic
than I'd realized—and the harlequin better built, more virile—a straight
Rimbaud—than I'd imagined. And another picture a weird inhuman
doll child by Cezanne. And Picasso's beggar and boy eating blue apple,
and the pubescent balancing boy clown watched by huge teacher.
Roomsful of good plaster casts of Greek & Roman classics—and an El
Greco Saint, and a Goya nun hand laid strangely sideways on the can-
vass—and acres of Lorrojin & some Pounin and a little ice skating
Auechanings and some sad golden Rembrandts—all his people wooden
eyed thinking of Death—and a Cezanne self portrait solid as a block of
ice—with little round objective marbles for eyes—and some calm sunny
Matisse—

(Yevtushenko last night had wall full of paintings—Cuban, Viet-
namese, gifts from Cocteau and Chagall and Leger & Picasso—and a

12. William Cannastra (1922–1950), friend of early Beat writers, including Gins-
berg, led a wild, rebellious life that ended when, as a joke, he attempted to climb out
the window of a moving New York subway car and was killed.

Soviet Union

great Max Ernst—and some nice Russians & dull Russians)—Then to Eastern Asia museum, not much there, I was alone, and walked down to huge multihistory apartment bldg. on Moscow River banks & went up to top roof—looked out down over Moscow—a huge building square yard below with police soldiers on file—and the façade of high newer buildings along waterfront, huge hotel under construction.

Near Kremlin—the many gold domes on Kremlin wall, and mixed in the city small villages gold brown wood houses lost among small solid official buildings of concrete—Moscow a "village"—then walked along river to Kremlin & up into Basil's little funhouse inside of domes—then on Red Square I wrote—Back in Red Square, the real beauty of the place on a sunny late afternoon—huge blue sky, the Basil Domes whose symmetry I now begin to see, the bright expanse of cobbles, small crowds gathered to watch the changing of the guard at the little red mausoleum—so highly polished it's simply pretty—a large red flag flying over the green dome inside the Kremlin wall, but it's the long expanse of space and noise of heels clapping on the cobblestones, and a faraway bell, and the long white palace Gum dept. store stretching out like a Versailles, facing the square—yesterday's billboards down, all but the wooden scaffold frame—The 16th century candy church sitting there as good as a time capsule—I retreat writing away—happy to be alone out walking—

Walked back up Gorky Street thru crowds, heavy hearted toward hotel to meet guide Nina—passing Pushkin statue stopped & looked up awhile, defeated. Iron or brass man with wild wooly hair, strange sideburn beard, looking empty-sad eyed down thoughtful also defeated—or bemused, a pathetic expression—standing there long time blue sky—I'd forgot to see everyone around as God, was seeing them as I thought they insisted, as Soviets—Felt lightness in my body & walked on looking people in the eyes more, tho still afraid. Odd sense of presence of everyone

Soviet Union

in Now movement with buildings around, crossing the big Pushkin statue street, young faces with fur caps & girls walking hand in hand holding net shopping bags full of cans and salami—

Up to hotel, no toilet paper, I tried to tell maid & several minutes later a mechanic with huge wrench was in the bathroom looking around confused.

With Nina off to Puppet Theater, large wooden inside [?] "cosy" she said, theater—"Divine Comedy" program, bearded God & archangels creating Adam & Eve and their troubles with the apple—I kept taking it personally—After all, Adam & Eve are alone on Earth as I am so shouldn't I eat the sex apple with Eve and begin the whole process of responsibility babies and would that in the long run lead to socialism?— And the ant heap huge dull apartments of Moscow—I really was amazed a moment walking past the Pushkin statue it said 1880's on it—all those buildings were little wooden houses—and Prince [?] statue further down Gorky Street, his knight on horse in chain—-mail armor— Founder of Moscow 12th century—"How wise he was to found Moscow near a good restaurant" his statue being next to the Georgean restaurant I went second night with Simonov and later with Yevtushenko— they both told me that Moscow Joke—Anyway 800 years ago little fort Moscow and now look at it with huge bookstores & central telegraph offices & vast crowds and astronauts. Where will it end on Jupiter?

March 25, 1965

Am sitting now writing in Metropole Hotel restaurant—huge room with antique green glass dome skylight marble baby-grabbing-goose fountain running in center, mirrors on every side, red marble pillars, a bandstand flanked by giant brass standing chandeliers, most of the customers seedy looking a few mustached sharpies, an older American lady fat in a green sweater writing postcards, service slow but not now "im-

Soviet Union

possible," a Russian with his passport in his breast pocket looks like my Uncle Sam—sitting across from me at little round table—he's been waiting 20 minutes with no plates in front of him, with sad quiet patient expression on his big face behind eyeglasses—The room so huge and brown that several windows from the hotel interior open up on the balcony from another floor of the building—potted palms at the base of the giant chandelier stands which are thrown around the room—a Mongolian face passes on clicking heels no tie—noontime and few customers & the fountain pisses away. I paid for my meal with intourist tickets $2.50 and the waiter hasn't brought me any change, about 30c or 50c I couldn't decipher from inscription on the bill.

But going back to last nite—Nina got taxi after puppet theater to Aksenov's[13] apartment in Aerodrome district—huge project where writers & theater people have co-op—& spent evening talking singing drinking a little, his wife talks English & was friendly even more than anyone days earlier—simply relaxed—her problems are sick mother & babies not Socialist ideology—so I complained my loneliness to her, she was affectionate—Aksenov told a dirty story about a magician homunculus drinking vodka which ended "fuck (or cock) the magician"—vague conversation they wanted to know what I thought of Hemingway ("Is it true he is not popular in Americas?"), Steinbeck, Arthur Miller, Edward Albee, the French New Wave, 8 ½ & Antonioni & movies—they have a limited gamut which means a lot to them—as I suppose I have a limited gamut of knowledge of red literature—or Russian anyhow—I explained I was bugged by Yevtushenko's put down of my explanation of self drugs sex and she Aksenov said "That's him that not everybody—" An actor

13. Vasily Aksyonov (1932–2009), Russian physician, novelist, and playwright.

Soviet Union

there, very sweet Catholic of Aksenov's new play opened that week "We won't know till next week if it succeeds or fails"—and chided me for going, to so many museums & seeing too few people—

March 25, 1965—1:30 p.m.

Red Square again, passing thru by Gum's fountain inside, the huge grey square closed off for Lenin's Tomb visiting day, so it's an empty expanse except for the long colored caterpillar lines a block away filing slowly into the tomb door between the soldiers—you have to walk all the way around to get to the clock tower gate, detour thru Gums. The sky leader or police whistle warning passersby & tourists from straying into the Square—a purely aesthetic decision to close off the Square & make a dramatic insect out of the worshippers—in fact purely aesthetic the tomb's open only a few days a week—for a few hours—so all the visitors concentrated in those hours make an impressive tribute (silent) to the Memory of the orange enshrined leader. A few pigeons flap off Gums roof—A father poses with his little girls for public photographs against background of empty square and the red spired revolution museum & a tower of Kremlin & the red pile of the tomb and the still moving life of visitors that stretch two blocks down past the gates of Kremlin into the snowy most-park below. Red flag flying over green dome always waving in the high breeze like an inspiring movie banner. Crowds thick in the side streets toward "Chinatown."

And turning back, down in the river valley behind Basil Dome, a 1920's view of thick iron black smokestacks nearby steaming heavily smoke into the Russian wind—giant cranes silhouetted silent in the grey sky behind the onion pink church-building a new hotel on banks of Moscow river.

Walked into Kremlin walls and along iron fence overlooking River—

Soviet Union

into church of old stone Tombs of Czars encased in glass and brass, thru Kremlin grounds out into long avenues to Writers Union, saw Romanova—still nervous with her, on my behavior, tho I disagree half the time with her presuppositions—Seems as hard Russian tourism to America as American to Russia—Intourist has a monopoly here & some contracted organization has monopoly there costs a fortune (in advance) to visit too. Check this?

Got 42 rubles spending money from Writer's Union—and then to Mayakovsky museum—a dark photo of him under the Brooklyn Bridge —his posters—in the room where he committed suicide I asked why? Lady Director and young scholars said three reasons—Fight Proletarian Writer's Union who rejected him (good man but just mistaken), failure of his play and unhappy love affair—I asked about note pinned on theater door (as described by Pasternak)—"You should have let us fight it out on the stage"—they didn't recall contents or whereabouts of that— "It was after a fight among literary groups, the party was not involved ... The party left it to these groups to settle themselves except that it asked for unity afterward, consolidation—It was not a political matter"—I was frustrated, they made it all sound so innocent—"Well if the party never intruded who arrested Babel"[14]—"Oh more than Babel were arrested, but that was later not till 1937 that that began"—He was just disappointed that on the first day of his exhibition there was nobody present from the Writer's Union—Surkov and the others came, officially only, on the third day—(there was a picture in the museum, giant group photo of that visit)—

The lights of Moscow moving backward, I'm writing on the train to Leningrad—Low apartments, night, street-lights blocks away across

14. Isaac Babel (1894–1940), Russian writer, critical of Communism, executed during Stalin purge.

Soviet Union

the R.R yards—"But you make it all sound so meaningless as if he were just a big disappointed egotist"—I got mad—and walked across the room & bent my head on his suicide bed & pounded on it in irritation. "He probably committed suicide because people were just as stupid then as you people are now"—and as I turned I saw Frieda Lurie!—standing watching me from the door—ouch!—terror! was this making "scandal?"—I would see how the poor man was hemmed in by bureaucrats weighing his gestures—cool it! which I did—the thought flashed by that if I don't make an issue further of my behavior, & cover it up by fast switch to some totally new exciting neutral area, it'll be amnesiaed, but the last fragments of conversation hung in the clean-painted bedroom, with glass top protecting his open desk—Oscar Wilde stories and H. G. Wells's Word History and many inkbottles of colored liquid, and mah jong set and Lenin portrait—on wall (with mouth open)—and a big thick pen, and notebook with last verses—(some revised lines crossed out, in pencil)—"His note said not to gossip so we have respected his wishes" said the lady director—and, 5 minutes later Frieda Lurie staring me in eye said "Of course Lenin heard a lady reciting these verses, and his first attitude toward M was disapproval because he didn't like the style but when he saw the *posters* he was enchanted, he couldn't stop praising Mayakovsky—and Mayakovsky wrote that he followed . . . he made himself *clean* by following Lenin's path—that he purified and simplified his poetry, so that it was direct, free of unnecessary complications, and could be appreciated by the proletariat—"

I was angry listening to all this. We went in and I read "At the top of my voice" for their tape museum and also "Death to Van Gogh's Ear"[15] which by now in parts appeared to me cheap in its attack on America,

15. See "Death to Van Gogh's Ear," *CP*, 175.

Soviet Union

so I threw in a few extra phrases implicating Russia more in the general conspiracy against delight. Read trembling into the microphone.

Then downstairs sat in office & heard activities of society described, we broke away—Alexei had arrived—and walked to theater saw Lermontov "Hero of our times"—and then by car from hotel to the Leningrad express, very smooth riding in 19th century style wagon-lits car with red velvet curtains & plush soft chairs & beds—joined in my compartment by an English-speaking professor of physics.

March 26, 1965—A poetry reading in the garment workers club in Leningrad—old building on giant square across from St. Isaac's Cathedral—upstairs a library like 1930, small room with Russian cardboard backed vols. of prose with Lenin and Gorki portraits on cover—

A big theater with stage inside, auditorium lecture hall, half the seats in hall filled, and on stage seven, eight, baby blue covered armchairs with soft backs—the poets—an engineer with thin greying hair—satyrical verse—about fool who found a bag of wisdom & who give it to? Titter in audience. A red haired 40 ye old lady in black dress—& long poem about students in dormitories—when she was young they shared grease & bread—the others sit & look at little notebooks—

Two handsome young blank eyed well drest youths in front row—

All these aggressive middleaged women declaiming his poem—very moralistic and healthy—enough to strangle a baby angel—

Now Vladimir, whom I got drunk with—2 poems about Pushkin—about what Pushkin felt within some verses "I remember the beautiful moment"—he has a business suit & is editor of magazine youth 300,000 copies—"My poems are wandering all over the world looking for me. Some people go to forest gather mushrooms I go gather poems . . . I'm not greedy I can show you where they grow"—

Soviet Union

"Bislovov Dru ... Tvoyvee ... Ispakoyves"—"Mama maybe that very man killed that my father"—"a Russian soldier: was guarding them & protected them from the crowd at the railroad station threatening the train full of German prisoners ... not because he was sympathetic with them but wise ..."

Now my Agayeev—a solid worker in suit & florida-hollywood rust brown shirt now reads quatrains in an aoiu "yuch" nem voice—his eyes look up occasionally at chandelier—He "loves two women & drinks vodka"—interesting sing song rhymed, he plays with a paper between two hands fingers at his jacket button while he intones—Audience giggles—"the last verse is about the neighbors"—against people who lead a monotonous life.

Now an older man in brown suit now holds hands behind back—"about different kinds of mercy"—Irregular verse—"the best poet"—

Another lady in black shirt "the dream is going to communism"—"Some different people got off the train at different stations called flattery or power but I decided to stay on the train to go to a place which is called communism"—Then a poem about 1930, time of the trials & how her father was beaten right on the same scars he got during the revolution—she has boots—remembering poem the time she first got kissed—and the love that flowers in the sunshine heat at Lochi seashore isn't deep as Love can be—

Now a younger beard kid in no tie brown jacket—to Pasternak "While the poet was writing his verses the savages were dancing some strange dances around him & Pasternak went on writing his verses."

"And the water erased the word from the sand"—

The curtains & backdrop of the stage a strange paper-velvet black.

A poem about Siamese twins?—or twins and why were we born separately? And some children's poem from green mss.

Soviet Union

Finally the chairman, with busy hair flying back from his thin face, like a 1930's orator in Newark, reciting *his* rhymed long 19th century poem.

I cracked the old rusty padlock
and opend the ancient trunk,
lifting the lid saw thru the bottom the red
Square, and Kremlin Clock & Wall, and tomb
and a long file of citizens moving on tiny cobbles

"Another London there I saw"

Long avenues, old palaces, old dungeons,
Great gardens covered with mud, an iron
fence on the Neva waters dirty ice lakes,
where Pushkin walked in springtime drowned
his heroine pique dame, the vast open space
surrounded by old low apartments where Dostoyevsky
trembled at the Eternal hole in the barrel of Czarist rifles
and left reborn, now a children's theater with Mickey
the Red Mouse, the giant dome and malachite
columns of St. Isaac's, Kirov's caricature
Christ and Holy Fools with magic signs & foetus
dynasaurs illustrating Scientific Method on
Mosaic floors that eye trick solid space & make
a vertical columned wall you can walk on dream into,

Soviet Union

the 300 foot pendulum hanging on iron wire, slowly drifting back and forth in elastic gravity overturning a matchbox—the student jumped in the magnetic circle to make the happy experiment and a black communist window guardian severely entered his Universe and placed the matchbox on its back & glared at the imp—"It can only be done in groups of over 12"—O Isaac Abraham Israel, in thy Palace thy will be done—Nevsky prospect & Palace Bridge covered with mist, with mist the golden spike of Peter the Great's Cathedral tomb, with mist the cold river steps where idiot Ilyich was led to Fox Nose doom rowboats one wintery dawn—the palace bank of Petrograd shimmering the last time in his eyeball—with mist Hotel Angleterre shrouded, Yessenin's[16] death room unknown, Dostoyevsky's Engineering school an old palace an old apartment of Pushkin closed for repair, a brilliant searchlight on the Bronze Horseman. Venice, Washington, Amsterdam faraway southern mist, the North City St. Petersburg's green Hermitage stretching for blocks along the iron railing where I stood with fur collar around my neck and fine snow settling on my hair, my nose open smelling the Finland Bay from the car window, dreaming of Gogol's forgotten overcoat, clerks in huge palace bureaucracies, Brodsky on some farm, Yevtushenko telephoning the guitarist from Moscow, a drunk with open fly in the street floor coffeeshop of Writer's Union—we looked out the window across the wide grey water to the granite fort walls faraway—How in Hotel Europa halfnaked dreaming back on the Leningrad day, the armored car in the museum courtyard, Palace [?] and the giant column of 1812, the spacious city & [?] high on the roofs of Triumphal arches, silent boots running across the cobblestones of history, an iron balcony

16. Sergei Yesenin (1895–1925), one of the most popular Russian poets of the twentieth century, was a possible suicide.

where Lenin pronounced his April thesis near a mosque coffee and 18th century rooms, I read to an old poet in Peru and answered poetical questions, I went poetry reading with 8 dull Leningrad bards, I supped in a new apartment with 3 philosophers and compared 12 social systems from Ind to Dane—home thru the empty snow-frost streets in a taxi and now to touch myself naked 1965 in Leningrad bed. It was a Tartar taxidriver in a grey fur cap that looked like Nijinsky alone in his cab at 1 a.m. on Nevsky prospect that woke my fantasy after all day talk—and the gold silk luxury of Hotel E and curtains drawn before the bed, and silence, and streetlights outside the window shining thru snow— the curved tire traces of the cab that brought me to the oaken door.

5 minutes later spread-eagled my legs up pushed against the wall my buttocks naked my sphincter stretching pulsing—flashes of Peter fucking me, Prague Turkish bath boy lifting my legs over my head, 1937 Haledon Ave dream ass raised to heaven to receive spanking,—rubbing my cock up & down with hand trying to get ass cheeks spread wider & wider even reached hand around thigh to pull legs further out & down, upside down—flashes of circus acrobat blown his own cock—I came splatting warm drops all over my brow and beard and eyes & lips. Dream Massonet & [?] record album "Prelude & Overture in Prague"—I was looking thru the whole stack of records like Yev. Looking thru his drawer full . . . telephone rang at 9 a.m. to wake me to go to hermitage—forgot dream.

Down in Breakfast Café of Europe Hotel, writing. while dressing & bathing I found myself thinking more about Brodsky and Volpin. Originally I'd asked Romanova and Simonov the first day, & their reaction had been indifferent, cynical, a light laugh. "I have not read his works"—"His translations are supposed to be good . . . but Yessenin-Volpin is sick—he is in and out of hospitals . . . I don't know if he is in town . . . his mother lives in Alexei's building . . . We may ask her if he is well enough

Soviet Union

... He is a fine mathematician but not a poet ... He may be working in Siberia—He was in a mental hospital perhaps he is now ..." I asked Alexei several times to contact his mother & ask permission to see her but each time I saw him he was indifferent to the matter "I may see his mother ..."

Here I asked (in Leningrad) my translator Nina to arrange privately some contact with Brodsky ... reassuringly, without scandal, since Lurie (saying she disapproved of their works) and Yev. both warned me it would be interpreted as "provocation" if I pursued the subject ... at the writers club yesterday Nina took the Chairman aside & asked him, he looked up, as if everything were normal, & asked the few others there if they knew anything—(Yev. had said he was to be tried 18 March ... or any day ... or may be free ...)—Everyone there said they "didn't know where he was ... the trouble is difficulty of finding out, no public record of trial... actually there was more interest in B in West than here in Leningrad ... I read a verse of his it was not bad, a black horseman, and the poet asks, who could be the heroic rider? And names several Soviet present heroes, but can't find one great enough to be the rider ... rather an apocalyptic poem ... we will find out, actually we don't know"—Savitsky was to call in the morning—Savitsky the Drama Critic with mustache who met us at train yesterday—didn't call, nor did younger poet with face burned off in tank during war—now has red hair round face beard—He said he'd call in Morn.

Turned out he'd called in day we out, & that nite reported in no news of Brodsky, nor his address. Nobody knows what court or how to reach his friends, or could not on such short notice.

That nite at ballet, Savitsky came with wife & so said. He said Sergei Orlov also had called & couldn't find anything out ... Nobody knew Brodsky personally.

Soviet Union

The Winter Palace—Pavilion Hal (small hermitage)—Marble interior staircase & balcony giant pheasant clock.

Francesco Francia—1500—all the eyes intelligent & friendly glancing in all directions and the child looking out like baby Buddha, globe in one hand, abhya mudia with other (Mad. & child)

Kirov Ballet "Legend of Love"—old Marinsky Theater—Arif Melihoff (story by Hilsmet)
—great Slavic barbarian georgeior Asiatic honkey tonk
dance choruses—same hall as Nijinsky danced, same school
(still continues) giant leaps & Mongolian animal splendor
Magicians and earthly sisters, but ending with a red hero
working on the water mountain—from a poem by Nayin Hilsmet,
ancient corn, actually Turkish snow.

Dream—Mar. 28 4 a.m.

On train passing thru territory ... standing and waiting in his long house, Gipetto the Jew (Cinna the Poet)—my flesh crawls—Time for Death—something still in me of that ancient skeletal strain—He lives on the edge of town in a big long chicken coop store—Naomi crawls thru the barbed wire of words—He's killed her, and thousands more, and buried them in his store. They are coming to get him like Marquis de Sade. But the one that knows & has discovered the existence in the country, the girl that knows, will tell the others and then a group of horsemen are taking a train back to get him first. He hides in the lights of his cottage. He offers her refuge. She accepts thinking he does not know. Ugolino. Who will kill who? They have discovered him, he has not

Soviet Union

hidden all the bones. The dead bodies begin speaking. He is trapped by their voices, which he saved. He tries to destroy the phonograph records. They are singing too loud like the skull of Poe. The train passes his window. He offers his hospitality. There is no one on the train, they are all hiding behind his sanitarium. At midnight they will seize him. He tries to kill the girl, but they know she is there alone with him. His thefts share his feet, he wears a necklace of gold teeth, he drinks champagne from the Mortuary. She has red hair & Pevdichenko is outside of Moscow.

I wake with skin crawling & look around the room? in summer palace—porcelain pillars in one room very delicate & beautiful & tall & thin.

St. Petersburg Leningrad—Cezanne's Mont. St. Victoire. Looks on palace square from Winter Palace.

March 28, 1965
All day yesterday and half today at Hermitage—Same minor Angelico, 2 da Vinci Madonnas—I walked thru museum an old veteran of Prado Toledo Uffizi Louvre Metropolitan Vienna Tate National Gallery Philadelphia Athenaeum Munich Venice Rome Athens Prague Amsterdam Chicago—so began this round looking afresh the paintings moving, like last gestures, in the Florentine primitives, I could finally notice—the meaning of the looks in the eyes of the Madonnas, the abbya mudras of the tiny christs, the cynical or penetrant looks of the attendant Josephs and Johns—the ashenhuman jaws of Jesus—the hermitage a vast ornate palace with marble & malachite pillars, giant rooms of complex parquet floor, great windows opening under gilt stucco walls on to Palace

Soviet Union

Square or Nevsky Bridge or the Peter the Great golden steeple in Prison
Island or the old Venetian Canal giant ice water of Neva—facades across
the river in cold blue afternoon sunlight—& there's Titian's Danse with
3 gold coins showering between her thighs, & Rembrandt's Prodigal Son
with one showoff & father's eye agaze aside—he has a haven beaten suf-
fered head—wino bowery skull—and R.'s old Jew with a nose so real
when I stuck my nose to the glass eye to eye like looking in a mirror I
saw the red pores on the bulb of the nose—Flora Sackin & crazy Rem-
brandt jr. with cherry saskin lips in prince's costume—Christ limp dan-
gling from arms helped down dead from cross his hip askew & grey—
Rembrandt's Danse reaching hand up to light with lost smile on her face
& old crone interested in the golden shower too—

Van Leyden all chequered and bright—one Canaletto procession near
St. Mark's the spot where I walked—a great roomful of 14 Gaugin's I
never saw before, orange & blue Tahitian fields—a room of Cezanne with
the great Mt St. Victoire wrinkled like a snub nosed Socrates blind eye-
less face—creases for its neck, and that giant-dwarf tree on the road
under his studio—the lady attendant an old fat woman made a gesture
to explain the top & bottom rottenness of the canvas—Cezanne rolled
it up to throw away—paint scratched off upper & lower border—and 2
Rousseaus forests—rooms full of Van Mier's and Steen, the landscapes I
didn't have time to look at Ruyshael—tho I expected old Dutch windmill
picture from my Paterson wall 1935 my archetype home landscape of
child nostalgia to turn up for red, & it didn't or I didn't notice—never
knew who fecit—Peter Breughel II a carnival market, with knife fights—
couple great Poussins organized with arrows pointing from upper right
background down to lower front foreground & arms & bodies plunging
down around & straight up left to center top again—a great cylinder
shape—

Soviet Union

I'm back in Leningrad–Moscow Express Midnight just left that city of huge avenues & canals & palaces & bridges & holds—& no brodskys—just Hermitages—

This morn before museum drove in clear March light blue sky thru streets over Neva Bridges to Pushkin or Czar's town—another huge palace, bombed out during war, & now slowly restored with wood drawing & shiny fine guilt ceilings—& Pushkin's old school where he read his first poem aloud—declaiming according to painting of him with arm upraised in military suit—and saw his litter dormitory bedroom, he could sneak into the next cubicle to snuggle under covers with his bosom friend Pushkin—thru the window space despite well partition dividing the two bunks—

And to cemetery where 80,000 Leningraders starved in war blockade are buried—vast lawn & statue heroic at end of a walk almost as long as the garden of Taj Mahal—

Night to a youth café, huge room like cafeteria, band playing slow soupy secondrate dinner music jazzy, 1000 young couples at tables talking quietly—glasstopped tables with knee obstructions, uncomfortable, & no smoking—Khrushchev could look around at the healthy Workers Society at rest & say "that's nice"—one or two cats with shades—talked to nobody—everyone stared silently when I crossed the huge room in turtleneck red sweater jeans yellow checkoslovak shoes bears & long long balding hair & my inevitable belly, horrible—

Nevsky Prospekt crowded all today Sunday—I walked up & down at odd hours afternoon & night—took a few photos—and that's that Leningrad.

Much talk with Nina last few days about "art"—"But the artist must teach the people" etc. she says. I tried to explain how, but it's a circular argument.

Soviet Union

Mon. March 29—Brite sunlite over sheets of snow, the train drifting at sunrise toward Moscow. A big red glass of tea. Hayfield & flat village in distant ice fields like a view in Averhamp or Breughel winter scene. Tall wooden crosses standing next to houses like flagpoles, radio antennae I guess. Frost on the benches of railroad platforms, entering Moscow outskirts.

New Hotel Bucharest 2.50 rubles a day, nice room with view of river & St. Basil's & Kremlin clock tower.

By taxi to theater, a reading enactment with guitars of Voznesenski's poetry—a little corny, a little chic, a little fresh, a little Brecht, a little broad Russian humor—the audience all young lovely normal girls and sensitive dumb looking young boys—nobody crazy hardly everything so *healthy*! At 11 a.m. it began—poems to stripteasers & Marilyn and one about everybody's nose is growing all the time—at the end strong applause. After a performance of poems by Voznesenski this morning at theater.

[...]

Kremlin Bell quarter to five, Red Square in bright afternoon sunshine, long shadows of strollers in the great perspective under the tooth row of "buttresses" above the Kremlin wall top—yellow buildings inside and the green domed red flag flying above—a dove pigeon above St. Basil's gold bulb top—the floor of the square rolls like the ripply top of Carib ocean transparent, a great bulge in the bottom of the Vista—stamp on the cobbles and see if the floor gives way to another universe!—Pale blue sky on the horizon over the building tops downhill across the river and derricks upraised in that—then bright baby blue the whole sheet of sky above, yellow light on the book from the sun & the shadow of my pen

Soviet Union

moving, the grey curb where I sat, flagpoles at attention in front of gums with floodlights although 20 feet up—the soft choir of many bells on the cobbles, a minute sparrow lapping beneath the Kremlin tower, a chap in a cap with a moth in his teeth—sits down on the curb next to me & a shadow passes across the page from a boy walking ten feet in front of me—crowd of several hundred silent across the square waiting at the gate of the mausoleum deep brick red shiny in the shadow—Workmen with huge black leather boots & fur hats & pleated coats clomp by to the tomb to watch the 5 p.m. changing of the guard—a row of small trees grey leafless for winter filled with sparrow chirps makes Parisian curtain of vegetable fur across the vests of Gum's—the Kremlin trees have delicate peaks & arches—it is the olden space so shivery—and the groups of children walking with teacher Being inside this vast symbolic space place makes life seem small—the clock hand's moving toward the golden XII and it's five. A telephone call down the valley in my hotel so I must go.

Tchaikovsky Hall—Moscow Symphony

The first violin draws his bow, and everyone fiddles together, the silver conductor stamps onstage, applause & the orchestra stands on its feet—sweet twiddle of violins, thump thump thump, and brasses introduce the Holy thunder of Death—Tchaikovsky's first, the strained hysterical homosexual hair and body waving a bloody banner on the planet, insistent, built of violin threads on the long pole of a trumpet—a skull opening its mouth to roar music—pacing up and down the room, heartache in the heart, all those blond trumpeters and white marble lips on athletes in the Hermitage. Who was Nadja Von Mech? Who held Hands? Who wept on a pillow imagining starry brass music?

Soviet Union

Evermore in the blue chairs of Tchaikovsky Hall in Moscow bend their heads as in prayer, Chin in hand, legs apart and listen. A giant insect— met everywhere.

In youth café—monk beard on a saxophone, the slow stately bounce, & the lovely echo on the clank plane. Many a youth & many a maid dancing on the wooden floor, modern lights hung from ceiling, plastic tables, hot dogs & peas, ham & cheese, caviar & salmon, young kids in babushkas, one couple doing an Afric twist, middleaged Slavic beauties drinking sweet punch & coffee, a wine bottle at the musician's table, the band jumping and most of the dancers swaying back & forth slowly a foot apart, a smart photog from a youth magazine with a giant-eyed camera, the saxophonist gaunt & calm, intellectual, from the behind with his sensitive fingers and delicate skull he looks like Jonas Mekas.[17]

NIGHT

Red Square the Clang of Shusky Tower
    eleven times echoed from brick gothic towers
GUM blinding spotlights on Kremlin battlement
    a range of neon zooming across arched
            display windows,
Electricity gleaming on cobbles, electricity
    like power station cabaret of red marble
    atop Lenin's tomb—
a lonely cop walking the asphalt street

17. Avant-garde Lithuanian-American filmmaker.

Soviet Union

by the tribune—long coat & black

    fur hat—I sit on the white bench—

orange lights in the arches of Gum say

    Gum—

a crowd gathered in the dark shade by

    Lenin's portal to witness

the hourly goosestepping change of the grey guard—

and rolled away like a tree when the

    bell finished echo—

gangs singing Ukrainian deepvoiced

    juvenile Vodka chants

    walking away to the Metro—

Faraway over Dark Basil's Dome the

    new hotel construction white in

    spotlight from the bridge—

a tourist with Swiss hat & huge camera

    strapped to shoulder walks

       whistling by—

How slow the legs of a couple move, her

    heels clicking, his legs striding

    quietly, two shadows together

    across the stone field.

The red flag still flying at night

    from the great Dome.

Red Square feels like the giant fortress

    of Asia Space.

Sitting in the snow at

       Kremlin Wall—

Look up, I stare in a circle

Soviet Union

the hands of the big
                    dipper
The chug of dynamos generators
    in the bloodlet skeleton
        of a white hotel
            unfinished.
Saint Basil's bulb Domes
    between the branches of
                young trees,
a few car lights on the huge
    bridge entrance
the white arcades of Gum's lit
    up for display to the ghosts
        of midnight—
my behind is chill in the
    cold dirty snow,
but at last my backbone
    leans against the
        Kremlin Wall.

11:30- p.m. on Moskooskaya Bridge
ramp, over the road by a corner
round turret of the wall—
    the lights of house in the
Bucharest Hotel,
    a great square apartment
sitting on the water, familys awake
At rows of yellow windows,
    yellow windows and streetlight
in the clear night air, wavering in the

Soviet Union

black water, row after row
—the upper stories deep orange,
trembling at the bottom of the river
six stories down.

Tues. March 30, 1965

In a small room at the Musical Institute with pillared white columns behind an iron gate—the old delicate voiced fat teacher at one huge brown piano, the young student in a brown suit sucking in his lips at another keyboard—the clang of Beethovenian Woes ring out and the answering tremble of heavenly European Soprano notes—on 3 chairs by the wall one girl and 2 other boys wait their student turns at 10 a.m. They go over the music phrase by phrase exploring and explaining— "This is pathos"—"There should be more melody, keep on with the movement of the previous part"—he raises his hand thumb & forefingers circled & looks thru his glasses—"The poolse! Pulse!"—He has a set voice like Jan Zabrana, they're playing Chopin 3'd Scherzo C Mol, trill by trill. The teacher bounces his ass to the rhythm & slaps his hand on piano in & out of time—what you can't hardly teach—old Schuman & Chopin and they sound like silent movie music, that sweet & sad— "Alyosha, you must appeal to your own heart—and even if you have no romantic feelings in yr soul *this music* can give rise to it"—The next student has a red nose & white shirt & tie, & looks stiff & self-conscious— playing with only his hands not his body—Mr. Guttman the teacher smiles & appeals & bounces with his body on the floor & smokes a papier-russo. "To be the artist means to *live* in the Image"—as he explains a contrasting passage. "Here the hollows instead of eyeballs, like a skeleton"—and the boys two students at the side play with each other's piano fingers and hold hands & watch the lesson.

Soviet Union

THE RED UNIVERSE

The Communist Party like a giant snake eating
        its own tail
its teeth are microphones, loudspeaker eyes,
          television scales

    Lunch with F. L. at writer's union—Random conversation—I keep wanting to talk about Stalinism & rise euphemistic "cult of personality" talk—She keeps saying "you don't understand our struggle . . . and the war . . . and our faith . . . Yevtushenko would agree . . . you have much to learn. . . ." I listen & occasionally ask questions.

    Then meeting with 20 professors translators and students, read a piece of Kaddish & Sunflower[18] & Organ Music[19] and N.Y. rooftop sketch, answered questions & sang Hari Om Ram Shiva. Nina said I sang too long—but F. L. asked me to. Meeting ended with Professor giving formal speech about poesy appealing to the heart and here perhaps they build a society not so lonely I said I felt lonely here, but I hope so. Then to Ballet Bolshoi at vest modern congress hall inside Kremlin Walls and lousy music ending on triumph note a la Shostakovich, the ballet creaky corn Spanish style from Lope de Vega but felt like bad Carmen with proletarian revolutionary massed corpse conclusion & the evil soldier's castle burning.

    Walking on Red Square in fine vast snowfall, drunken kid with bandaged head spoke English asked for match, "This system not so good"—

18. See "Sunflower Sutra," *CP*, 146.
19. "Transcription of Organ Music," *CP*, 148.

Soviet Union

and he's a puppeteer from Puppet Theater I saw—25 years old and kind of sweet looking—drunk walked metro underground passage under Moscow Hotel to cross the giant streetcorner below Kremlin, & his friends English speaking very gangsterish youths wanted to change money, coats—I gave him my "American" handkerchief since he wanted my coat—walking past police in Red Square later he persuaded me to change my grey threadbare-sleeved seam-burst jacket for his Bulgarian blue unstylish suit jacket—finally I did, in an archway of GUM—& walked across Moscow Bridge "all young Russians think like Yevtushenko." "Khrushchev not like Yevtushenko . . . Khrushchev go"—He made gesture of kicking Khrushchev off Moscow Bridge at night in the fine rain—"Khrushchev was Dictator . . . Stalin was very good man—Khrushchev get big, Stalin get small . . . all Russianmen say "Stalin & Nation"—Food Cheap—Khrushchev, food expensive—Stalin like peasant—Marx–Engels, Lenin, Stalin—people love Stalin"—

"Stalin no dictator? What about many people in jail?"

"That not Stalin . . . Stalin's friends . . . men around Stalin . . . Stalin not see"—

"I think Stalin see," I said.

He didn't want to come near dark hotel door—I leaned over kissed his cheek, Russian style, he pulled me over & kissed my other cheek warm wet-lipped kiss, very pleasant to feel. "Send me Beatles record . . . I give you peasant Tzigane records here . . . I have many things here, but want American music—Great British Beatles"—

Wed. March 31, 1965

Morning birds grey sky the machine kiss
    thru the city air—apartments & TV antennae

Soviet Union

Overlooking gold bulbdomes of Novedevchy and the
    black marble crosses and pugnacious stone
    tombs of Soviet Heroes—

Mayakovsky has a new monument, a baby
    hero podium of Dark Shiny Mineral
    Like Lenin's tomb, with a red slab in the
    middle
Framing his bust, with deepset Communist
    farseeing eyes, a sour determined
    expression on the mouth, thick bushy
    hair, and naked cords standing out
    of his neck as he turns his head
    To look

At Macinery OPU Beria NKVD
    the proletarian writers union Sequeros'
    Mexican blanket on his suicide room
    wall—
around the grave small fir trees, my sneakered feet
    are cold on the wet asphalt—I face a pile of old snow—

On his right the Bust of 2XYAOB
    the general on his left the holy black
    Cross of Mun ТРЕТЬ{}КОВЕ

—pine boughs pine sprigs heaped around
    the marble podium where his sister and
    mother lay underneath black slabs—

Soviet Union

It was all done many years later to deceive
  the public—1893–1930—

Not a monument to be proud of Vladimir!—
  You should have sent a letter to England
  Denouncing Stalin—my pen
  now dry—
"They will laugh at my bitter word"—says
  Gogol on his grave—

"The Clever Man is the throne of Feeling" (Chap 12, 1 13)
"The truth makes the language sigh"—(Chap. 14, Verse 34)
                    [...]

Gogol surrounded by 2 inches of water mud &
  broken ice—a black column,
  a white smiling ironic statue—a
  funny expression—

"Not only laughing is true also true
  Is the confession"—Jehovah—Chap 8, Verse 21

On the column "To the great Russian master of Words"—
  From the Government, Sept. 9, 1951.

"Sometimes I feel like Zeus walking thru Red Square"

Then to Writer's Union—Andrei Serg. my translator—walking up &
down in the lobby "Mayakovski ... in his last days he was watched by

Soviet Union

the police ... how do I know?—an older writer told me ... he is now dead ... I won't mention his name ... He visited Mayakovsky in his apartment—Mayakovsky looked out of his window to see who was there...."

We sat had lunch in the huge mahogany room—a Mongolian fat gentleman very intelligent looking & his Mongolian lady there too—& were joined by a tall balding young faced dark-bearded but shaven scholar who knew Huxley's *Doors of Perception* and was Indologist, Cybernetics expert, as well as Iranian & Oriental culturist—wanted copy of Vajra-Chabra Sutra—absolutely sweet—I sang him fragments of mantras—He had conspired with Andrei to meet me at lunch & we giggled & talked about Wisdom & gurus & Shivanidas & burning ghats & Sanscrit & he said the older Orientalists were all dead ... In Mongolia they have no contact with Tibetan Lamaism—the situation in Tibet?—Shigatise Chasa & the third great Monastery under Chinese direction however inaccessible areas of Tibet, 200 active isolated monasteries practicing as always in the snow & lone—It all continues—Difficult if not impossible to make contact thru Russia—"Tibet is closed"—. And my poetry can't be published with dirty words.

Then to Frieda Lurie's office & discussion of my program—sudden realization that my visa time is up & if (as she says) it's not possible to make a deal with Intourist to spend rubles here, I *won't* be able to extend my stay—So I may have to leave—Voznesensky's mother phoned him in Crimea & told him I'm waiting, he'll come back before I leave he said. He knows & wants to meet me, & knows I have few days left.

Then to a student amateur dramatic group in University humanities bldg. for several hours—read Magic Psalm[20] & The Reply,[21] explained

20. See "Magic Psalm," *CP*, 263.
21. See "The Reply," *CP*, 265.

Soviet Union

poems & talked for several hours answering questions "The answer my friend is lost in the wind, the answer is lost in the wind ..."—Explained avant-garde movies, problems of consciousness, drugs—Composition spontaneous poetry "beatnik" history & the word & Kerouac as a genius—they all want to know what I think of Albee and the Centaur—and Miller—I indifferent don't care & say I don't read their work, I read Dostoyevsky—Then after to Composer's Club, we drank vodka & I asked about homosexuality, said I was bisexual & wanted to know the Laws—so we got drunk & talked about what does it feel like to sit in the Center of the Universe & be Zeus.

Earlier today on phone Alyosha said tho he had not been able to find out anything about Yessenin-Volpin's mother. Where is she? He asked & nobody knows. I remember Konstantin had said she lives in the same building as himself. "But doesn't she live in the same building as your father?"—"Oh No you must be mistaken"—he answered. "I asked my mother & she knows everybody in Moscow—she doesn't know where Yessenin-Volpin lives."

Last nite in bed masturbating—sex fantasies that went all the way back thru Prague and Peter and Neal to 1944 Hal Chase[22] and earlier to Paul Roth[23] 1942. My interior imagination seems to be fixed at that level, & in ecstasy goes back further sometimes to age 6 or 7 the dream scene on Haledon Avenue, being punished by street gang with my pants down hit on my behind with sticks.

Yevtushenko's Russian hand in composer's house—Verses of Pasternak—and Lermontov?

----

22. Hal Chase, a Columbia University student in the 1940s, introduced Neal Cassady to the core group of Beat Generation writers.

23. High school friend of Ginsberg.

Soviet Union

With Russian poets Vasily Aksyonov, Yevgeny
Yevtushenko, and Robert Rozhdestvensky

If I only have enough pen to carry the thought—the remembrance—
tonight Thursday, April Fool's Day, April 1, 1965. I did go by cab after
a shorecall from Aksenov—to the writer's union, and met there, as I en-
tered the lobby to give in my coat, Eugene [sic] Yevtushenko, who was
there in a sweater—I saw him & ignored him, to give in my coat to the
inevitable cloakroom guard—he called me, I went up & kissed him—
Russians kiss each other, a very good feeling—and he said, wait, we will
leave with Aksenov—I sat in chair, he disappeared inside, came back &
told me, we will leave our clothes here—I checked my coat & long red
& black scarf & camera in my coat pocket—and we went into room to
sit round table—Aksenov, Yevtushenko—I had met Voznesenski earlier
in day in antechamber of Frieda Lurie's office—he had pockmarked
young face, I kissed him also & kneeled at his feet while we made a date
for Saturday I sayd "I have been waiting for you for weeks—he said "I
have admired your poetry"—he has not so long nose as in photographs
and pale face, a fur cap and a coat very informal like a young man's un-
serious coat—unlike Yevtushenko who looks mature—it was in this of-
fice or antechamber of the Writer's Union—Vorovsiy, Nina my inter-
preter said, there is Voznesensky—there were 2 men crossing the portal
—I rushed up enchanted—addressed the wrong one, looking in this
face—and looked sideways at the others, recognizable from photo by his
innocent visage & eyes & nose—"Voznesensky, yo estoy Ginsberg"—he
didn't recognize me for an instant—then I realized he understood & I
kissed him, aiming at cheek, his aiming at my mouth—he was returning
that day from Crimea—his wife was "terribly" sick—"We have a date
for Saturday"—I thought that was too late since this day was Thurs—
but as he sat down at round table by window I knelt at his knees to give
him my address—pale skin, fur cap, cold face, cold heart, young, too
young to remember everything, the lady from Writer's Union taking
him aside to talk—

Soviet Union

"I admired your *poesy* poetry"—

"I have been waiting for you for weeks." He scribbled addresses—I said we meet—I said, "Franceski, Engleska, Ersmol?" He said "We will speak English, of course" with authoritative diction under his fur hat— I suddenly realized he *did* know excellent English—Aha! great!—yes!— When we meet?—Saturday we have—I showed him my schedule program datebook in front of that window on Tolstoy's statue, and we agree to meet at 3 p.m.—he wrote his address in my book but said he'd pick me up at my hotel 3:30 the day of meeting—Then he said he had to go— I left him—he ran out & came back, some girl had words with him, I hang around and watched—then he left, running to make appointment "My wife is *terribly* sick."—

Then I went to hotel, phoned Gal Yevtushenko's wife, & back to Aksenov's mother who spoke no English—after long conversations—Aksenov phoned me said, come 252 Ave. or St—I took cab—arrived who entering door give my coat—a saw sweater of wool of Yevtushenko, red— He told me to wait—I sat down in lobby on chair—then he told me to give in my coat—I did, with camera in side pocket—and inside restaurant began the evening, a beautiful boy Sergei & [?]—whom I'd seen before in coffeeshop—(signed on wall Rafael [?], Yevtushenko said "A beatnik"—

We sat at round table, he asked me what happened in Cuba. I explained at length, details of Lacra Social—

He said—"We have all been waiting for your scandal.... if you by 7 April have made no scandal you can stay—don't worry we will arrange...."

"You understand this is terrible situation—You do not understand ..."

We talked a lot in writer's union café—I explained U.S. laws & trials—

I asked friend Hamlet (actor Kayahov)—could his play be

Soviet Union

(next day) April 2, 1965

successful yet? He'd said last week that he'd know in a week if Ak-senov's new play in which he starred was success or failure. I thought he meant criticism in papers. "It isn't playing now . . . we're waiting to find out if it's approved—we'll know in 2 days."

Sergei and I tried to talk—has handsome fine face young—"How old is he?"—"29" said Yevtushenko, then checked—"26"—we were talking in Spanish, Yevtushenko's interpreter Aksenov there—

This is all fucked up I got so drunk I couldn't clearly write or remember last nite and now 24 hours passed, the crucial details not fresh—I'll remember what I can—"Exactly what happened to you in Cuba"—

I was describing Cuban experience so when I got to "Will you say maricon so I said to these journalists etc."—He interrupted me with paternal wounded look "Allen, Allen—why do you say thing like that! Do you want me to translate that!?"—Sure—"Unless you feel there's something. . . too much . . . indiscreet"—We fumbled around for a few minutes. "I'll translate *anything* you want but Allen, Allen!"— "But you can say anything you want in front of us . . ."

I described how journalist questioned me about what I'd like to ask Castro, and I'd replied one why persecute homosexuals?

Yev said, "Ah Andre Gide did same with Stalin—you know his letter?"

"No I don't—is it published?"

"Yes."

"and so these 2 young friends were in jail overnight & let out next day"—

He looked at me sighed "Ah, we've known times when people have been in jail 12 or 20 years . . . so one night in jail doesn't frighten us, that's child's play. . . ."

"I'm used to making scandals without paying consequences"—I explained.

Soviet Union

"Ah one scandal here we have to pay 20 times what it costs you in trouble—for one small scandal here a whole life can be finished . . . caput—" he made a gesture, horizontal with his waist, fast, no word.

I described legal trials over book censorship—he said "You live in paradise."

Sometime during conversation, "Don't tell anyone what we say here—we can talk with you as brother . . . You are like one of us."

"I have Cuba in my heart—I know every corner—I was there 8 months—3 visits—"

By this time there were about 8 people sitting around table in corner at Writer's Union, drinking vodka—I wanted to talk with Sergei the Visage—

"He has beautiful face" & Yevtushenko translated that—when we met (Y & I and Aksenov) we all kiss—sometimes on the lips—old Russian custom. But I explained long time about Cuba—When I came to capital punishment "Ah that's serious—"was Y's comment—earlier points had been sex & pot.

I told him about letter I'd written to Ylena & Simonov[24] about him when he was in trouble "If Communism produced such fine men as Yevs & Voznesenskys then I accept Communism—they were good propaganda"—he raised his hands and eyebrows & touched his heart—"They never told me, they never said a word—. . ." Kazahof actor said "Very naïf" and I agreed, "All I could do"—But Yev. Said "That kind of naïf is good . . . It would have meant something beautiful to know then—that someone cared."

We left in 2 cars to go to House of Composers—In car I talked with Sergei who gave me names of other Russ experimental poets—and

24. Konstantin Simonov (1915–1979) poet, playwright, and eventually (1967–79) head of Union of Writers of the USSR.

when I asked about Y-V—said, "I can give you his phone"—Sergei long blond hair & square set face high cheekbones fair handsome, slightly rough skin & delicate features—Russian Rimbaud face—almond eyes— He tried to say something about "The Esperanto of the basic substance of art passes thru all the jail-bars of the world" which Yev. translated into Spanish for me but stopped in middle laughing—"He always talks in such metaphysical figures I can't translate—his mind is too fine—He reads too many books—he's our intellectual—he writes criticism—he says that architecture and painting flourish but here criticism is not yet born."

At restaurant door we were stopped—new rule only composers allowed in—Yevtushenko stepped forward & leaned in the glass door discussing it with the madonna of the management—I hung back & watched & looked in Sergei's eyes & gave him my book & pen to write names and addresses in—A little girl Mischa was with us all along. "She's the most beautiful woman in Moscow . . . I'm in love with her . . . Gala's home . . . You must promise me to tell Gala my wife that I was with you all night . . . You must tell that story"—Yev has childish charm, spoiled child, conscious of his authority & so plays child to give other people advantage over him, to pet & love him not to be distant or fearful—to get close & mother or brother him—more intimate, a variety of gentleness & politeness—I suppose most people think he's silly & love him, he in this sense encourages disrespect.

He was looking at my notebook, came to a page with Russian name for medicine against Crabs written on it by Alyosha—"Don't show this to anyone—you mustn't let anyone see this page," he laughed, but he was serious.

A table we ate cold relishes, sourkraut, pickled mushrooms, sweet preserved pickled apples, salads & olives & drank vodka and wine—Yevtushenko against the wall on my right, Kayahov actor on left, other poet

Soviet Union

across from Kayahov, and facing me Aksenov and Sergei Visage & the girl—ah, Sergei looks like the blonde actor who played Nevsky!— but smaller & rather beautiful delicate hands—we started scribbling in the book, making pictures I my three fishes, Aksenov his soldiers marching & one long individual walking away. Sergei a drawing of fishbone & head, vodka & glass, the Russian table—Yevtushenko kept raising his eyebrows & nudging me to look at the beautiful little girl he was wooing—

"Don't tell Frieda who gave you this phone number—this you should not talk about—Alex G. was in jail for 2 years—he just got out recently in '62—Better not mention this to Frieda at all."

We drank a lot—Yev—"You must go to Siberia—Moscow & Leningrad is not Russia—Understand the first capitalist was prehistoric, the first man who had an extra bear-skin to trade—the traditions of capitalism are ancient—Socialism in Russia is only 40 years old, a baby, the first steps, each little step is an experiment—"

"I hate the Russians—" Here he stopped & warned "don't please repeat what I say"—"I was born here & raised here my family my life my country—I half hate and half love—It's a country the biggest in the world, old slavery, they're used to slavery and the psychology of the people hasn't changed yet—Lenin never foresaw this, never understood this problem—The Plan was all in his head, it was theoretical—it was an idea to begin, to try—meanwhile we suffer for our mistakes—enormous suffering"—

We were getting drunker & he leaned against wall sitting in his chair in the intimate side room—Jap style a little—of the Composer's House restaurant—"No composers come here just friends, there are never any composers here"—

Aksenov in his cups very sweet quieted everyone, Yevtushenko began to recite—I remember this moment very clearly as silence settled in the

Soviet Union

room, everyone at table listened intently, I watched his profile—a curious Russian rhythmic form of speech this poetry very akin to the impulses of actual speech codified into what sounded like triads of lines the end of each triad rhymed, with much internal rhyme at endings of the triple sections, and each triple section broken into waves of three, with extra syllables unaccented uncounted, just the pulses—a sort of dactyl in effect—dactyls with extra syllables trailing—

His voice got stronger while reading & powerful intensity came thru, elation & energy in very hard solid blocks of triplicated syncopation—almost ecstatic—a message—The childishness of face disappeared & political man emerged—old roar—I could see fine spit fly forth from his teeth as he bit off words—I was looking into the lamp, his profile against the white stucco wall, face grew more deep flushed as he recited from memory, perhaps 10 minutes, a long passage that deepened in seriousness till the cords stood out on his neck, the voice came from upper chest & throat, he jutted his jaw forward to emphasize some terminal declarations—Sergei listening occasionally smiled, shook head & clapped his hands in agreement & wonder—Yev's fine blond hair a wisp hanging over brow and nose like thin Bob Hope curved up, grew handsome in face, a manliness like Declaration of Rights & Injustices of Man—the word veysmir Universe or world I caught—I sat in wonder photographing the scene in my brain—a vast sad movie—at the restaurant table.

When he had finished, the waitress came in and kissed him—everybody else by then gone from the restaurant—and the cook too came in and smiled & patted him on shoulder—all happy and appreciative & distinguished—lovely that waitress in black dress, a friend with ear at portal hearing the Russian poets drunk over Vodka & pickled mushrooms leaning against the lamplight speaking forth in staccato declarative cadences—

Later he recited some verses of Pasternak he liked—about Christ—

Soviet Union

"Thru too great abundance of love you tried to embrace too many people in the wings of the Cross"—

Meanwhile Kozahof the actor, and the girl had skipped off—Yev turned to me and said "I am defeated"—

We drove home, on way I sang a little and read him Moloch section of Howl in car, in soft intense voice, singing the lines melodiously to emphasize rhythm as he didn't fully understand the English words—

Had spent the morning at Intourist, at Visa photographer on corner of Metropole Hotel—passport photos take a week, we got special treatment, it only took 5 hours—at Polish Embassy & then coffee at Writer's Union & then to Joe & Annie's, rode the Metro myself alone from Prospekt Marx stop at foot of Kremlin to Sokolinki stop—

All afternoon there talking about the family, who did what—made up family tree—I told Joe I'd asked about Beria or Simonov and Simonov said it was nonsense to think Beria an agent of Scotland Yard. Annie said, "Well I guess those people know more than we do"—We sat over tea in their one room, a window a little open to let in freshair I was smoking—I ate some potatoes & fish & stringbeans with butter—They offered me rubles if I needed any to stay—But the problem is Visa extension not rubles.

April 2, 1965—

Woke hungover by phonecall, washed & dressed fast to meet little furhatted Nina in her black boots & coat in lobby—we rushed by cab to embassy & got visas finally cleared, then to Foreign Literature Magazine, I gave long description of U S poetry Pound——>Creeley prosody consciousness sex legalities etc.—Said they'd give me rubles owed from old poetry—& publish some new—

Then to Dostoyevski's house, he with wart on face "a good fellow . . .

Soviet Union

not our best poet but good friend good man ..." said Yevtushenko—&
talked about Vienna and Berne conventions & Frieda Lurie interrupt-
ing like a housewife with worries—sat at table and Aksenov came in,
then Yevtushenko, we ate fish and potatoes and crabmeat & drank
vodka, Aksenov's wife came—

Yevtushenko—"If cognac had bubbles I'd drink it, I can only drink
champagne ... Yesterday you called me a narcissist but I read in your
book poem about making love to yourself in mirror you are also"—

(He'd asked me at supper last night what they thought of him in
America, what critics said?—and I gave long measured explanation—
Voznesensky a better poet, Yev a stronger political force—Both with
huge responsibility—Yev a narcissist etc.)—

Rostevtiensky brought out Oxford book of Russ poetry with photo
on cover Blok & Yev—He smiled & rubbed his breast—I said "It's like
setting up a triumphal pillar on Red Sq. that anthology will still be a
text in 50 years"—He kept rubbing his breast, smiling like spoiled
child—"More ... more , .. I *need* that ... I like to see that."

I notice his skin very pale & almost white trans-lucent, delicate fea-
tures, blond hair & perhaps slightly thin haired skull, gaps showing
scalp between locks of fine straight hair—their thin fingers, pale arms
in his shortsleeve wool pullover shirt—He wore big red knitted wool
sweater both days—and almost beardless shaven face, pale hair almost
invisible, hairless arms & very smooth skin—a rare body—

"To understand us—You realize the intelligentsia of the 19th century,
were aristocrats, they had no future, they finished themselves—then the
revolution took many—then in the 30's the cult of personality killed off
the best poets and intelligentsia—then the war—you realize how many
million died?"—

"20 million?"

Soviet Union

"20 million—imagine—we are six of us here, if we all were killed at once the earth would feel it a little, yes?—perhaps?—but 20 million! What Russia went thru! then again after the war in the 50's more trouble, in cold war—more Stalin—So that we are the *first* generation of the intelligentsia—Here the whole population have been slaves before the revolution disorganization—now everybody reads—the culture is more widespread but shallower than before—but by the third generation, then the *greatest* intellectuals will emerge—You understand that in 19th century we had the greatest intelligentsia in the world, the most advanced—do you know that?"

I was confused but nodded yes anyway thinking of Dostoyevsky Tolstoy—Tchaikovsky—OK—

"If Communism comes true, then by third generation we will have a population of intelligentsia—and really great men!"

"You are one of us, here we are together old friends talking—as if not stranger"—

I nodded a little embarrassed but happy. "I had many fantasies of you for years but now that we are sitting together it's like a vast sad movie"— He inquired of translation of that phrase & exchanged ah's with Roz and Aksenov—

China? "Let me repeat your Tolstoy's dying words—I see a yellow peril raising itself up in future—I'm not supposed to prophesy—this is between you and me—but I will prophesy anyway—that in the future, Russia will once again as against Hitler be the victim & bulwark that saves your nation and the West"—

"Well, let's you & me go China together" I said—

Yev "They'd execute me! I read a Chinese article, I'm referred to as a lackey of imperialism & an agent for US capitalist aggression—I could never get a visa—it would be easier for you—they'd execute us together— ... I heard on radio last nite, Chinese broadcast, accusing Russia of supporting American aggression worldwide scale—helping stifle revolution everywhere, Congo Cuba Vietnam."[25]

"I like Chinese food I don't mind if their menu fills the universe" I said.

"I could do without it—not many people except specialists here know much Chinese classics—I know one poem"—he quoted something Oriental about silver branches & moonlight—Aksenov laughed & said "Yev's full of shit, that's Japanese he doesn't know the difference"—Full of shit no some Russian expression I didn't catch—

I had to leave, brought out camera & we took a few photos—talked maybe we go to Brotsh—"We can get your visa extended"—Yes? But never talked concretely on that.

Then to auto plant, I talked to small group of literary club, read a poem, burning grounds tales, listened politely & they read a few poems—head of Club a nice old Jew friend of Gorki—Faihesh Yiddish & when I said "A Bissel" he was delighted—here it's a sort of secret password to acceptance of being Jewish—still don't understand that scene yet—When I toast "La Chiam," Yev always seems to think it's a big charming political joke declaration triumph of some sort as if honorific.

Then to Bolshoi Ballet—end of second act Prokofiev music suddenly

25. *The following text was included by Ginsberg as a note to Yevtushenko's comments:* "There is a Chinese general Po Chu I who is pro-Soviet—They send him to a work camp for reeducation—but everytime there is an official function they bring him out, dress him up in his uniform and put him in place on the line of review or at receptions—If anyone attempts to converse with him an aide interrupts 'Do you want some bread . . . or caviar' and leads him off to the buffet—So a friend of mine is a diplomat—they are honest and realistic among themselves—drinking with a Chinese diplomat asked him why they preserve this general—"In case there is an improvement of relations with Soviet Russia we will need a man with a clean record"— "The Chinese are supreme Machiavellians"—

Soviet Union

awesome, as the 12th hour sounds & the illusion vanishes—and end of opera the Good Fairy stands waving wand triumphantly at Moscow audience as curtain closes—a very odd statement for Prokofiev to make—the last lovers—united trumpet cadenza very slow & piercing—great like Tchaikovsky—suddenness of the spirit of feeling there, 2 tears rolled down my cheeks—and the curtain closed on the Lady Fairy Princess moving glittering wand—as if saying to Moscow folk that despite godless atheistic materialistic stupid Communism—Wow the end of the Universe will be transcendental glittering MAGIC!—

Home & writing when at 1 a.m. door knock, I was scared—cops like in Cuba?—it was the same kid I'd met nights before & exchanged coats with drunk again, with an English student friend. He'd mended my grey coat & it looked chic on him—he began kissing me on brow on thick on lips, hugging me, I got a hardon, he took me aside & hugged & kissed me "I like you"—and then drunken slav still, "You button down shirt—I want." I sat with them half hour, they left me half bottle of Vodka, I gave him some jockey shorts but hung on to my blue jeans & button-downs & animal skin suede jacket with hole in sleeve—

March 4, 1965 [*sic,* should be April]—Saturday [*sic*—it was Sunday]—

A papier-russo, clean math, and the curls of my fingernails in an aluminum ashtray at Downstair Hotel National.

At hotel 3 p.m.—waiting for Voznesensky—he called phone 3:30—"Allen?—Andrei—I came to your hotel in 20 minutes—yes?—half hour"—

I went downstairs after singing hymns for myself awhile, & was bearing camera on Kremlin when this cab came—I turned, he raised his hands as if covered by gun, I shot photo after delay adjusting the distance.

Soviet Union

In cab, a small girl "I introduce you my friend—she translate."

"Can say anything in front of her?"

"She has no official connection."

2 a.m. Dream—

I am at Kremlin wall or wall of some school or military camp—As I walk out between school lockers a young kid walks straight into me puts his hand on my throat and forces me back down supine on a couch— "You are under arrest. We will let you go from here, accompanied and silent to Japan, where you will have an interpreter and guide a young man who will walk in front of you at all times and protect you from intrusion by others. You will accept this situation and speak as you are instructed beforehand. Is it agreed?"

I said "No wait a minute you can't do this it's not even practical, my name is Allen Ginsberg, people will know the difference—readers or friends will stop me on the

street—"

"That will not be a useful attitude"—he said pushing me down by the forehead—"for the transport a needle will be desirable—you will feel no pain—" He asked another young friend to get needle—from locker perhaps—

Aide began plunging the fine long strong hypodermic into my left breast—supposed to knock me out—I woke up.

Sunday, March [April] 4, cont. He asked if strongest rhythm came with or without drugs? I said, both, it only happened 3 times maybe, once with and once without and once half & half.

I read aloud, softly, Part II & III of Howl for him to hear rhythm, he said "I don't fully understand the words but I was with you in the sound."

Soviet Union

Then he asked friend to play piano—"This is something like what you are doing—the powerful rhythm"—

We were still drinking white clear vodka and getting a little drunker in his living room. I went in bathroom to pee, he showed me the way— I kissed him in the hall—he said "I am glad to see you—we are both poets above all else, we are together that is supreme"—In the bathroom a little kewpie-doll attachment to the toilet-paper box.

In the room I began chanting mantras omomom Buddha Dalini— then Gopala Gopala Devaki plandina Gopolas—He said "I liked the first one better"—I never really sang much tho, still it was deep voiced & rhythmic impressive—

Later: "I have to go out to theater"—Same performance of his poems as I'd seen several days ago—"Would you like to stay here or come along?"—"I would love to come along as I am not left alone"—"We won't leave you alone" he laughed. But I was serious. In the car I started weeping—"You look beautiful now" he said "This may be the only time we see each other, you have no idea the trouble I went thru to get here— it was very difficult, and I am unhappy that I can't stay more than a few days, I am free to stay longer but trouble with visa bureaucracy ..." That's why I was weeping, plus vodka, and the excitement of riding to theater in car.

Performance same as last, a chic gamin in cap with triangular black-board on which she wrote names of poems as they came up on the empty stage—filled with same performers whom I'd seen in Lermontov Hero of Our Times—She swung the black triangle back & forth like pendu-lum with tick tock of clock strummed by actor with guitar—at end of recitation Voznesensky stepped forth, in sweater & suit jacket & pants, one foot forward, looking at audience, very casual & sincere, his face flattened in the distance of the stage—& recited a few short poems—one old Farewell to Architectural, another new poem—his style more con-

Soviet Union

versational than Yevtushenko & less impressive, but very firm voiced, still a recitation from memory and not fresh knowledge—then much applause & he added "We have here Allen Ginsberg a great American poet one of the founders of Beatnik movement and a good friend of our country—I will recite a poem translated into English by one of his friends"—and reciting "Fire at Architectural"—

Much applause very steady and continuous a manisfestation of faith—the evening audience mixed young and old—

I found later this Bill was presented informally at first a dozen times, at odd hours, after regular stage performances—then finally put on separately, sort of sneaked thru into official status.

We went out, he found me a taxi, I said I knew how to go home alone—disappointed we were not going back to his house—"I'll call you Monday"—so I went to Hotel National & had long meal alone.

The girlfriend translator of his spoke also some Hindi & Urdu—she'd been in India several times—was leaving the day after tomorrow another trip—Said she'd glimpsed me once walking on Benares Street—someone had pointed me out to her as the American poet. As taxi left theater she said to me "Namastiji."

Sat. that night, the young kid I'd exchanged jackets with knocked— 2 a.m.—Sober this time. Night before he'd come with friend both drunk—kissing me, showing his drunken muscles—a puppeteer—and trying to talk me into giving him my blue jeans & button down.

Tonight he came alone—we finished the vodka—he started after my pants & blue jeans again, asking to trade— he muttered in Russian "Amerikanski Mantekilla"—I guess meaning "Americans are too damn fat"—I got back in bed, he sat down & sang American songs—talking about button downs & Glenn Miller, an obsessional hang up on Amerikanski. I grabbed him & pulled him down next to me & kissed him, he said "I like you" but I was all Slavic tenderness no hairy genitals.

Soviet Union

I think he understood what I wanted, but he said he had to go home to his mother & get up early to work so he couldn't stay overnight. And left, promising to return in a couple of days bringing me a present of some records.

Sunday, March [*sic*—should be April] 4, 1965

Woke & tried to phone Alex G.—couldn't figure out the right phone number from Russian scribble—kept getting ladies speaking wrong Russian. Then to Intourist 11 a.m. arrange polish train ticket—at hotel 12:30 Alyosha Simonov met me with actor friend & car & we drove out to the country toward Bella Akhmadulina's[26] house—wrong road & passed yellow house white pillared in the Leninsy-Gorky suburbs, set back a mile in the hills overlooking barren snowy valley—where Lenin died.

"Can you help me phone Y. V?" "Yes" he said—"I simply have not had time as I told you—not seen his mother"—"Well I have the number now"—and showed him—He shook head abruptly & changed manner when he saw Alex G's name. "I don't want to have anything to do with this man"—"What's his story?"—"You know all our scandals and you don't know this one?" he laughed.

Seems A.G. had run an underground magazine—against the law—had printed Yessenin-Volpin & other poems, poems by Siusky against Stalin —("In those days we lived underneath a God")—Had written "dirty" things—so Alyosha heard, but had never seen the magazine 1958?— called in on trial, implicated writers whose work he'd published without their permission—"dirty"—""Was he in jail?"—"I don't know, I just met him once or twice, & when I found out his name I avoided him."

26. Bella Akhmadulina (1937–2010), Russian poet and translator, former wife (1954–59) of Yevtushenko.

Soviet Union

Other Gossip—Fadeyev (?) suicide, had done so much harm under Stalin, was RHPP (Proletarian Writers Cult) that after '56 he couldn't make his way back. "He had convinced himself that all the evil was for the good of Communism—also he forced himself to write things he didn't believe—also he drank heavily. People in that position drink a lot, it's a pattern ... Dr. Zhivago, maybe published in 5 more years. My mother thinks it's good, I don't personally ... My father rejected it for Novy Mir when he was editor—my mother says I have to read it again carefully, it's best on 2'nd examination—I don't know"—

Serg. had said days ago that Mayak. was followed by police last days. How did he know? An older poet, friend of Mayak.—told me—he's dead, I won't mention his name— "They came to Mayak's house and Mayak went & looked out window & joked about it"—

He'd read 1984.[27] and Koestler Darkness at Noon[28]—beginning of 1984 he thought was good description, & *Darkness* accurate picture. Trotsky? "I read many books by him—He's not dependable either"—the documents aren't yet published that would clear up that history he continued—he'd seen some that slightly contradicted Trotsky's versions for instance a statement by Trotsky that Stalin had fucked up some battle front till T. removed him & took over—another military diary said yes but Trotsky had done even worse when *he'd* taken over—

"The final relation between the Commune and the individual have never been defined, even in theory—I've tried to investigate this subject—But in Marxist theory this hasn't been taken up."

"It's the key question," I figured.

"Marx said ideology 50 years behind Economics. We have almost 50 years of socialism so by 1967 we should have an ideological revolution."

27. Novel by George Orwell.
28. British novelist Arthur Koestler wrote *Darkness at Noon* (1940).

Soviet Union

Finally on snowy country lane amid fields and woods, a wooden gate—Girl in black fine dress and white apron came out without coat into icy path to open latch—"Bela"—She had upswept red-orange hair and fine reddened cheeks bright lips—a red head with fine red head complexion—young body not thin not heavy, big breasts and nice womanly ass—The house a large wooden country house maybe 5 rooms downstairs, big kitchen—we went into living room & sat down not knowing how to begin—She brought out lemon & caviar & sardines on plates of bread, and a large silver-glass bottle of Vodka which had music box inside that began chiming on table—a number of small paintings & drawings on the wall, one large buttocked woman squatting washing a naked pubescent girl. Some old black negroid statues on the mantelpiece, familiar but not Afric—Her husband a big headed grayhair man & I talked desultorily about London—he's a novelist (scriptwriter)—I described U.S. filmmakers Lower E. Side scene vaguely to him—It's out of context here—There's no social function for personalized avant-garde expression—nor sex art—hard to begin explaining.

She came in & sat down—With her a lady friend an artist, very fine elderly face, who showed me drawing of Raskolnikov in sharp-eyed agony—and a soft voiced lady English teacher intimate of the household—once a friend of some persecuted artists—

BA wore an emerald cross—"Are you religious"—Her lady friend interpreted—"Bela is certainly in a way religious, she has an aura about her … she is so kind to everyone, she gives so much love—She is a very beautiful soul, a religious soul, without defining a system of beliefs"—I said I was sort of religious & had had various experiences of mystic nature, and had she? The other day she'd felt a sense of foreboding, gathering of evil—she'd brushed back the hair from her forehead to let God in—Next day her father in law who lives in the house—with an old white small sharpeyed mother—fell ill—taken to hospital, serious. It was hus-

Soviet Union

band's birthday yesterday, the family & friends had all gathered, still gathered today, many people, smell of tongue cooked & steam coming from kitchen—"We'll eat in half hour"—

I talked about psychoanalysis—All her maternal relatives had been crazy one time or another—always in institutions—I told her about Kaddish poem a little—"Many people who are mad write Bella letters"—

She sitting there said "At one time I used to gather all my magic power in this little green ring I wear . . . but then when I saw how difficult it was to live in this world, how much suffering, I gave up my belief. . . . But I'm still fond of the ring" She had two rings on her right hand, one a black dull jewel, the other a green face carved in jade perhaps—a bearded ancient face—Whore?—I meant to ask but never had chance later when I thought of it drunk.

"I went to 4 analysts looking for the right doctor"—

"Leader?" She laughed. Explanation, it had been mistranslated Leader. No, I explained, the right doctor who'd be nice to me, give me candy.

She's been to doctors too, but they were all too cold, & weren't really kind to her. The last one she sent a poem in advance, warning him, a poem describing the cruelty of doctors with their golden instruments. He'd sent it back saying it was nonsense, he'd never met a doctor who had golden instruments. So she never went to him.

Aura of gathering of lady saints, kind magic, spiritualism, witchery or old Russian lady sensitivity in the household, centered on Bela—She sitting there round eyed & very mature looking, tending table and kitchen, occupied like middleclass lady completely normal—The artist lady & the sensitive tall trembling-voiced English teacher friend all sitting around ah!ing and oh!ing and saying "da" and "Krasnya"—Yes beautiful—"You have come to the right household if you are interested in mystic experiences—There is something good and spiritual about

Soviet Union

Bela"—said the English teacher with thin preraphaelate lesbian face beaten in by the '50's, her hair drawn back on the side like a man's but longer.

So we defined God as desire and talked about that in harmony & then to Alyosha sitting there silent & practical & asked him *his* desire?— "To get a few weeks rest, & finish my work here so I can go away & take that rest" he said mock grumpily. But the lady artist took him seriously and objected—"No you have closed yourself off from us, you have closed the possibility of conversation when you give us so superficial an answer."

"Whatya mean?" he said—they argued in Russian. "He's really angry," I said to the trembling lady—"Yes see how harsh he is"—she answered.

Bella described a letter she'd gotten from a madhouse in Yugoslavia—because her picture looking like a ski-hooded madonna, thin faced way published on cover magazine—she brought out brown rotogravure magazine to show me—"Naturally I didn't know Yugo, so couldn't read it but showed it to some friends and asked them to translate it for me—They started reading it aloud—some people got embarrassed or thought it was shocking, and left the room, critical—It said, "My wife Bela, I have always loved you, not forsake me, return etc. etc. I am forever your devoted husband etc." I went to Yugoslavia & wanted to look him up but couldn't—I would have gone in to hospital and said "I've returned" & that would've cured him . . . He'd probably prefer his ideal Rotogravure and been bored with the reality—He could've rejected me & kept his ideal satisfied, we'd both be free of each other"—

At supper we talked a lot, I asked her to describe Russian prosody— She'd said she'd written early free verse with her friends—talking about Voznesensky "I feel closer to him—He keeps reserve, he's very human, but is most modest about his inner nature—" . . . "Rosdevtiensky is not a poet"—"You realize that as we grew up the language was exhausted— There were no real words anymore, it was all official language, irrespon-

Soviet Union

sible—I had to find words that came from my own throat—Now I write in any form, we have conquered all forms and can transmit inspiration in any medium we choose to"—

She recited one poem, charming, and then at length a long interesting poem about *Rain*—It as translated line by line after each stanza—She looked to one person's eyes after another, & then in distance aside, while reciting—came to stanza of children's cloud silver chorus ending mocking on *Bread* with flushed face and excited eyes gleaming childishly spritely, harping the stanza out of her mouth, I saw her cheeks red—(Voznesensky reciting his lower teeth only were visible in his face in theater)—& lips red, the syncopate rhythm of the stanza child-celestial, a note of pearly realism I hadn't met in human imaginative Voznesensky or godly Yevtushenko—

She asked me to read, I sang awhile & intoned some Howl musically from memory—then chauffer had to go home, so we drove back, I was silent most of the way.

To Technological Auditorium poet Lamuelsky reciting—old high backed benches, wooden, that Moyah, spoke to—

and to theater club where ate with random gang of producers lawyers & middleaged actresses, talking French, eating chopped liver.

Sunday, March 4 [*sic,* should be April].—

Then morn sat writing & noon to U.S. Embassy met cultural attaché—lunch & gossip—he knows Yev & Vos & Lurie & others—

Then at Writer's Club with Eugene [?] poet—talking Gnosticism all 3 hours—then to house Marguerite Alghier—talking about Parra—

Then to Lily Brik's apartment—Mayakovsky Suicide?—He wanted to stay himself, not be a bureaucrat—He talked about suicide as far back as 1916—called her up & insisted she come over to stop him—the note on theater door? Meant he was sorry he couldn't finish the public battle, not that he was forbidden to. Followed by police? Not at all, this was all before Stalin's bad time—that started later. And he didn't want to grow old. Not politics, nor love, were reasons. We talked about Cocteau, Aragon & Elsa Triolet—

Mayakovsky very sexy—very tender as lover—very gentle, never raised voice, in private—Klebnihov not sexy, or secretly so, but outwardly sexless—She had Mayakovsky portrait of Klebnikov on her wall— [?] & Yev. Not poets—publicists, or young—yes a true poet—

And she had painting by Leger & [?] and Russian primitives—we sat late and talked, I read her Kaddish rhythms and sang mantras, she recorded—old European apartment filled with mementos & paintings—we ate caviar and raisins & blue cheese and talked French.

Home later, Yess-Vol called, talking rapidly on phone in French—we made date to meet 11 am. At Mayakovsky's statue next day.

The Russians are trapped in Russia.

7 April 1965

All morning at hotel writing, postcards from Moscow, Alex Ginsburg phone & in long halting conversation in pigeon German I explained what time to meet me with Y.-V.

Then waiting for Nina to call about magazine rubles due me and today's departure plans, time grew late, I phoned the Writer's Union & said I'd be there that afternoon 3:30. Sergei also phoned and made date with him at 4, and Sergei Tchudahoff I phoned to meet at 5.

[...]

I took taxi late—arrived 11:05 and Yessenin V a young middleaged man in grey overcoat & brown French style beret waved briskly and walked up, extrovert & courteous, speaking in rapid stuttering French. Little kid in green cap with rosy face was Alex Ginsburg. I'd remember

I'd heard of Alex Ginsburg years ago an underground Russ poet? For days I'd been trying to reach him on phone, not remembering the earlier association that just came to me this night before. He'd finally got my message & gone over to Y. V.'s house to tell him Allen Ginsberg was looking for him. Tsk, Tsk, he said on phone, when I finally got my name across.

Alex went off for bottle of wine—I noticed that Alexandra Y. V. pulled out big ruble bills—5's and 10's—so he wasn't broke—

We walked up and down in front of the Metro station at Tchaikovsky Hall and talked, waiting for Alex to come back—speaking in this nervous French, he answered lots of my questions rapidly & amiably, perfect understanding & openness I'd not encountered much in anyone here before—Had had 2 periods of hospital—"Were you crazy?"—"I consider the Society was crazy & I was sane"—First time 1949–51, second time 1959–60. The same troubles again in '62? I forgot. No shock—half the hospitals are prison hospitals, half regular, he was in both. And he got out, in time, his mother helped, brought presents. Doesn't write much poetry now—working on a long theory of basic logic with many moral & political implications. Will return to poetry when task's done. He would explain later how he got in trouble. Now things not so bad—worst period 1936–7—than after war '45, then as soon as Stalin died, within a month the whole cloud lifted. By Hungary Revolt time, another small wave of repressions. Now things aren't so good, but by no means very bad, as before. Were we now tailed by police? Doesn't make any difference, all they can do is question me and I can tell them to go to hell. It's a bureaucracy, you can deal with them a little now. I'm mainly concerned with formal legal procedure, questions of logic & law—that's the one thing so confused & corrupted here—Basically fighting for my rights, interested in constructing an unbreakable sodality of logic applicable to social problems & law—legal procedure,

Soviet Union

Alex G. had got lost, we went up street looking for him, finally decided he'd meet us at the house so we went down into beautiful white subway & talked—I showed him Howl—he read lines aloud to himself intelligently—"This line's funny," I said & he nodded—

He explained Alex'd run an underground magazine Syntax, but hadn't been sent to jail for that—they got him on another small charge—faking a passport identification booklet to get into school cafeteria—a common procedure, but they tried to get something on him & used that.

Had he known his father? "Died when I was 1½ years old . . . he never saw me, they were separated, one went to Moscow—the other to Leningrad, then she went to see him but he'd gone to Leningrad & next thing he committed suicide. The reason? Probably an accident—he wrote an 8 line verse"—"A good poem?" Tres *very* good"—To die is nothing new, to live nothing new, either—then wound rope round neck jumped off table or chair—but didn't die of suffocation—his neck broke—Yessenin-Volpin leaned head forward & indicated neck-spine with his palm of hand, with his beret on his head.

Now he has job—only last few years—teaching a small group of mathematicians—they meet a couple times a week & he gives a little lecture on logical problems—

He explained he'd gotten into trouble for things he'd said in '56 in Paris or outside Russia, talking about Stalin or illegality of procedures. He'd been rebuked for that in some newspaper—He went to *sue* the newspaper as they misreported what he'd said, and there were no witnesses anyway—the girl who reported his remarks wasn't even at the meeting—Several years later he was arrested on that charge—perhaps—"Defaming Russia"—that led to Bughouse one time—or was one incident starting his troubles—.

How many people taken under Stalin, 20,000,000?—Who knows—10, 15, 20, maybe more maybe less, there's no statistics, no witnesses—

Soviet Union

"And if it's only 10,000,000 does that make any difference," he laughed gaily in the snow. We were near outside his Metro station.

His house a house modern white apartment in a project in Moscow suburb near the Metro station—He lives on first floor, we went toward it thru mud streets, Alex waved from the window. His wife a plump little friendly girl younger than he—Said his mother wd/be coming—Sat down in his study with Alex & talked—I slumped way down near floor in beach chair—He had lots of books, & English logic texts, Quine, on his desk, & Russian texts—His work, opened the desk & showed me a huge pile of neat papers with figures all over them—

An older mss. of his on logic would be published soon. Then he hoped in a few months, half a year, to finish his work on Social Logic, whatever it was. He tried to explain it to me, in French, but I got only the most general idea—an examination of permission and forbidden in Society. What's permitted and what's forbidden defined once & for all, no more legal ambiguity.

I talked about drugs & sang mantras & explained Burroughs' cut-up, interrupting all this—saying I thought conceptual thought was a vicious circle, & quoted Diamond Sutra.

He said yes, it's not the entire universe, but this human form needs repetition, for comfort's sake, therefore rhythm or pattern or concept or language—but that had to be examined & made stable & dependable. Therefore work on basic logic. He asked me to send him books on codes of criminal procedures & systems of laws, original texts—for comparative study. I explained our censorship trials & how they worked—latest Supreme Court decision on Henry Miller.[29]

Agh. I'm tired of transcribing all this—

29. On June 22, 1964, in a 5–4 decision, the United States Supreme Court overturned an obscenity judgment against Miller's *Tropic of Capricorn*.

Soviet Union

Before I left his house he explained it was easy to find him—on every major square of neighborhood center are citizen's directories—all you need to do is go to the booth, give family name, age, & profession & they can give address. Nobody like Frieda or Nina did this for me.

Began looking up laws on Alex Ginsburg's case—No law against possessing mimeo machine, but some technical laws & fines against it another way—gotta be licensed or something—But Alex was jailed on totally other charge than running his magazine *Syntax*—poems by Slutsky and Yessenin V.—they got 400 people in on his "investigation"—Yessenin V. fumbled on the right word for this first stage of legal procedure—

Yessenin-Volpin got on another charge—called in because someone'd given him invisible ink which he'd destroyed, too dangerous—let go on that, but then began sending mss. or complaints to magazines—so they arrested him again & put him in bughouse.

Said he was kept there & the judgment of his sanity was whether or not he'd make a statement that the GPU was correct in its actions in his case. He got around that somehow—verbalizations—and did get out.

We took photographs—Ginsberg & I looking each other in the eye—Ralph Cheysey & Louis Ginsberg—Lots of Ginsburgs in Moscow he said—G asked me about Stockhausen happening, was it filmed? And wanted me to send the score.

They took me to Writer's Union in Cab—

[...]

There with Irena Grodenitze talked over possible return visit—then to street met Sergei—

"Well all this time you've been surrounded by police—it *is* a police state"—

Then inside to coffeeshop with Yevtushenko & Aksenov, we sat & drank champagne & got tipsy & intense and argued—I told him he was really polite not masochistic, his ability to let people walk over him.

Soviet Union

His face pained & thin, marks under eyes "I have this only last few years" pointing to crowmarks over his nose on forehead. "Voznesensky a mystery—like soap in the hand always slips away—a machine without personality for making great poetry—I lived in same room with him 22 days in New York & he was like wet soap"—

His long poem "I got the decision today"—"From the 'Credo'" I asked, remembering his earlier image. He was surprised I had understood & remembered & laughed—"Yes, from the sky—from Heaven today—it'll be published—they just decided they approved—Now I have to begin worrying for real—what public will feel—Took a year to write & a year to revise & get published"—

Boulata A. came over—in from Leningrad—thin fortyish face, mustached. The floor was covered with champagne making its green plastic sticky—Yevtushenko popped open his bottle, spurty foam all over floor, he was turned away from the small coffeeshop cafeteria table. I explained about young kid who changed coats drunk & said Stalin was great—that he'd sang me akuljava songs—Yev turned to Bulata & translated from Spanish—? "That's not such a compliment when one of those change-clothes people sings my work"—I said "He was a good person—gave me good Bulgarian coat, bottle of vodka & sang songs"—Yev kept translating, repeating laughing, "a Bulgarian coat!"—

Later "I am masochist with feeble people—with higher ups I am different hombre"—

"What kind of tactics with them?" I ask't.

"I want to murder them . . . and I do, slowly in another way" he looked at me with sudden apocalyptic steely false blue eyes, a little drunk.

I pulled out camera & photographed his face while he had that slightly degenerate blonde pain-eyed expression. I started to take out chango beads to give him—found they were broken, in my bag, beads spilled all over wet floor.

Soviet Union

We drove all to Journalist's house, couldn't get in, so back in car to Actor's house, everyone welcomed him, we sat down with champagne & caviar again—modern décor—talked about family life, he plays around but gets jealous when wife does—I described me & Peter sharing girls— "I'm too normal . . . perhaps too bourgeois—get celoso—jealous . . ."

And Voznesensky'd told him I told V that I wanted to make it with Yev but Yev wouldn't—I corrected that gossip—No, I wanted to talk & felt rejected on sex & drug talk—

And if I come back "we'll take a trip to Siberia—Brotsh Hydroelectric Dam"—via Mongolia—"You don't know RussiaMoscow & Leningrad's not Russia"—. . . "You make great mistake not visiting painter—I gave you his number—Best painter in Russia"—He halted & waved hand— "outside of Siberia, anyway, that's another matter—I would have taken you but didn't want to force my company on you"—

He said that several—"actually a misunderstanding" I explained—"I was thinking maybe you'd call & take me"—

"If you were here we could take Siberia trip—but I have a few weeks business to straighten out"—He'd spoken of those few weeks several times before, I guess affairs connected with Bratsk poem—"Tonight I have boring work to do—I'm moving to new apartment"—There had been empty cardboard cartons in back seat of his car. "I spoke to Gala on phone, she wouldn't accept any excuse my not coming home to pack— dull family life work—except if I were out with you, she gave her approval"—

Home walked upstairs 10:30 and there was Yessenin-Volpin waiting in hall—surprise—He came to my room corrected some notes for Prager volume of his—and we met Nina downstairs—I wasn't sure it was safe to introduce them, but did—Frieda that afternoon had inquired if I was disappointed not meeting him & Brodsky—I'd lied & evaded & not mentioned seeing him that very morning—this conversation had taken place earlier afternoon—so now I was caught in lie—

Off to R.R station Belyroussin for Warsaw train— and then Aksenov & Yevtushenko came up still high & friendly ebullient to see me off.

"Mr. Yevtushenko, meet Mr. Yessenin-Volpin," I said in happy deliberate voice—Yev looked blank and startled a minute, in the gang—then shook hands & they conversed familiarly in Russian—I got kissed & kissed Yevtushenko on the neck, holding him tight—he laughed— "Chico!" and pulled away startled again—Train moved away & I waved goodbye to all of them—hanging on steps—Ah, Yev, Yess V, Nina, and couple other vodka drinking amis—on to Warsaw!

Soviet Union

Auschwitz death camp, April 1965

Poland

APRIL 1965

Ginsberg's decision to visit Poland before returning to Czechoslovakia was a sound one. As he told Peter Orlovsky, he was hoping to visit as many Communist bloc countries, including East Germany and Hungary, as financially possible before returning to the United States. Poland offered attractions to someone interested in Communist influence on everyday lives. Ginsberg also hoped to visit Auschwitz and the Warsaw Ghetto. It didn't hurt that Andrei Voznesensky was going to be in the country for a week; Ginsberg arranged to meet him in Warsaw. The tour harked back to Ginsberg's earlier travels, when he was alone and visiting places where he knew very few people and had to rely on his wits and curiosity to fill his hours. After a period that found him keeping busy schedules in Cuba, Czechoslovakia, and the Soviet Union, the slower pace in Poland would be a welcome respite.

Russian Railroad Station at Brest—The dining room huge high ceilinged, pastel marble columns shining like the Moscow subway stations.

On bridge over River, standing still, looking out train window at Warsaw for the first moments—orange setting sun, a boatful of blue crewmen practicing sport with oars—and the peaked roofs of old town red & brown, very tall on a hump by the river, a domed Church in front, rows of new grey apartments & in the mist from high [?] tower of a 19th century skyscraper. An old Polish horse clops by on the bridge dragging an open wooden wheeled dray.

In a cave in Warsaw—black curved walls with names scratched in the plaster—a young architect with glasses smiled when his friend's lovers kissed—I just remembered I was Mischa Auer in San Francisco—The time Lucien[1] & his girl embraced in a booth in an Italian restaurant on Grant Street Vesuvios perhaps—1964—Time passes—the first recollection of Micha Auer mugging & smirking like a sad deprived pederast was from a movie in Fabian theater in 1937 or before—Paterson—and it might have even been *Naughty Marietta* with Nelson Eddy who's a dead name—and the polish Jazzy dance band is playing—"Yesterdays"— No!—the piano tinkles [?].

Dream April 8, 1965.—Warsaw—Hotel Europe.

All day in the side room upstairs lobby in the theater—hotel, a gal reporter official and her friend a fat necked weak editor, are trying to "help" me with an old difficult manuscript I want to publish—they have been poring over it, trying to perhaps make sense of it or cut out a middle section that goes on too long with mere babble—I get back & they hand me the onionskin pages of the original—Magic Psalm[2] or the psilocybin part—torn apart in three, down the middle—

"Well we worked on it & we do *like* your poem but we feel it would be better for *you* if you did more work on it"—I look at the pages and it shows no real indication exactly how to remedy the text—It's just torn discreetly down the first third of space from the margin, and then torn again 2/3 of the way across the page. (Of course a cut-up's possible but

---

1. Lucien Carr (1925–2005), central figure of the nucleus of Beat Generation writers, met Ginsberg at Columbia University, encouraged him to read the works of Arthur Rimbaud (a major Ginsberg influence), and, most important, was instrumental in Ginsberg's early friendships with Jack Kerouac and William S. Burroughs.

2. See "Magic Psalm," *CP*, 263.

that's not what they're after)—I get mad "Oh well it's so easy for you to talk, all you do is work all day and come up with a vague suggestion but *I* have to write the poem and *I* have to sit down and re-compose and that's impossible the way you set this up it could take months and there's no time—I'm the one that's doing all the work here, you're no help"—

Dream ends there, had begun earlier on streets and in hotel lobbies, with some young girl, we all rented rooms or cubicles, I was going to send something to Flossie Williams—

Woke early, last nite arriving in Warsaw had walked streets people staring at my long hair, uncomfortable in strange language, the city all new rebuilt no central place to go—found a jazzy cafe & had beer & wine there that upset my stomach—wandered upstairs & blundered into Hatha-Yoga class run by a thin aggressive blonde girl who spoke French with me "Oh I've learned it only from books, & I do so want to meet a real Indian who can correct me!" I sat on chair & watched 20 girls spread legs & breathe & take peacock & snake positions, & murmured very nice & smiled & left—Walked all over old town past coffeehouse where pianist was playing nostalgic old jazzy—"Loverman"—and on main street found great crowd in front of Church, services over, I went in saw many young people kneeling serious for confession.

Spot

Head is wobbly.

💙

April 8, 1965.

Woke 6:30 and went out walking in empty morning light, thru great open squares toward 19th century style modern Soviet gift skyscraper Palace of Culture—giant sexy statues of blankeyed idealized laborers

See from *Siesta in Xbalba*[3] the dream "What Men do women can do"—"*No fate more terrible*"—

—and giant muscular women with shot-put cannonballs uplifted on their touch arms, huge workmen thighs and gyn aprons—and the laboring men naked chested muscle-rippling in rough concrete down to the lap, covered with cement drape—or bare breasted except for overall tops thru which ribcages and visible folds of abdominal musculature press tightly, the thinnest sheerest veil of overall over that phallic-belly bulge —one great stupid-faced workman statue carrying a volume on which is carved names Marx Engels Lenin Stalin—"a historical place" said the critic friend of Mr. Spender—and it's a useful building with vast view of Warsaw—I stood & watched a giant insect steamshovel feed dirt to an ant truck in a hollow beneath some toy brick buildings blocks below my perch on the stone balustrade 30th floor mist & smog spread over the suburbs and Vissa River—huge rows of unfinished apartment boxes lining the avenues, great white spacyness, and clusters of old red pre-war high-peaked houses scattered thru the out-spread city—

Passed an ancient brick house being demolished by tiny workmen climbing cornices and walking in roofless rooms of pink-walled flats open to sky & passerby curiosity eyes—

Then walk down neat walls & shopwindows of mainstreet reconstructed new surfaced—

Met with English speaking [?] Kachoo who spoke of Auden & Mary McCarthy—"Czechoslovakia is where we were years ago—first wave of

---

3. See "Siesta in Xbalba," *CP*, 105.

repression, which lasted longer there, giving way to wild freedom—which gets pushed too far—after that things settle in & close down again—nobody believes at all in Communism here now—it's not U. at all—the tension is real—and we begin to think what our children will think of us"—

Second time I heard that—this is an advanced stage more than other socialist countries—and that the Czechs "will learn"—their present freedom will settle into a big drag later—and nobody think *within* Marxist terminology anymore except the police.

Then with professor chap—taking about roles and identities. "I'm a civil servant" he kept repeating.

Then to Writer's Union met Barbara and Wollo and Slusky & talked about Yev & Yes. Volp.—and began arranging visas—-& they said same thing about stages of socialism—"We all have to help each other"—"Things close down, we had a stage of Beatniks after Stalin's death, after '56"—

"But the fight now is to preserve traditions not destroy them as Marxism is doing—So the young men dress sensibly socially—and their resistance is in the preservation of their inner identity." Mr Kachoo over coffee.

Barbara has a nervous tick in the right hand side of her face—a young girl fashion director, in suede boots & sporty wool dress, very fine manners, who spent all day on telephone arranging connections for me.

A Polish clock—black horse raising front hooves over the clockface.

April 10—Lost track of time dates—let's see—nothing exciting happening—big open streets, low buildings, apartments—Morning I woke & went down to breakfast, there were crowds of people on streets with flags, students and young "workers" all dressed well lining the main street outside my hotel—huge grey retouched-looking photographs of Brezhnev & Kosygin the Soviet leaders and Gomulka and several others nameless Polish middleaged faces set upon the public buildings—B & K were visiting Poland to renew 20 year mutual defense pacts—They were leaving that morning—I didn't see them—the populace came out— neither screaming nor sullen, just quiet and nice to see them off—

Made phonecalls & went to Writer's Club—arranged extension of visa—now I'm Guest of the Ministry of Culture—one week free hotel bill & some spending money 1000 Zlotys—all morning and early after-noon meeting French poets at the Club—then with a gang of younger poets by cab out to an apartment in suburb—we drank & I was interro-gated about my ideology, a long translated dialogue—I fought it off— I fell on the floor—I answered mentally—too dreary of me—we got a lit-tle drunk—Rimbaud in French on the magnetophone—one kid with cracked dark eyeglasses kept kissing me & saying "Communism is shit." His girl objected—"He's exaggerating"—the doorbell rang & militia came in, a neighbor had complained the noise—police stayed 15 min-utes, not unfriendly, taking everybody's name but mine—"You see, po-lice, police, this is Communism"—"In the US we'd all be naked or smok-ing marijuana, the police would've been a *real* threat" I said. The fuzz left & we all went around sh sh'ing each other—then home midnite cab.

I had stopped in lunch at US Embassy met Halberstam[4] there, last seen in Saigon, and groups of Culture Affairs officers—

"It's a goddam police state" said Halberstam—"never saw a country like this where there's a total split between populace & government"—

I'll give a lecture at the University.

4. Journalist David Halberstam, *New York Times* reporter, future Pulitzer Prize–winning author of *The Best and the Brightest*.

Saturday

National Gallery—

Poe-Ryder like portrait by Antonio Kolberg (1815–1891)—called "Portret mtodego mezizyzny"

These specters that have come to rest on plastic
    stools,[5]
These young specters with leather gloves, are
        flitting thru the coffeehouse
        an hour,
These specters with scarred faces or little chin beards,
Young specter girls with black stockings and delicate heels,
Young specter boys with short blond hair combed neat
        over the skull—
O Professor Chopin your statue with romantic sideburns
        and waves of hair over your pink ear
        against the smooth plaster wall of the reconstructed
            cathedral—
These new specters with legs crossed and scarves and
        Italian shoes, talking so intensely
        with smiles
    over the small low tables,
        That specters crowded together at late afternoon
with the high soprano of history chanting angelic

---

5. First draft of "Café in Warsaw," *CP*, 358.

thru the hi-fidelity loudspeaker—
and in the background, the perspective walls & windows
      of 18th century streets
curving down New World Avenue to the high
      pedestal column of Stanislous III with
      his sword upraised
watching over Polish youth for 3 centuries—

O Polish hearts what have you suffered since
      Chopin wept into his romantic piano!
The rubble of old buildings coming down, the last
      few pink and blue bedroom walls from
      before the war,
Before the tanks what I know not, iron
      tracks rolling over bone and cobblestone,

before the gaiety of all night parties under the
      air bombs,
before Auschwitz' black bodies, before the
      first screams of the vanishing ghetto—
one or two old bedrooms stand open to the workmen
      of the sun afternoon—
Now these specters gather again to kiss each other's
      hand, girls to kiss lip to lip,
To sit with fine gold watches and red with
      hair stylish from Paris,
To sit by the yellow wall with a large brown
      briefcase, and rest and stare thru curved
      shining eyeglasses over a cup of liqueur—

Poland

To meet and smoke 3 cigarettes with thin black
      ties and nod heads over a new movie—

O Specters sitting before the clean new
      walls of murdered Warsaw
thy Christ and thy bodies be with you for this
      hour, while you are young,
in the New postwar Deva heaven stained
      with the sweat of Communism,
thy loves and thy white smooth cheek skin, soft
in the glance of each other's eye

Peace time is here with us now, peace and the
      classical soprano singing from back time
      thru the wall,
O Specters how beautiful your calm and your
      shaven faces and unswept hair,
how beautiful your round faces and eyebrows
      and pale lipstick and pastel soft cheeks,
how beautiful your love for each other, so
      patient, so courteous sitting thinking
      round the low plastic tables, together
      reading the art journals—
how beautiful your absent glances, waiting
      alone at table with long eyelashes,
how beautiful your entrance thru the blue
      velvet curtained door,
      gazing laughing into the overcrowded room
how you wait in your hats, and measure the

Poland

faces and empty seats, and turn and depart
for an hour,
how beautiful your meditation at the bar
waiting for the slow waitress to prepare
thy hot red tea, minute by minute
Standing as minutes pass, as hours ring in
the churchbells, as years make your
temples grey & turn you blind—
how beautiful you press your lips together,
blow out your cheeks & sigh, or pass
forth smoke from your lips, or
rub your heads, or lean together and
notice this wildhaired madman
who sits weeping among you a stranger.

Ah! Today I saw, in the courtyard of
drab new apartments, the strange-eyed
children of the new age,
playing with sand, gathered at beaches,
carrying white wooden swords,
myriads, innocent to themselves by small automobiles,
guilty eyed gathered waiting in front of the Iron Ghetto
Monument,—
they begin again, and enter forth into the
street & courtyard of the universe,
two by 2 hand in hand—exploring
the new built neighborhood—
As if it were the Ancient Warsaw of old,
except they pass a battle scarred Church wall—
We all go forth and don't know where, except

Poland

for the skull we see in the movies,
or a book on Auschwitz or Belsen, or
a dead aunt lying on a hospital table
in Newark,
or an exciting moment on the street—
a beautiful eyed longhaired girl in
a black coat
and her tall lovely husband in his Palm
Sunday suit and gloves
wheeling their baby along the sidewalk by
the windows of the new built grey modern
apartment house
in the open street at noon, where the
night fires of 1945 made
shadows when they were newborn.

Is now to make rhythm cry in Warsaw '65. The sexless streets of
Moscow.

------

2 a.m. Warsaw April 12, 1965. Monday a.m.

Dream—We went into a Sunday gift shop—me and Naomi-Elanor—
There was music playing from the deep Victrola—The music hath charms
as in my ancient dream of spectral music said Aunt Honey[6]—Elanor's
dead & Naomi's dead—they never knew Soviet Death—So, in the dream
I'm holding Naomi up in my arms in a street waltz—and Beethoven mu-
sic is chorusing upon the cobblestone Navy M City Square anew—

6. Hannah Litzky, Louis Ginsberg's youngest sister.

The intense beauty—[?] Bundershaft!—a terrible beauty is born again, I'm holding the mother lady up, whirling in the Jazzy Dance—to the door of the phone shop, to listen—"A terrible beauty" is born—

The woman waits for me, the woman needs me to hold her up to hear this ode to Joy, ode to life dances on—

8 a.m.—Dream & wake—Some vast political parade with Leaders—I'm on a cobblestone square (maybe Red Sq. or Union Sq.) walking naked with my head above water, a floating head— someone that I know, perhaps Halberstam is on the Square—It's my "protest"—demonstration for something or other—

I sneak up gangplank to ship, or scaffolding where the Leader's making a big public speech in company with other Leaders of small countries, Israel or Egypt—He's Al Aronowitz,[7] and I'm listening to the speech with other correspondents, hidden behind bunting and a pillar—Aronowitz concludes "and so in search for peace I want to express my confidence in Mr. Shah & Mr. Stein, Mr. Ben Gurion too, for as leaders they are . . . they are . . ." he hesitates . . . "they are . . ." and he can't figure how to finish his sentence. I wait awhile & then say aloud, peeking at him from behind the bunting—"They are . . ." he repeats . . . "peaceful people"—I prompt.

We meet to go off the platform—Aronowitz says, "They weren't peaceful people that's why I couldn't finish that way so simply"—"Oh" I say, "I see—I'm sorry"—I realize he was only trying to be honest and worked himself into a sort of trap—just like Aronowitz. And wake.

7. New York journalist, author of groundbreaking *New York Post* series of articles on the Beat Generation.

Poland

April 12. Yesterday took car ride around Warsaw with Halberstam & Barbara H. Explanation of the War Uprising & razing of the city—radio Moscow gave the signal, & uprising began. The Russians were on the other side of the [?] River in Praga—and then didn't move. Slowly the Germans wiped out the Polish Underground "the flower of the generations"—The Russians waited till Warsaw was completely destroyed and all the leaders & fighters of Underground killed, then entered—The Russians did it deliberately, not wanting any anti-Communist Polish opposition or underground to deal with in postWar takeover.

We went by old 19th century promenade street & great delicate Water Palace from afar thru Park gates, & across river to Praga, crowded streets & Montmartre markets—then around looking at new architecture—Stalinist & post Stalinist more modern style—then to the ghetto area—now a vast greens and surrounded by new apartment projects, and monument showing old & young Hebrews with wild eyes & Torahs facing invisible Legions of Destruction—a gang of children gathered on the great stone platform under metal bas-relief. I started crying—Whatever had happened was completely invisible—a whole new Universe had emerged in the same place in space—nothing left of all that ruin or suffering except the monument & the few visitors— Then walked back alone by Old Town curved reconstructed streets humming Beethoven quartet feeling sad—all the beautiful desire that must have gone into rebuilding a whole city exactly as it was traditionally—lovely men!

In coffeehouse wrote strophes on that, ate in Jewish restaurant gulfilte fish no [?]—then with young poet & lady friend to visit recluse poet Miron—dark dark room, him in bed under huge bolster, intelligent face, tuberculosis, room hung with ikons & museum fragments of puppets—secretive handsome young man attending him, old expressive aesthetic friend visiting putting me down as a show-off in Polish—I didn't under-

Poland

stand conversation. Later the lady said "No not married, he likes young men" I read his poem in French "The elect as self elected."

Read Robert Lowell & Randall Jarrell poetry at nite. Lowell very solid reality & everyone's tired of my troubles.

Monday April 12—Woke early & wandered around buying pastry & coffee, then to Ministry of Culture got guest-money and letter to Police. Hours later the police were telling me "come back tomorrow"—I left angry. Found I could go to Berlin on same air ticket.

Wrote letters & phonecall from Herbert's uncle—went with him to his house, he's an American retired back here after 19 years photo technician—curious optimistic energetic old man, who survived 11 months concentration camp as a fine dentist. "The Germans admitted that kind of good workmanship even in an enemy." His wife in half blind stupor, high blood pressure Don Allen anthology[8] on his critic friend's shelves (sublet apartment)—

Home I reread James Schuyler[9] "light bouncing off UN Bldg."— good sensual pix N.Y.C. nostalgia for life there & that fineness of perception—reread Corso poems—very strange & mysterious pure mind, like thinking old useless dollar bills from another era, classics seen with new eyes, vegetables.

Mailed letter and on street met Lu Sota from RV—date to film me tomorrow—he told me about his Negro boy-girl friends in Harlem. Walked him to his office downtown to huge Soviet space square sur-

---

8. Donald Allen (1912–2004), founder of the Grey Fox Press, edited *New American Poetry* (1960), which included contributions by many Beat Generation poets, including Ginsberg.

9. American poet James Schuyler (1923–1991), 1981 Pulitzer Prize winner for *The Morning of the Poem*.

Roland

rounded by grey square buildings, coffee houses on ground floor. "Roxana & Alhambra cafes for boys, who want money."

I went on long walk down huge wide Soviet architecture street, and saw many wonderful small things & had many feelings & impressions but now home am too fatigued & the moment passed. Could have written well. This constant yoga of transcription requires such patience time energy & withdrawal from the actual scene to meditate & scribble slowly.

I went past all the shops, restaurants, cafes, faces staring at my head, withdrawn on Marzalhowska Avenue.

All the cashiers in all the *small* stores.

In Church, great files kneeling waiting for Confession, an old white-haired priest leaned over in booth listening to the monotone silence, behind the scene under the giant Cathedral columns a velvet drape & behind that the sharp sound of wood being sawn. A [?] scene.

To make a list of small details!

Finally back to Palace of Culture Square, and the huge Moloch building with red lights on its edges standing in vast space under the sky—an odd music from that slab & spire—and tramcars & crowds hurrying by—

One strange doorway with loudspeaker & Beatles music, I passed it once & on the way back saw a young couple looking into photooptikon glasses fixed into stone portal of the passage. Looked in—It was bright afternoon looking down on the canyons of NYC & Empire State!—I couldn't figure why, and why the rock & roll blaring into the air in the passage—went inside & found an odd little magic theater 2 ½ zlotys—sit on chair look into stereoscope glasses see a series of Kodachrome slides of NYC—Rockefeller Center skating rink, St. Patrick's, views of the Narrows Bridge, sero views of Empire State & the light glinting off U.N. Bld.—Oh Schuyler!—the prophesy in those poems—the huge nest

Poland

& power of NY visible in this drab Warsaw theater—Times Square at dawn, a few cars—Times Square at night, all the bizarre great nights—Forests off Manhattan seen from Empire State down to the cluster of Wall Street, Battery-bay-waters beyond, & piers—and the flats of Greenwich Village—Chinatown neons, a festival on Mulberry Street, Central Park seen from Rockefeller Center roof, & flat Harlem beyond—What a vision! And Beatles & Rock & Roll *She Loves You* fortifying the nostalgia from a tapemachine loudspeaker attached to the round magic-eye—all this in a sort of Times Sq. honkeytonk theater way inside alley in courtyard off main Warsaw street—

Emerging I saw that single Soviet skyscraper of Central Warsaw & the great Communist space around it. Poor, and the shopwindows filled with precious commodities.

Lines and ques for meat, cans, bread, seats at restaurants. Everywhere the inefficient cashier in the middle of his shop at desk, filling in huge report sheets.

Alhambra Café—small crowded velvet wallpapered, low chairs—fresh groups of winter coated arrivals at the chic cloakroom door—and the tables, Polish whores looking like 1930 Berlin, heavy eyes & lips, worn, Bouffant hair & one or two old modish lesbian girls—all gossiping & some—One strained face with large lower eyelids and bleached hair, cigarette hanging from lips; one stylized 1920 doll with small face and boyish bobbed hair, looking like Valeska Gert—amazing collection of pre-war types all suddenly concentrated in this one polite coffeehouse. I sat at low table—having stood at door waiting and gazing at the small crowd, till a tall thin sad blond hair gave me his almost invisible beckon of the eye to sit at a free stool at her table with a gang of other redhaired girls—who wanted to see my passport to prove I was not Polish in disguise, an imposter American. I drank tomato juice and sat half an hour, no beautiful boys & all the girls were sad.

This Jerosolimskie Street a sort of new built 42 Street, the Stereop-
tahan Theater; a café where three drunk women were dragged by police
thru archway in the same building to huge courtyard, and a crowd fol-
lowed; the boy-girl whore café Alhambra; the hustler's Roxina Café,
closed for repairs; old hotel Polonia that survived the war (in 1948 all
the Embassies each had a room there—) with giant dining room & men's
and women's barbershops on the street behind cut plate glass—

I had walked first up & down both sides of Marszalkowska—Signs of
Soviet hand, the giant boulevard, vast sidewalks, special department
stores, centrals, for food, for clothes, for watches—buildings recessed
from the boulevard, with archways passage into large interior apart-
ment courtyard perspectives, children gathered to play at dusk—in the
boulevard Squares, four giant lamp posts like divine extensions of 19th
century crystal palace mentality—torches to light the Commune—and
many more restaurants on this main drag—cloakrooms as everywhere
from Prague to Moscow, except here you pay a Zloty for service and you
got to have the service—the petty cashier everywhere, in some restau-
rants and watchmakers and shops first you pay and get a ticket, some-
times line up in front of the cashier, then you go get merchandise. Diffi-
cult for me not speaking Polish as often I don't know what to order in
advance, as in the milk shops at breakfast. But the labor's divided—one
serves, and one sits and fills out papers & watches over the money.

Intense solitude on the walk, hours & hours, and young people star-
ing at me contemptuous or giggling at my rare hairy appearance—I
passed several barbershops but was too shy to go in, wanted to shave
beard & cut hair, but mechanical inertia very great—half dozen people
sitting waiting for free barber—and didn't know how to ask for hair-
cut—Still I now have crabs all over my body—all week picking at them
and finally got a greenish liquid destroyer but still not free—and several
days ago found a few animals in the skin at the edge of my beard—and

Poland

not sure but my skull doesn't itch too—had spent several hours that week picking clean my breast & left armpit hair. A huge depressing problem I haven't completely attempted to solve in Polish. Probably souvenirs of Prague—I discovered them in Moscow but with all the paranoia and hurrying there did nothing but worry.

The great movement, however, after walking thru all this bearded history, new boulevards & memories of old deaths & rubble—Bookshop windows full of giant black volumes of Auschwitz & Warsaw destruction & photos of staring boys of 1943—and now the Stalin-Soviet arcades and apartments and wide pavements and no English–Polish lexicon to be found for sale—and all the cloakrooms & cashiers—the familiar Times Square smell & sound in a portal across from Palace of Culture, and the Stereoptioptik, and inside, giant energetic jazzy skyscrapers of New York City. I walked out into the quiet dusk & wrote a hymn to NYC in my thoughts—my field of vision filled with the one lone Stalin monumental wedding-cake palace on its spacious plaza, a provincial, idiot stoneworld monolith trying to pass itself off as *the* high civilization—"oh look at that impressive huge building they gave us—aren't they the end?"

Recalling Schuyler's nostalgia poems about New York, & Frank O'Hara's city world centered on 53'd & 5th Avenue—the chic shopwindows, martinis, lunch poems, money, taxis, subways, rendezvous, light glinting off skyscrapers, down in the Wall Street canyons—that rhapsody in blue from the '20's, John Marin, William C. W. thru the Negro '60's, the domesticity of that synthetic universe my old home.

Tues morn, April 13, 1965—

Downstairs in hotel for Breakfast, in lobby, bearded tall dark glassed fellow came up and shook hands—and several of his companions all huge Vikings with beards, a group of Danish poets and prose writers on the way to Moscow & China—They gave me their address, said, visit.

Poland

10:13 a.m. to Milicia to renew visa, had been there yesterday at 2:30 p.m.—"Come back tomorrow my chief is occupied" ... knocked on door room #9 this morning—"Wait 2 minutes if you please"—The French-speaking young clerk sitting in his office, the window light grey behind him, bending over a glasstop desk empty except for a glass of strong red tea—staring into the shiny glass, vague eyed.

"Let's go home!"
"People are dying at home!"

(Home is house) but people are dying there.
Recurrent bar conversation. Warsaw.

"Let's go!"—
"Where?"
"Let's go home!"
"People are dying home. Let's go to R. R. Station."
"Let's go home!"
"Home? Never!"
"Let's look down another glass!"
"Let's have a new glass!"
"Chlushniem Bolushniem"—"Drink means think sleepy"—

[...]
Thru unlimited energy until the age of 38, I had traversed the earth once, and crisscrossed many countries—Mexico first so near the US southern border, and visited again for half a year some half decade (or less) later than the first month's enterprise—then later boy sea in Arctic

Poland

Ocean—and had made passage thru Atlantic to Dakar and consulted a witch doctor when I was even younger in the year 1946—But now to continue in accurate history of my travels, I did ship from N.Y. to Tangier, & resting there a while to see the American poet Burroughs and poet Kerouac & proseists Bowles[10] & painter Bacon[11] of [?] England— I did go on to Spain—and thence thru Italy to Venice and southward, and by train thence to Vienna City in Austria, where canvasses of Breughel were brought forth, thence to Munich only a week, a confused vision of Hitlerean Art museums, and afterward to Paris, a week, and Amsterdam a month, via Bruxelles, then a year almost in Paris—8 months where I met L. F. Celine & the poets Michaux Duchamp & Tzara & Perret—then by London M. Spender Auden & Mme. Sitwell then alive—& by Paris to America where I rested a year or so at my own home.

Then I sailed again forth on Atlantic to M. Burroughs residence via Paris—resting a month there, thence to Cannes St Tropez and Aix—and by boat Marseilles to Tangiers, stopping over in Casablanca by force to cure Corso fellow poet's discussed passport—but to Tangier, horrors of love lost there and a moment alone on a roof—and shipped via Scylla & Charybdis to Greece, several months examining marble breasts of statue men of Antiquity, and by rocking boat to Israel, the white soft advice & beard of Martin Buber[12] "You will remember what I say"—To Red Sea then via Tanganyika to Kenya, and a month's bus to Nairobi,

10. Paul Bowles (1910–1999), an American composer and writer, lived as an expat in Tangier, where he met William S. Burroughs, Allen Ginsberg, Jack Kerouac, and many other Beat Generation figures.

11. Francis Bacon (1909–1992), an Irish-born painter.

12. Martin Buber (1878–1965), Israeli philosopher, whom Ginsberg met on his way to India in 1962.

high on boulevards of Mombasa—then boat to dear Bombay—to Delhi and Himalayas to learn the mantra of Maha Shivananda and long time from Calcutta Benares Ganktrok—till by plane via palaced Bangkok & thence—Saigon in Vietnam the Buddhist conspirators with meet mouths—Cambodia & Ankor Wat's motorcycles & old palaces covered with trees—I went back to Saigon by plane to go, stopping a moment in Hong Kong, then Japan to sit in Kyoto Monasteries & be quiet in my stomach—then to the place called Canada & by car to San Francisco again & by plane to N.Y. where I rested another year—and flew off to see my ancient smelly Mexican green parks—to flew to Cuba with free plane ticket & thence after police expelled me to Prague the story brown old city of Czechoslovakia, and by snowy train to Moscow where I spoke with poets & shivered on the spacy vastness of Asian's Red Square—and there by choo choo to Poland Warsaw destroyed & rebuilt where in a bar of the Hotel Bristol I now record these Marco Polonian travels to (Spot?)

Drunk last nite with Irridensky and wrote that at midnight or 1 a.m.—taxicabs thereafter over Warsaw Singing Hari Om with too much vodka in my head I blacked out and woke next morn on the rugged floor of his girlfriend's house in suburbs—headache.

That morn I'd post with police office & got papers extending visa—

Broke off 2 days ago writing. Well I got visa that morn till 20th April then made TV tape for Mr. Lasota who'll cut it—I started talking about Polish censorship. Finally it's autocensorship that makes the machine function "smoothly." I knew if I went too far he'd edit it out. Trapped.

Evening went with [?] of US Embassy to a jazzy cellar & got drunk a little & talked at random—then all of us moved over to Actor's Club—nice big mahogany room with Titian-esque paintings on the wall—a couple Embassy folks, broken Polish talk, vodka, Barbara half looking

Poland

brave with half her face paralyzed, an actor, a wit-musician, later bore-dom—I went out singing & met drunken Irridensky on the street & with him went to Bristol Hotel bar across from my own Europeski Hotel—Midnite to 2 a.m. more vodka & we couldn't even talk, he kept kissing me on the ear—finally in taxicabs to his girlfriend's house.

Next morning by cab home to hotel with Irridensky, I went upstairs & washed & then to jazzy magazine round the corner, they wanted to talk about N.Y.C. scene, & publish another poem—last year'd reprinted U.S.–Polish translation of Howl from Exile magazine—and a young kid there who's written a little social introduction—we talked about pot sex—and then home met an American professor & went with him to Warsaw University & lectured for 2 hours exhausted, Whitman——> Pound——>Williams Olson: Stein——>Kerouac: prose composition——> action painting——>action jazzy——>mental contemplation——>Zen——>Tibetan Mantras——>Prosody——>consciousness etc.

Then to Stern's house with Halberstam of Times, supper & vague talk, about Poland.

Dasota says workers life is better. Halberstam says chickenshit Stalinist police state.

Then to Marilla's apartment, blond girl artists with young poetry friends, lives a block off reconstructed quartet Latin village style old Warsaw Staremesto main square—more wine & more explanations—"No ideology." To philosophy students—one actor—philosopher 25 years old attractive & spent time gazing in his eyes but we never talked much openly, partly I too shy to make a social break in this scene, but asked him to call me—He's a large energetic muscular cat with rough head & jester-acrobatic snap-finger athleticism—reminded me vaguely of Neal. "Where you live?"—"Outskirts of Warsaw with my mother. She's waiting up for me. Unfortunately I have—no girl—or boyfriend now waiting for me." I thrilled a little at that but took no special notice. And home at 3 a.m. naked I lay in bed masturbating imagining him fucking me.

Phone rang 9 a.m. Thurs. 15.—Herbert's uncle—wanted me to visit hospital with him, so took cab & talked to calm intelligent doctor— Moscow medicine? "I have impression their scientific research is generally very poor—They have killed science—most of them are technicians, not scientists—therefore less contact with outside experiments—and no discipline or regimen of creative work—A few fields very good—but as in arteriosclerosis they are 25 years behind—still preoccupied with cholesterol—the idea of science has atrophied—as technicians they run across problems they aren't trained to solve, and so fields of personal experiment diminish in boredom."

Next day—transcribed—

(Had dream that morning of the same tall boy—He was naked sitting next to me with a huge erection of meat—and slipped his giant whang down between his own legs, sat crosslegged and slipped it in up his own behind, with himself. Then he started coming all over my face and chest —spurt after spurt of distasteful cream—spurt after spurt like a faucet, I was surprised to see so much white come jetting out of him as out of a tube. A rough meat.)

(7 a.m. waking)

Change! Change! Change! open up the ear! open up the eye! open up the belly! open up your ass!

Went after hospital to Kultura magazine office to keep date with old editor to translate my poesy—he didn't show up—Walked across street to U S embassy & had lunch & met same Ruel Wilson I'd once met in

Poland

Paris café years before—"I didn't recognize you, you look like Jesus Christ?"—"Things worse than when I was here 4 years ago—a phase of liberalism to 1958–59 after '56—And then close down—people depressed and the salaries too low—chicken once a month"—

Went upstairs to renew my passport and put in extra pages: conversation with visa attaché I'd met in bar several days ago, who once was assigned to Peking, till 1950—Says Formosa is like old China—"I wouldn't mind being sent to Hong Kong"—acts as translator for Chinese-American talks here in Warsaw over the last years. No publicity, so nobody'll get into a publicity spectacle. The conferences don't mix socially, never drunk together. Chinese students in Warsaw a few—but don't have much social life—they work all the time, trained to study.

Then I walked toward the Europeski Hotel along the curved reconstructed 18th century perspective of low roofs, book and antique shops of Novy Swiat New World street—selfconscious in my monster hair as I'd been for days on the street—till a moment of change came along & I straightened my back & began breathing freely in my abdomen—a sense of pleasure, free in leisure to walk along the stage scenery of a beautiful ancient street crowded with new people, military coats and frowns, old ladies trudging along with narrowed eyes, young suave businessmen with briefcases and resolute mouths, and the eyes everywhere, eyes of ugly young students walking hand in hand—each passing glaring in my eye—I gazed back in each, happy, and breathed more easily, a sense of lightness entered my body, I avoided all thought of the presence of the moment, and met eye-glances and smiled, forced smile a little, then after awhile a euphoric happy smile, and as one workman passed me gaily slightly drunk leaning forward in the street in blue over-alls smudged with industrial paint I winked as we gazed amazed eye to eye and he waved and laught to me, two souls met passing by a streetcorner in all the traffic of weakness and woe on the way to work—I burst out

Poland

laughing, happy striding solid down New World street and began know-
ing my appearance smiling broadly at everyone who gazed at me, so that
the atmosphere changed for 5 minutes around me to an Easter holiday
avenue with buses and packages of shopping delight—joy everywhere
except for the tortured faces of some passersby so introverted they did
not look out at the live bodies & souls of the afternoon approaching the
corner of Bristol and Europeski Hotels.

At 4:30 p.m. an silverhaired Jewish editor who kept saying he was
alienated took me to the house of Anatole Stern, early 30's futurist poet-
essayist survivor of the wars, a friend of ancient Lily Brik—and widow
gossip—so I sang Tibetan songs and Eli Eli & om tara totara turay so-
ham tara tara tara to his wife, a rogue lipped old witty dame who spoke
French—"oh, Rogievitch, je comprendia tour!" And Stern's doctor was
there, this Futurist is dying of cancer and doesn't know it yet. Himself,
fine featured & smooth silver hair, curious & intelligent and as usual ar-
ranging new literary information (prosody! peyote! jazzy!) into the con-
test of his Futurist Movement histories—

Then after to Actor's Club Supper with [?] Piatrowsky who'd helped
me by telephone for a week, without a rendezvous—He had a list of plays
from Café Cino & La Mama and Leroi Jones for me to tell him about—
Paul Foster?—But I was bored—Later walking home with his wife along
Novy Swiat he explained he'd been 5 ½ years prisoner of war—And
now—"I try to get along, I have my young Venus to please me, and I
translate plays—Poland? Very good theater"—

Saturday April 16, [sic]11 a.m.

Woke late yesterday, wandered thru old town square to a small [?]
little restaurant and had breakfast beef & kasha—then writing, sat a
long time at the table, then walked back to Writer's Union & sat com-

muning with Anatole Slutsky, a bright eyed smiling grey haired old Jewish poet—who'd been in Russia 5 years during the war, "Partisan"—He drew a picture of a fly on the newspaper, to show me what human life was like—"very light weight"—He laughed. "I have 3 Stalin medals ... Poets make good Partisans ... History decides what we do"

To hotel, just wandering around streets remembering the euphoria on New World street, & recapturing it at moments—then to Jazzy magazine where Joe the editor gave me a book on Warsaw Ghetto I'd asked for—huge grey pictures of starving bellies & Jews scrubbing the streets with toothbrushes—"Have you met anyone here who was in Warsaw Ghetto?" No, I hadn't—I'd met survivors of other scenes—We were sitting late in afternoon in his darkened office—(I'd also been in Europeski Hotel drinking vodka with Iridensky & a German lady editor, talking with her teenage daughter about Baudelaire 3–6 p.m.)

I was at his desk with the book in front of me—"The lady at the other desk you saw the other day—is my wife—and the young man who wanted to meet you, who was here with you & at the Jazz Club—is my stepson"—There was something curious about this, I couldn't figure why he hadn't introduced them in those roles before—"This is my day of confession," he said smiling, awkwardly but very kindly—And started telling me his story—In the ghetto during the fighting, in an underground bunker, a lady friend who didn't look Jewish had crossed over the bridge after and got him papers, he was prepared to run away, he lived under the rubble, the Germans were systematically dynamiting, toward the end they drilled a dynamite hole over his head—nothing happened but that night he realized "It entered my head like from God—my body was cold with fright—I felt nothing"—that he'd die in that cellar or escape—so he went out that nite thru the Wall—Stayed several days on outskirts of Warsaw with friends, but had no money no resources—left for work for the Germans in Ukraine—(answering a newspaper ad)—Saw his sister in hospital at Lvov (where her husband the director was later shot for preparing papers to escape to a Russia hospital)—She told him & old dying Jew had seen his brother's picture & said he'd been shot nearby; and seen his picture & said he was under another star & would see the light of day after the war—Then he went on & worked on roads near Stalingrad. "The great day came when the German Wehrmacht looked like 1812 retreat"—Escaped to a village where they dressed him up in peasant clothes—but he had no papers so it was life or death by accident, if the German or Rumanian soldiers, who were still in and out of the village, examined him—Finally the Russians entered & he reported to them, told his story, and wound up on the Black Sea & elsewhere traveling around as a press correspondent—and after the war, go home to Warsaw—and now lives in an apartment with stepson & wife near same spot on Earth in old Ghetto area where he used to live.

Well, it's better this way, rebuilt, more space & air healthier for children. A difficult world. But the trouble is salaries are too low, impossible for average salary to make ends meet—meat, shoes, clothes—not to say autos—are out of reach.

The main economic complaint I hear everywhere—wages are too low to afford reasonable support to family life. (And long queues today at the vegetable & meat stores. Saturday before Easter, I went out for a walk & breakfast on New World street.)

Then later last nite to Bristol Hotel, Irridensky again & Peter Hall & an Englishman boy Bethel who'd translated Brodsky for BBC & held & sniffed his vodka glass under his nose like a big fleshy undergraduate—Said Brodsky's poetry was good—contradicting claims of the Russian officials like Simonov & Romanova—We ate caviar & vodka, drank & Iridensky pulled out 500 Zloty movie money and paid a bill half the month's wages of a shoe worker.

Poland

Easter Sunday April 18—Warsaw

Went out walking 11 a.m. on Novy Swiat & had some scrambled eggs in milk shop & wrote, suddenly had to shit & left shop looking for a bathroom on New World street in and out of familiar jazz club alleys closed— finally entered Music School building & found a John in one of the corridors. Immense pile of sick brown & wiped myself with this journal.

Then at noon to Peter Hall of British Embassy, & some British Council gents there who'd been in Indonesia & said Bali was fine for touring—and knew Beatles disk with high feminine tender Woo sounds at the end—and new Rolling Stones "They can take monotony to great sensual heights," said the young trilingual blonde British diplomat. Irridensky there, reading Paris Match, the conversation before the morning window about Beatles. George is the queer one and the new Swedish ambassador who's "saturnine."

Then to hotel to meet a poetry kid with broken dark eyeglasses & frizzy hair, & coffeeshop with him talking all afternoon thru an interpreter a young tall student friend. Mostly about Polish communism, complaints—the mental attitudes restricted, censorship thru P.K.P.W.W. —worst on theater & prose & not so bad on poetry—Brodsky's poetry he read & liked, in tradition of Blok—Couldn't be printed here, was printed in Paris—His friend spoke university English very gently and slowly as the afternoon darkened & the coffeehouse chilled with a drizzle out the windows and no lights turned on & all the young couples slowly left, we sat drinking tea & smoking cigarettes while he complained & complained till six o'clock. And the Writer's Union, all the older writers adapted to the politics of that kind of institution and the younger more ambitious literary gents could use it, getting power by judicious attack on antisocial tendencies of experimental souls. I don't remember that he said anything very precise, only that he seemed to have an open mind. But asked me not to "quote him to anybody" by name. Why? He'd have

Poland

difficulty getting into Writer's Union later when he'd published the necessary 2 books.

Then to Marilla's house, I ate baked potatoes and sour cream & horseradish—big jar of white sharp [?].

Which reminds me that American Jewish kreplach, in soup, is similar to wonton, and only when I'd eaten pilenyi at a stand-up buffet near Moscow Bridge on a plate with no soup, did I remember eating them in Calcutta with no soup, but soy sauce—and in Himalayas eating meat wrapped in dough like Ravioli—So keeping wonton ravioli is Asiatic in origin. Central Asiatic wonton of Chinese wonton that by Poland have degenerated to slightly fried tasteless pilenyi in Jewish restaurants in Nove Mesto Warsaw but maybe bought in Chinatown N.Y. alleys delicious or frozen at yr. nearest supermarket. Acculturation. Such a nice Jewish dish, all the way from Peking.

—and a Marilla's house, conversation with unshaven intelligent formalist married poet Gonchorovsky—"There are brilliant poets" said Voznesensky but I see no sign. but Gonchorovsky wanted to take lamp & cigarette and make a 3'rd image of their white "Lexical imagery" whatever that meant in French translation from Polish, something seriously intelligent. But he thought he had a duty to society, he said after I described Lower East Side movies.

Home by car, an Italian girl visiting Poland who had a German Ford with a built-in phonograph set. First time I saw that. Playing rock & roll on a hi-fi speaker in the rear window. Let me off at Hotel Bristol & I crossed the street, midnight.

And picked another crab off my cheek, had crawled out of my beard while I was describing my New World Street moment of aethereal eyes—"I entered into other's eyes"—to a Polish sociologist at the party. Again, masturbating in bed, going back to Cuba to fuck little Manolo.

Poland

This morning washed shirt & brushed teeth—finally realized after almost 39 years that proper brushing is up & down including the whole gum to the root upper & lower—and walked out, aimless, at 10 a.m. along prezdemieskie to the old market square of Stace Mesto—walked across bridge over [?] in a drizzle with scarf wrapped around my neck, looking back saw reconstructed façade of mediaeval Warsaw peaked redbrick church on the hill above river—into Praga side of Warsaw, into churches crowded for Easter Sunday noon—last night long lines into the street at all churches downtown, everyone filing in to see display of white Jesus body dead below the Cross, which is hung with his white loincloth—and into Russian Orthodox church—ancient Russian choir, deep tranquil music, basso & soprano trill extended for minutes while everybody stood under the small dome and watched the sacrament—one old bubba had to be helped up a step to take a wafer, and helped down again to a bench where she sat powerful & old—the inner door opened & priest with dome-cap glittering and vestments as I'd seen in Kremlin Armory Museum came out & distributed liquid from a silver cup, with a spoon to the old dignified Russian souls who gathered up pressing at the marble stairway to the Inner Sanctum—a hush over the crowd—blackrobed Russian saints staring down from the gold backgrounds of the walls—strong saints in chain mail armor with black beards & black quiet eyes—and a manly Christ proffering a gesture of peace—The choir in the balcony entering in the silence with long slow phrases of familiar chant mood-music invocation—and silent again a few minutes—then repeating the adoration—then silent again a few minutes—then repeating the adoration—then silent again—then humming in the vacancy basso profundo and lady voice in Russian—like human clockwork, to remind the silence—I stared around, Christ seemed acceptable, I don't know

Poland

why he ever seemed alien, except his monopoly—but no less beautiful than Buddha Vishnu—on the portals ikons and on the pillars Marys, eyes all over & gold fine halos and meat peaceful strong eyes—invoking Easter silence & stone hush—great dignity of noon in Warsaw, and for a moment my eye caught & fixed the eye of the old lady in black in the middle of the crowd like on a stage in a Bolshoi opera, weak & wrapped in coat & old fur hat, survived all the wars, still on church altar steps this Easter, helped down on the carpet by her lady relative, both of them poor in old clothes, her face in the middle of the crowd & her old eye looking down toward the floor to see her foot way.

Out walking on Praga main street.

The moments return[13]

like a thousand sunsets behind the tramcar
   wires in the open skies of Warsaw
the Chinese peaks of the Palace of Culture turning
   black in the fading orange light—
like the spark off the insect antennae of
   the rolling iron trolley—
Blue in the mind, red brick side street
   sparks of Newark by the Cigar store—
Bullet holes in the old rusty apartments—
   Man grey hat cane limping at dusk
   along the black avenue—
And Christ Under White Cloth lay in the chapel—
   old ladies high voices fragmented in the

13. First draft of "The Moments Return," *CP*, 360.

Poland

Polish choir—trembling fingers on the

long rosary—awaiting Resurrection—

old red fat Jack mortal in Florida—tears in

black eyelash, Bach's farewell to

the Cross—

That was 24 years ago on a scratchy phono

graph Sebastian Sampas bid adieu to Earth—

I stomped on the streets to remember the

Warsaw Concerto, hollow sad planes

crashing like bombs, celestial tune

In the kitchen at Ozone Park—It all came

true in the sunset, on a deserted street

in a later Warsaw—

The moment's return to the twilight of the

Gods—old avenue gables might be Berlin—

the music fading to another universe—

And I have nothing to do, this evening, but

walk furred in the cool grey streets—

remembering Mahler's symphony I used to sing

in New York—a melancholy man alone—

or the mood of Indian music on this planet,

Ali Akbar Khan's sarod call lasso—

microtones familiar to my small living

room a year ago—

reverberations of blue taxicabs arriving at the Park

bench—The old familiar light inside the car—

"a hairy loss"[14]—my beard in misery, I am

14. Jack Kerouac described Ginsberg as "a hairy loss," a phrase that Ginsberg found to be particularly astute.

a strange man with no language to these
  young eyes of laughing boys—to
  myself—
in bed naked, eyes closed, in ecstasy memory
  opened to another room in Havana Manolo's small black
  body—
or back thru many empty streets to a corner of
  Paterson where I submitted myself to
  The will of blonde infants—the earliest
  Tender dream—
Now sitting on a street corner of Jerusalemski
  in Warsaw—rueful of the bald front
  of my skull and the grey sign of Time
  in my beard, behind
the moment's return as I am to die, still
  not knowing the God I desired—
"What I come to is partially done, partially
  kept"—the knowledge of this streetcorner
  in the physical world,
the passing cars, a timid pain in my heart for a
  moment, the few when this body is destroyed
  warm this moment—
as headache or dancing exhaustion or
  dysentery in Moscow or vomit in N.Y.
reminded me of the great pain of Death—
  How can I bear it?—or maybe
  release from Knowledge at that moment—
This knowledge that makes children leap
  in front of their mothers in the
  Church courtyard at Easter—

Poland

"As to the Tebor's sound"—the poem
    returns to the moment,
Oh! The Metropol Hotel abuilding—the
    same old moment—thin crowds
    waiting on tramcar islands under the
    streetlamp—
A great day of the Universe—the cry of the
    tramcars on Jerusalem—
My now to completely come home to my dying
    body & live in this moment, my vow
    to record—my cold fingers.

Now I shall sit and wait for my own
    Lone Presence—
A pretense, Hope, Prayer, defeat—"I will
    grow old a grey and groaning man"
—writ 17 years ago—the first psalm—the
    Moment returns to itself
I also return to myself, the moment and
    I are one man on a beach on
    a crowded streetcorner in Warsaw,
the sky a familiar dark blue, red dots on
    the high-cornered tower,
Under the yellow lights a wide avenue,
    traffic light red and the long tree tramcar
    rests,
a young man twirls his umbrella, a motorcycle
    passes exploding, families gather in the
    moving doorway

or walk slowly across the street an Easter Zoo—
    I breathe and sigh—What shall
    I do this evening?—At last there is nothing
    I have to do.

But my soul is imperfect! I'm unhappy! I'm unhappy!
    What do I want? I'm lonesome, the
    tenderness of a little boy to my body! What
    boy? What old pearl breasted perfumed woman?
"Give up the desire for children" said the
    tall bony white bearded Guru—am I
    ready to die?—
a voice at my side on the bench, a
    gentle question—the good young face
    under a pearl grey hat—
Alas, all I can say is "No panamay
    paruski"—I can't speak.

"Lumenous Propaganda!"—propagandas lummosas.

April 19, 1965, Mon.
    Dream: In a car travelling thru mountains of Albania and Rumania—
Looks like Bolivia valleys with façade of mountains behind, or trip thru
riverbottom up steep road in Cuba to Minos del Frio—I'm looking back
from the rear of the bus-truck, on the open sky, the crag peaks—maybe
there's gypsies in the mountain, something romantic & old thru mem-
ory?—
    I get back & see Jack K. "Ah Jack, I just saw Rumania! It was sad! I

Poland

just went thru a *valley* in Rumania"—Just the idea of a valley in Rumania makes me weep in the dream—"weep" figuratively speaking not literally—even—

I also did something in Rumania I don't remember.

Out thru grey streets rainmist Monday morning searching for a cheap restaurant—all closed in the neighborhood—last day of Easter. In Tourist Home hotel the big empty café—sitting and waiting minute after minute for the waitress, who's at a side table conversing with friends. And minute by minute for eggs. It takes an hour for a breakfast.

Carl S.—Communism feels like your mother—the size of Red Square.

"There's no way to beat the game." in politics.

Evening. A meeting in Sala Congressowa, 21st Memorial to Warsaw Ghetto massacres. At noon, wreath laying at the monument.

Verglis—"I am a Jew—I am a Soviet man—Warsaw Ghetto—Viet Nam. Warsaw Ghetto—Napalm Pentagon—Warsaw Ghetto—Washing tear gas"—

A huge 19th century hall, delegations from Folk Societies of US led by my cousin Sam Pevsner "All the speeches in Yiddish, 1930's sounds—"alles ... Yiddishe menchen"—but now irritate me—you can't beat the game—Verglis, I'd never heard of, supposedly a controversial figure, Soviet showpiece Jew—or Jewish editor spokesman, library frame glasses & red hair thinning in front—reminded me of Willard Benininger old High School liberal friend of Louis'—who later had nervous condition brought about by world political disease—Verglis last night saying "Voz-nesensky Yevtushenko friends of mine good boys but nothing new—Klebinhov did it all"—slightly drunk. "If you translate Yiddish literature you will be world famous," he said to me like Ancient Mariner ending longspeech. Turned off. "A *nice* speaker," I can hear the old Bronx ladies say.

Speeches & then art—a violin solo accompanied and a famous Polish Yiddish lady actor reciting a speech like Mollie Goldberg, and a piano Chopin solo on the vast stage—and then a group of younger kids rehearsed to sing a few sweet Yiddish songs & recite poems in similar style to Voznesensky nite, but less swinging & existential—This YMHA Paterson recitals of high school patriotic pageants—22 years after Warsaw Ghetto chaos. And all the old Jewish left-wing ladies in the audience said "That's nice."

Earlier had just bathed, & wandered around, and ate, and waited, & went to memorial Noon wreath laying at monument to see the crowd, and then pleasant late afternoon with Joe Jazz mag. & his 16 yr. old son a soft-voiced blond thin kid with sweet sweet manners who spoke halting English. We talked about first memories. His earliest was of [?] in schoolyard, a grove of trees, one large branched wide trunked tree, where playmates swung, and there he saw them hang white cat with black spots—the cat leapt and cried but it didn't do any good—Recently the cat came back in dreams.

Desk clerk in Europeishi Hotel looks & moves like Gregory Markopolis—

Poland

20 April 1965

S. last nite American girl from Radio Poland came to my table in Europeshi Hotel to ask me for a few words on the Jewish ceremonies of the day—"Hypocrites," I said irritably, not knowing why, annoyed with Verglis—and my cousin Sam Pevsner's wife's smugness. "Oh I met the most lovely couple yesterday, a young Polish engineer & he's so happy here . . ." and the conversation fell briefly on the gossip of the Polish underground wiped out & Warsaw destroyed with Red armies on other side of river.

"Oh no you are misled" she said "the lousy Polish underground conspiring in London . . . the Red Army was tired . . . Radio Moscow only gave signal to *prepare* . . . the leaders were misled . . ."

I lost my temper & told her it didn't make any difference. She offered to lend me an "impartial" history book. Immediately I regretted opening my mouth, especially in irritation, as I had to apply for visa renewal tomorrow. However any gossip would probably filter thru police—if any gossip—days later. Still I felt bad. How do I know what happened?

This morning to Joe Jazz to get letter usable for visa renewal. Said he was with Polish army on Vistula bank exactly that time, and story was correct "Everybody in Warsaw knows it. . . Polish general—Berliner?—gave order to aid the Underground, & attack across river—He was immediately deposed—The Polish soldiers stood & watched Warsaw razed." . . . No permission given for London–Polish [?] to use Red airbases—they had to come from Italy & dropped supplies in the wrong place so 80% went to the Germans—Joe watched it from across the river and says the story's true. "Joseph Stalin did not want any opposition."

I typed him Prague Big Beat[15] poem & went to pick up my visa, at police again easier, come back tomorrow.

15. See "Big Beat," *CP,* 357.

SPORT

On the Warsaw stage, burlesque, straw hats, flappers, shimmies, furs, striped jackets, top hats, cigars fuming, ladies rolling their eyes, pinkies lifted, faints just in time, fake diamonds glittering in the audience, horse trot, heaving bosoms, my yiddish mamma, feather boa hanging to the toe, long black earrings, a rose in the lapel, a final waltz that whirls the old songs away under a photograph of Nazi bombers in the grey photograph sky—the drunkard that leaned against the proscenium is sober, & the mooooooustached dandy draws the ragged swastika rex postcard curtain across the stage.

A happy theater—the scamp bag collecting pickpocket, the black hat bureaucrat, survivor in striped Buchenwald coat, dame in a man's coat, the rags of tin can eaters, & bop comes on with Leather & Levi, & red tie & work shirt the asses wave in time, the hammers & sickles clang & sing, Warsaw takes style, the blow up of Maribahkovaka's modern buildings end the scene with applause & happy madness, the bureaucrat in his suave clothes skidding back & forth opening & closing the curtain for socialist applause.

---

21 April.

Early ate breakfast, picked up passport, saw huge atrocity photos at Jewish Institute, taxied to Kultura typed up café & street poems, received 800 Zlotys, went walking to radio station read poems aloud, on tape, strolled thru Water Palace small excellent marble rooms, then the park with brush-eared little red squires I never saw before, climbing friendly on pants legs & skittering back & forth on ground approaching & retreating. Then to Ludmilla's house walked—she told story of her

Poland

wartime in Chesteslaw—once taken by Gestapo for question, but the co
had seen her mother & gave her the right answers (translating her Pol-
ish into German for the report & arranging her replies to be innocuous)
sent her to the gate out instead of Auschwitz the next morning. And to
her living room we corrected translations.

And I had 2100 Zlotys in my pocket, plethora of Polish moneys, and
1000 more tomorrow—never had excess cash like this before—changed
my R.R. ticket to stopover at Cracow—and trolley home along Jerusa-
lemski Street by the high culture palace ("wedding cake")—and walked
to Bristol Hotel to check for Voznesensky maybe arrived—and ate dig-
nified meal, trout in Jelly with horseradish, overcooked Chateaubri-
and, potato puffs, mushrooms sauté, pear-pineapple compote & foccee.
Black market rates $1.25 but I had all this legal Zloty to spend, sitting
alone at Bristol under the potted palm.

[…]
[April 23, 1965]

I came back to check at Bristol, Voznesensky'd arrived—went up-
stairs, he'd got my note—was standing in room just arrived, in company
several Polish friends—a critic of Russian poetry, tall & with scalp show-
ing in back of head, tho young—some burn or wound,—and his Russian
wife with who'd been friend of Vos in Moscow—young girl—an older
short lady, lively, Vos' Polish editor—He introduced me and explained
who I was, kissed me, I was embarrassed at intruding—He picked up
my note—"I have a letter here from the most great American poet"—
"Do you know what 'Wow' means?"—I'd written I'll wait for you wow—
so I shouted wow & he laughed. "Will you like to come eat with us?"

He was to be Poland perhaps a week—he judge at a recitation contest
in Poynan at fair "That was the excuse we used to get him here" his ed-

Poland

itor explained—"Did you have trouble getting Polish or Russian Visa"—
"Russian" he answered. "Only till the end of April"—He looked rueful—

We walked down wide Bristol Hotel staircase to lobby & out onto
Avenue, toward Navy Swiat—I explained—"It's New World—like Le-
ningrad"—He nodded agree, right—"only smaller—the perspectives"—
"There's Chopin's heart in Church"—I pointed out.

"When I die and they build my monument, I leave instructions not
to bury my heart but in my monument bury my fuck, for poetry is made
by fuck"—"Ah," I said "yes—cock—fuck is the process, cock the organ"—
"Oh yes, cock—cock—They bury my cock—What is cock?"—"Rooster"
I sounded cockadoodledoo to illustrate—He smiled recognizing—"Of
course"—

He talked in Russian, I separated & tagged along, chatting in French
with the editor girl—occasionally he turned to me & held me around, or
slapped my shoulder, giving attention since I was silent. He wore blue
raincoat & light blue pants, black Italian style crude shoes, and a pale
grey cap with button on the back—fine face like a typical new generation
young smart kid on the town in Russ-Poland, well dressed, indistin-
guishable from any happy student or young architect on the street, ex-
cept for a redness in his nose skin, and his nose is biggish. He kidded
with the girls, playing gentle coyote style withdrawal games in Russ-
ian—They'd say "Oh you" & laugh at him.

Critic friend's apartment—6 floors up—smooth plastic floors—we
ate, I was hungry, & mostly quiet, waiting. They mentioned Brodsky, I
heard the name & asked what had happened—"Nothing new, he is still
away, still not free—we are waiting."

He said he'd been in Leningrad giving "concerts"—"make money?"
"No I do it for applause—no money there"—and in Leningrad they'd
asked him about me—that I'd lay down on Mayakovsky's bed?—I began
to explain, no, I hit the bed, never finished, language difficult.

Poland

"Why do you like Mayakovsky?" he asked me. "Because idealism in *At Top Voice* like Shelley—a vision of communism that's transcendent— then die my verse, that's tragic & beautiful—not like the light of long dead stars—and in conversation with sun—at first I read it as mystical sign—but then I still liked it later as just poetic bravado and the transparent factories"—His critic friend translated my answer.

Did he hear about train station meeting Yevtushenko & Yessenin-Volpin? No.—I explained what happened. He said "He is mentally very sick?"—"Not at all" I answered—"Not at *all*—He told me his story, he tried to sue the police"—We had to translate the word sue, when he understood, Voz. grimaced, a joke. "He's a logician I said—and everybody said he's mad—Simonov Romanov Alexei—they're all mad—an old conspiracy to your old story"—"Yes that kind of story is an old story to us"—

"I liked him"—

"I never met him" said I—

"And his mother's friendly:—"I know of her"—

"No I only know of her"—

"Everybody said she wanted to protect her son from seeing people but that wasn't true either—she was good friends"—

"It doesn't matter that his poetry's bad," said Voz.

"Is it really *bad*?" "Yes."

"It has quality of irritation that I like" I said thru translator, and I explained briefly Volpin's logic-analysis of Soviet la. "He is mathematician?" said Voznesensky. "Yes, yes" I said.

They talked more Russian—He raised his wine glass to me "We are brothers"—and we awkwardly drank—

"How is your heroine?" laughing at me. "My what?" I said. "Your heroine?"—but I was sick of explaining the difference I had last time at his house and he hadn't clearly heard—

He's leaving for Poznan early tomorrow, and I for Krakow—we made

Poland

date to meet again in Warsaw on the 26th—and this nite to the theater to see the review of songs I'd seen days ago—& I had ticket for After the Fall—So we walked out on street—He was conversing with the girls—reciting a small rhyme that made them laugh—"It's un-translatable," he told me "about fuck cock."

I explained what cunt was, & cock & cunt in Chaucer. "Old English poet"—"Yes I know Chaucer." That's nice surprise, he knew who Chaucer was.

And took cab, they left me off at Palace of Culture for my theater. Perhaps we'd meet at Krokodile tonite. If not Warsaw on the 26th— "On the 27th I give my concert here"—he said. (He had asked me on hotel stairway if I'd given any concert in Warsaw. I said no, he was surprised & asked why. I explained "Too difficult, and I've been mostly alone here—I've been writing a lot" & showed him this book full.)

"Ah, it is *difficult* to be a poet" he said.

"No I'm happy—for two weeks I've had plenty solitude walking on New World Street."

"I'm never alone. That's the trouble," he sighed.

"Are you with delegation here?"

"I am the delegation—I'm the head of my own delegation, myself." He was gay about that, a sort of bureaucratic triumph. This was back in hotel room when I first came in.

He asked what Polish poets I'd met—I said, few—Herbert & Rogievitch out of town. Did meet Grahovias—"He's interesting"—and he asked me about Rausinovitch, who's also in Krakow.

Does he know of Anatole Stern? "Ah Stern, he is not a good poet but he is a great . . . ah" he search for a word.

"Historical figure? Essayist?"

"A great translator. He is the best translator, *my* Polish translator— he was my guest in Moscow—and his wife"—

Poland

"Very witty."

"She likes to take clothes off naked when she drinks— ... But Stern you must go to him and say you are the greatest translator, you must translate all my poems ... How is Anselm Hollo[16] as a translator?"

He apparently didn't even remember our conversation about that on the elevator to his apartment in Moscow.

"Very good ... inaccurate but alive!"

At supper I mentioned Irridensky—He didn't know of him, & asked his lady editor friend & translated her answer "a good writer but a bad man."

"He drinks," I said cheerfully.

"He killed a woman."

"What?"

"Not kill—he drinking—they beat her with a machine." Confused translations.

I never got the complete story on that. I said, "He's like the character drunk young man in Scott Fitzgerald."

"Khrushchev is now writing poetry."

"What?" I asked.

"A month ago ... some Western journalist—he answered 3 questions—one, yes, yes, he made retirement it was good decision of Party all satisfied yes yes two yes yes yes the party is following steps of Marxism-Leninism yes yes three now in spare time he writes poetry, for his family and friends, he reads them, he writes poetry ... it is surrealist."

The first buds of Spring
   yellow, rain on grey stone

16. Anselm Hollo (1934–2013), a poet, was Ginsberg's Finnish translator.

Roland

perfect, old, from before the war
 black pillars and gold-bust
 polychrome altar at St. Mary's
the dim trumpet sounding from Medaeval lips—
the student's jazzy cafe humming with velvet,
and a blast of New Orleans from the Krakow
 Jukebox Workman's buffet—
there sits Christ with his bearded father
 two men blessing the world
 continuity springtime to springtime
one beard has died, the other lives forever—
I kissed the dead one's wooden feet—
the other lives forever,
 the little buds emerging by magic
 from the dead twigs of every tree
and the music of resurrection song
 from every head in the Church—
Krakow Krakow, old mahogany,
 chandeliers, round bright mirrors
 in the long ancient coffeehouse,
  amaze, the old men talk mustache,
  the young rise courteously from
   marble tables for their hooded girls—

The leaves rise from the trees, the rain
  dooms the bare branches to life,
Easter's over, it's mid-Europe, a hidden
  corner the war never bore bomb,
all the tombs are intact, delicate marble
  knight and stucco hew composers—

Poland

Myriads set in the walk of the churches,
  dark heads looking out of high pillars,
    the unforgotten, the good
      ancestors who built a place that stands.

The castle on the hill, the cathedral in the Square,
  And all the statues on the roofs stand remembering—
and a handsome iron pole with gaunt cheeks
  and youthful thighs crossed, meditative eyes
  glancing down on the cobbles
guards the bath of flapping doves.
This eyebrow, with skin
    to be flaccid pale bloodless
  me dead
So—as all must, it's a shame,
  Depart, after all, & not come
    back anywhere—
A strange thot in front of
    the Polshi Hotel mirror.

26 April 1965—

Last few days wandering around Krakow—H [?], poet, his house a
big room studio, Daniel [?] a drawer of fantasy comics, in and out of St.
Mary's cathedral every day to see Wit Stotz altarpiece & stained glass,
sitting at cloth palace café in Krakow main square drinking coffee, tea,
in small old Mead shops with brown walls drinking hot sweet wine, one
night drunk at Student's Club on Square, and with my beard won the
longest beard contest two bottles of wine, another night at [?] nightclub
giggling at Katz girl & Wadislav thin faced intelligent journalist camp-
ing together—we wound up at his house 7 a.m. dawn light I naked in

bed him making love to me an hour slowly I relaxed despite my drunk-
enness acid stomach the soft pleasure of absolute passivity till I came &
slept till noon today—To all the museums, one white faced Mary & child
of wood with pink polychrome cheeks, an odd Da Vinci body with a Wes-
sel and the last Rembrandt landscape varnished gold-brown, Wavel Cas-
tle just wandering thru the rooms looking at tapestries of Noah and
Adam—Met a few American students who said they were bored in
Krakow—Decided not to go back to Warsaw but just stay here in old
streets and sit in café a few days and do nothing.

28 April Krakow—
    Floodlight yellow beams in the dark
        air building top Vase ornament
    the trumpet call from the church
        tower, eight o'clock
    McKievicches black statue clutching a book to
        his hip
    stands on a pedestal in the evening,
        shopwindows lit with a little blue neon,
    and the clatter of the café, the long café
        in the cloth palace arcade
    where I sit in my body a pleasant feeling after
        a dawn drunk and naked eyes closed
        hands and lips caressing
        the head of my prick & my belly—
    and a long walk thru the low streets
        of the grey old ghetto, by brick
        cemetery walls,
    in and out of antique bookshops and
        Gothic cathedrals

Poland

Looking at Christ heads hanging from black
　　crosses in the gloomy chapels
under vast pillars and heavenly roofs, giant
　　Marys and tiny bearded Gods—
All pointing to the Crucifixion, all
　　weeping over the rock tomb—
I have nothing left to do, but go
　　home—or see Berlin
and sit in a café the same café and feel the
　　same pleasure and the same doom—
How beautiful the new faces of young men, or
　　how they bow and speak low
voices filed with tenderness in the soft light
　　of night
For their bodies are new to them, and their desires
　　not known yet, bellies of bicycles
that quiver at the fingertip—thoughts of Krakow
　　and springtime eve—
the hair on my round belly reminds me of death—
　　and this long New York apartment years
　　to come—
and what to do with myself now, Allen? And
　　what to do with thee now?
Nothing to fear, nothing to hope, money and the body
　　are in the bank—
Is it women? That I don't look in their faces
　　anymore?
and all my illuminations, were illuminations, but
　　now—
Well they'll always be Me and Desire—tho now

desire's only a pleasure buzz of sex in
my legs and chest—in this café.

perhaps to rhyme.

29 April 1965—Wroclow—Poland
The ill fitting pants of Poland-Wroclow student coffeehouse.

As I walked down deserted Wroclow
night street
a blonde dummy in a white dress raised
her hand in the shopwindow—
I looked into the lighted crowd thru glass,
men & women standing in sleazy
new clothes—
I saw their expressions and they said—
staring sadly at the street—
We are silent because we have nothing
to say like Cezanne.
Their hands gestured in surprise. One man
had his wristed twisted backward,
making a hoy sign down to the white
plastic floor.
One young blue girl opened her palm to
hold pussywillow for Easter
and stared at the wall. A portly man
with red hair stared up at god in a vision
completely stolid. Behind them
men & women with price tags,
motionless waiting for the busy day.

Across the street a row of girls
   stept up close to the invisible
window in cloth coats. Pinkeys
   lifted, hands poised in balletic gesture
But the eyes—gazing absently cast
   down—their male friend
had a handkerchief in his brown jacket
   I looked straight over my head
    into the street.
And across the street, another smiled.

In Tram 30 April 1:45

Not forget to write down what happened on Auschwitz ride—the boy-scout master's story of his seductions—and his impartial analysis of Warsaw Destruction—and the signs at Auschwitz—and the boys they picked up—and the queer guide.

Then Wroclow—all evening at the Railroad Station. The Queer gangs, the boy with the tall body & black bangs, the Blond tough drunk beauty hitting his fist in his palm, & at last the three racing car drivers—one boy so young & big & strong & of face so exquisite I stared in his eyes.

Poland

Czechoslovakia

AND

England

APRIL–MAY 1965

The May King, Prague, May 1, 1965

CZECHOSLOVAKIA

Ginsberg arrived back in Prague on April 30, in time to witness the next day's May Day celebration, which promised to be a display of a thawing in Soviet–Czech relations. The traditional Czechoslovakian gala, which featured the crowning of the May Day King (Kral Majales) and Queen, had been suspended after the Soviet takeover, but the substituted events, focusing on workers and Communist ideology, had drawn protests in recent years. The old tradition was being reinstalled in 1965, and Ginsberg wanted to witness the pageantry. But he was not to be a mere observer, and his participation wound up leading to his expulsion from the country.

Unfortunately, only a few journal entries, written after the fact, exist. Ginsberg's main journal was either lost or stolen; whatever the case, it wound up in police custody. Ginsberg tried to recall the events, but his journal ends abruptly, as if he lost interest in the exercise, and resumes when he was on the plane bound for London. On the positive side, he wrote about the events in letters, one of which, a lengthy, detailed description of his entire trip, is included here, inserted after Ginsberg's original journal entries.

May 4, 1965
Roccoco Theater

Behold the new Hero
Standing in the glitter of
   Microphones

His mouth open,
  with the call—
He stamps his young feet
  in black pants
into solid Time—at his hip
  a huge guitar
aluminum mirroring the spotlites,
  polished black wood
issuing diamond notes that fall
  out into our applauding
     hands.

Ivan dives poet drunk at Viola later.
Lost small Czech Notebook. Several poems copied out previous.
Dr. Roujeck—

May 5—Events—

Arrived Prague morning April 30—left bag at station & found out of way hotel in the morning thru Cedok—Then went wandering around town, phoned [?] no answer, then to Writer's Union got letter for visa extension & then met Y. on street, we went & had coffee, gossiped—Yan in Tatras— then lunch with Hayck talking about trip—then to J's house, he sick, said hello—back to hotel a phonecall from S—do I want to be King of May contest sponsored by Technical School—he come & be Viziez—I said O.K., is it all right? What does it mean? First Student May Festival in 20 years, first beauty contest for May Queen & first Kral Majales in 2 decades. So he'd meet me at hotel next day 1:30 to go to fair grounds. Phoned Mr. [?] number & told him to send message meet that

Czechoslovakia

nite in Viola—And on street met Andy Lass—who said he'd had intuition I'd be back—Viola program new, Howl brought from Bratislava premier —went & stood behind curtain entrance to Nite club to listen—strange slow intimate reading, no energy, stolid snob audience applauding.

May Day—Andy came to pick me up 7:30. Am to go see Mayday parade, brought friend Marxist theoretician friend K K chief liberal intellect critic—we walked to Wenceslas talking history theory Trotsky— "Certainly will be rehabilitated writings—we in 1945 never dreamed what would happen"—Explained the mode of his censorship blacklisting—sold his car to live off—big ladies man—We marched in huge quiet parade down past band—stand where stood Novotny & fellow gang— Theo explained significance of grouping—who was there & why that meant shifts of power—

Ideological Committee had met with his Philosophy Institute to argue out his case, 3 days in a row, his friends supported him so I.C. was forced to have him fired—

In '56 he'd been sent out, this faculty dispersed, to do study in provinces, after poet XX Congress articles—In provinces he wrote more, published '62 & in '63, he was bounced again—"revisionism"—the main tendency of progressive Marxism—Yugoslavia quite free in this respect to say anything. Ideological & philosophical language & discussions very important in social balance. We sat in outdoor café with young girls & drank lemonade & ate frankfurter after the Parade. Then I went with Andy to my hotel—passing Jan's house to leave message I wouldn't get to student riot at 6 p.m. by statue in park across River—

At one o'clock knock on door while I was stretched out resting and opend door—in come some huge band of students in parasols & top hats, 1890's dress, wescoats, canes, with Jesters, trumpets,—M. C. was young Jewish fellow I'd met last visit here, called in to translate—"Mr. Ginsberg we have honor to beg your presence in procession to the Crowning

of King of May and to accept our support for your candidacy of Kral Majales & we humbly offer you crown & throne"—a little cardboard gilded crown & they sat me on a chair with red drapes—I got out my fingerscymbols & statue of Ganesh & chamois old coat & was carried down in elevator to a truck parked downstairs—there we rolled off singing & drinking beer to Technical School thru streets, announcing our presence—I began singing all mantras & asking what was happening—very confusing—arrived at courtyard of Tech. school, big crowd of students, another truck with Dixieland band waiting, cases of beer, many girls, signs "Ginsbergum Kral Majales"—D. didn't show at all—There I gave first speech "I'll be the first kind king & bow down before my subjects. I'll be the first naked king"—and quit talking—

Half hour there, assembling people & playing Dixieland & we set out thru streets, winding in and out of traffic till after five blocks we'd gathered several thousand people in our train—I kept getting up & singing Hari Om Nomo Shiva thru loudspeaker—

Letter from Allen Ginsberg to Nicanor Parra, August 29, 1965 [1]

Dear Nicanor dear:

Got your letter from Santiago July 9 and am now up in the Northwest with Gary Snyder an old friend poet who's been living in Japan studying Zen Jap tongue and Chinese for last 8 years. We're camping with sleeping bags in forests and beaches and preparing to climb snowy glacier mountains for a month. Then back to San Francisco and October

1. See Allen Ginsberg, *The Letters of Allen Ginsberg*, edited by Bill Morgan, 300–309.

15–16 I take part in anti-Vietnam war demonstration and maybe end up in jail or maybe not for a month or so. We'll see. Happy to hear from you. I had some very mad adventures since I left Cuba. I even spent a few evenings till 4 AM with Alessandro Jodorowsky in Cupola Café in Paris. But anyway to begin where we left off.

8:30 AM after the party at the Havana Riviera where I last saw you in your pajamas giggling I woke up with knock on my door and 3 *miliciano* entered and scared me. I thought they were going to steal my notebooks, they woke me up in the middle of hangover sleep I'd only been in bed 2 hours. Told me pack my bags the immigration chief wanted to talk to me, and wouldn't let me make phone call, took me down to office in old Havana to a Mr. Verona head of immigration who told me they were putting me on first plane out. I asked him if he'd notified Casa or Hayden [*sic,* Haydee] and he said no, they had appointment with Haden that afternoon and she would agree after she heard their reasons. What reasons? "Breaking the laws of Cuba." But which laws? "You'll have to ask yourself about that," he answered. As we drove to airport I explained I was simpatico with revolution and embarrassed both for self and for them and also explained that my month was up, the rest of, most of, the delegates were leaving that weekend anyway, wouldn't it be more diplomatic and save everyone entanglement if they left me to leave normally with the rest for Prague, and why act hastily without notifying Casa? "We have to do things fast in a revolution."

When I landed in Prague, I wrote Maria Rosa long letter and mailed it at my port explaining what happened and asked for advice and said I won't talk to reporters etc. and would keep quiet so's not to embarrass her or Casa or Cuba but thought ultimately I'd have to tell friends. It would get out and look silly of Cuban bureaucracy, so perhaps best ask Hayden to invite me back, at least formally to erase the comic [expulsion] and so have been in contact with her and Ballagas ever since. Saw

Czechoslovakia

[friends] in Prague and later in London and they opined the police were using me to get at the Casa. Meanwhile I hear there's been increased wipe-out of fairies in university and finally this month Manuel Ballagas wrote that Castro at university had spoken badly of *El Puente* and now *El Puente* is dissolved and he's depressed. I certainly didn't know what I was getting into consciously but I seem to have been reacting with antennae to a shit situation that everyone was being discreet about. I doubt if things would not have come to a head without my bungling. I mean it would probably have ended the same way if I weren't there, the hostility and conniving was in the works all along, that was what I was sensing and yelling about.

Well anyway in Prague I found I had royalties for a new book, and back money due me for foreign Lit. mag and a years back royalties for stage performances of my poesy in Viola poetry café, enough to live well for a month and pay for 3 days intourist and train fare return to Moscow via Warsaw. Met a lot of young kids, heard all the gossip conducted myself discreetly, sang mantras all over the streets and literary offices, gave a poetry reading and answered questions of audience of 500 students at Charles University. They let me loose, I talked freely, the walls of the State didn't fall, everybody was happy, sex relations with anyone male or female is legal over age of 18 (in Poland all over age 15 is legal) and I left for Moscow. See, when I came I explained to Writers' Union friends what had happened in Cuba to forewarn them so they wouldn't get into trouble over me. I also tried to be as little abrasive as possible and confined my criticism to ideological doubletalk instead of saying directly what I thought in my own terms. So that worked out fine and I went off in a train to Moscow. Spent the first few days with Romanova and Lurie and little girl interpreter and got a weeks invitation, saw Aksenov *[sic]* and Yevtushenko night after night and briefly one day with Voznesensky and visited Akhmadulina country and his Buba and

Czechoslovakia

Ginsberg in a reflective mood in Prague. He spent a great
amount of his time in the Iron Curtain countries studying
their social and political environment, only to conclude that
they were no better than what he found in the United States.

Aliguer who remembered and asked after you. I had hotel transferred to Bucharest below Moskovsky a bridge and passed thru Red Square every morning and evening and wrote poems in snow by the wall and stood there at midnight watching the guards and yelling Slavic lovers in GUM (largest department store in the world) doorway, fast 4 days train to Leningrad Hermitage, saw my old cousins in Moscow ("It wasn't Stalin's fault, it was Beria. Stalin didn't see, and Beria was in the pay of Scotland Yard" explained my uncle—and K. Simonov commented "Yr uncle is a very naïve man"). Yevtushenko was godly reciting drunk one nite in composer's house after midnight profiled golden against wall his neck cords straining with power speech, but at first meeting very funny. "Allen I have your books you *gran poeta nosostros mucho, consego Hay mucho escandalo sobre su nombre, marihuaniste, pederaste, perro yo conosco no es verdad.*" "Well, er—*pero is verdad Pero yo voy explicar*" so I spent 15 min., trying to elucidate scientifically the differences between effects of alcohol marijuana heroin ether laughing gas lysergic acid mescaline yage etc. His gaze wandered, he had a headache, popped a codeine pill in his mouth, and finally said, "Allen I respect you very much as a poet but this conversation demeans you. It is your personal affair. Please, there are two subjects do not discuss with me: homosexuality and narcotics." Despite all this comedy I saw a lot of him while I was there and he was very open and simpatico with me and took me out a lot of evenings and his wife and I were all drunk in the Georgian restaurant and he came to train to see me off the last day with Aksenov— another weird scene as that very last day I'd succeeded in contacting Yessenin-Volpin and spent all day with him at his house talking philosophy of law, relations of individual and state. He's working on big project to define socialist legality inasmuch as they put him in bughouse for complaining about police treatment. His sanity certification depended on him signing statement that police had not abused him at one point.

Czechoslovakia

He has fine sentimental sense of humor and human mind—in fact because of his position as sort of writers-union-rejectee he has more recognizably real sense of social humor and reality than anyone else—at least by my heart's standards—very reassuring to see a completely natural mind working on basic emotional reactions rather than thru the medium of what's socially acceptable for the season. So there was Yessenin-Volpin the comic pariah at night by the train door and up rushes fur-collared heroes Yevtushenko and tipsy manly Aksenov and they stumble on each other and meet socially for the first time and I waved goodbye from iron door as the train pulled out for Warsaw. I'd not had a chance to meet much younger people or even give a reading there—toward the end they let me meet a group of Univ. Satiric Club theater youths, and there were a few formal conferences with select professors and editors at Writer's Union and Dangulov's staff at Foreign Literature Institute and Foreign Literary Club but no opening for big poesy reading like kindly Prague. So I sang mantras to anyone who'd listen and Romanova listened and all the girls at Writer's Union, in taxicabs.

Quiet month in Warsaw. I stayed alone mostly or drank with Irridensky a young rimbaud-ish marlon brando writer at Writer's Union and long afternoons with editor of *Jazz* magazine who'd printed my poems, a Jewish good man who'd been in Warsaw Ghetto, escaped, and covered rest of war as journalist with Russian Army and stood across river from Warsaw at end and saw the city destroyed by Germans and nationalist underground killed off, apparently Stalin didn't want to move his army across river to help them because he didn't want competition in postwar control of Poland. Then a week in Krakow which hath a beauteous cathedral with giant polychrome altarpiece by medieval woodcarver genius Wit Stolz, and car ride to Auschwitz with some boy scout leaders who were trying to pick up schoolboys hanging around the barbed-wire gazing at tourists.

Czechoslovakia

Then by train thru Poland to Prague again April 30, and called up friends to walk with on next day May Day parade. Students heard I was back, and this year on May 1 afternoon they were allowed to hold Majales (Student May Festival) for the first time in 20 years—last few years students had battled cops with dogs and fire hoses, so this year Novony President had stepped forth and restored the old medieval students fiesta. They have parade to park and elect candidate for May Queen and May King, and the Polytechnic School asked me if I'd be their candidate for May King—each school proposes one—so I asked around if it was nonpolitical and safe and writer friends said it was OK so I waited in my hotel after marching in morning May Day parade past the bandstand on Wenceslas Street with the Chairman of the Ideological Committee and the Minister of Education and economics and shoes all waving down on the crowd—and a gang of polytechnical students dressed in 1890s costumes and girls in ancient hoopskirts came up to hotel near RR station to get me with a gold cardboard crown and scepter and sat me up on creaky throne on a truck and took me off with wine to the Polytechnic school where there were hundreds of students and a jazz band crowded in the courtyard and I was requested to make speech— which was short "I want to be the first naked King"—and we set out in procession thru the backstreets of Prague to the main avenues downtown. By the time we'd gone half a mile we had a crowd of several thousand trailing behind us singing and shouting long live Majales, stopping every ten minutes for traffic and more wine and so I had my cymbals and sang every time they put the bullhorn loudspeaker to my mouth for a speech—mostly sang a mantra Om Sri Maitraya—Hail Mr. Future Buddha—a mixed hindu buddhist formula for saluting the beauty that is to be. By this time there were more and more people and by the time we moved into the old square in old town Staremeskaya Nameske where Kafka used to live there were floods of people crowding the huge plaza

maybe 15,000 souls and I had to make another speech "I dedicate the glory of my crown to the beautiful bureaucrat Franz Kafka who was born in the building around the corner here." (Kafka was published finally in Prague in '61) and the procession moved on past the House of the Golden Carp where he wrote *The Trial*, which I pointed out to the crowd and got drunker on beer and sang more and louder, finally we crossed the bridge over the Vhava River people lining the bridge and the huge dragon-masses of cityfolk following before and after our trucks and Dixieland jazz playing ahead and citizens sitting on the cliff ahead watching it all with their children—everybody in Prague who could walk came out spontaneously. When we got to the park of Culture and Rest there were over 100,000 people and half a dozen rock and roll bands and everybody happy and amazed. They'd only expected 10 or 15 out that afternoon. So finally at 3 PM the medical school candidate wrapped in bandages got up and made his speech in Latin and the law school candidate in kings robes got up and made a long sexy speech about fornication as his campaign speech. I got up and sang Om Sri Maitreya for 4 minutes and sat down, and finally was elected May King by the strange masses. So realized it was a politically touchy day and behaved myself, wandered around soberer than any one else with a gang of Polytechnic students. Meanwhile in this Garden of Culture and Eden the Chairman of the Ideological Committee and Minister of Education were wandering around complaining. I had slipped off to be alone a few hours and listen to music, I later learned they were looking for me; that night we all reassembled on the podium to elect a May Queen, I was sitting in my throne looking out at the crowds and floodlights and opened my notebook and wrote a poem and dwelled in my Self for a yogic fifteen minutes. Meanwhile the bureaucrats had given an order to the Student Festival committee to depose me. I didn't know that, suddenly two brown shirted Student Police lined up in front of me and the master of

Czechoslovakia

ceremonies spoke a few sentences into loudspeaker saying I was deposed to be instead Prime Minister and a Czech student would be put in King's place, and the police lifted me up off my chair and put me on the side with the May Queen judge and a drunken Czech student who didn't know what was happening was put on the throne where he sat for an hour confused and embarrassed. But the crowd thought it was just another student prank and didn't hear or know the difference everybody so drunk anyway the gesture was too late and small to be understood and May Queen was elected but I didn't get a chance to marry and sleep with her as was tradition for the night. In fact I was supposed to have the run of Prague and do anything I wanted and fuck anybody and get drunk everywhere as King, but instead I went to the Polytechnic dormitories with 50 students and we sat up all night singing and talking— along with a couple of business-suited middle-aged fellows who brought some Scotch and a tape recorder. Said they were trading officials but I supposed they were agents, perhaps I'm paranoid. But anyway we made them welcome. Meanwhile I figured I'd better leave in a few days so at Writer's Union next day made inquiries about whether I had money in Hungary, next stop maybe, and waited for telegram answer, and student magazines and had some secret nighttime orgies here and there and went to rock and roll concerts and wrote poems—and suddenly lost my notebook, or suddenly it disappeared from my pocket. And (All the capitalist lies about communism are true and vice versa) descriptions of orgy scenes with a few students and an account of masturbating in my room at the Hotel Ambassador kneeling on the bathroom floor with a broomstick up my ass—things I wouldn't necessarily want anyone to read and for that reason have never published my journals so as to keep them raw and subjectively real—but nothing illegal and nothing I wouldn't be happy to have read in Heaven, or by Man—embarrassing in a police car

or a politician's—fortunately not detailed like in Cuba or Russia as I was enjoying myself too much to write anything but concentrated Poesy. That nite I went to Viola and met the two business suits who gave me vodka till I was drunk and went out at midnight singing Hari Om Namo Shiva on Narodni Street. Police car picked me up asking for identification—which I didn't have since the hotel had my passport for registration. I explained at station I was May King Tourist Poet and they let me go. I really wasn't so drunk just happy. Next nite however, since I saw I was followed around all day by bald plainsclothesmen, I stayed sober visiting the Viola, and left with a young couple to go to allnight post office to mail postcards to you or someone and as we turned midnight corner on lonely street a man came up from around corner, hesitated, saw me and suddenly rushed forward screaming *bouzerant (maricon)* [fairy]) and knocked me down, hit me on the mouth, my glasses fell off. I scrambled up and grabbed them and started running down the street, the couple I was with tried to hold him, he chased me and had me down on the ground again in front of the post office and a police car full of captains pulled up immediately and I found myself on the ground with 4 police rubber clubs lifted over my head, so I said OM and stayed quiet, they pulled me into police car and we spent all nite in police station, telling the story the couple I was with said what happened accurately, the Kafiian stranger said we'd been exposing ourselves on the street and when he passed we attacked him. Finally I asked to call lawyer or U.S. consulate and they let me go and said it was all over, nothing more would be heard of it, I was free. Well I reported all that in to Writer's Union and Foreign Literature mag. friends and decided I'd better leave town, tarrying foolishly for Hungarian telegrams, still, and next day I was followed again and in evening to remote café with student friends on outskirts of town was picked up by plainclothesmen.

Czechoslovakia

Ginsberg and Pavel Beran in Prague

"We found your notebook, if you come to lost and found with us and identify it we'll return it to you and you'll be back here in half an hour." So I went to Convictskaya Street Police and identified and signed paper for it and soon as I signed the detective face froze and he spoke. "On sketchy examination we suspect that this book contains illegal writings so we are holding it for the public prosecutor." Next morning at breakfast downtown I was picked up with student friend I knew slightly who volunteered to stay with me that day make sure I didn't have troubles and taken to Convictskaya Street again, same plainclothesmen, brought upstairs to office with 5 pudgy-faced eyeglassed bureaucrats around polished table. "Mr. Ginsberg we immigration chiefs have received many complaints from parents scientists and educators about your sexual theories having a bad effect on our youth, corrupting the young, so we are terminating your visa." They said the notebook would be returned by mail, maybe. I explained that I was waiting for Hungarian telegram, and if that didn't work out had plane ticket for London so could leave on my own the next day, and it would be more diplomatic and spare them the embarrassment of exiling the May King if they left it to me to go voluntarily. I certainly didn't want to get kicked out of ANOTHER socialist country. And it might be difficult to explain to the students etc. Deaf ears, incompetent bureaucracy again. So was taken out to hotel and sat in my room with detective all afternoon and not allowed phone call to Writer's Union or U.S. Embassy or friends and put secretly on plane for London that afternoon and pretty girl I knew who receiving LSD thereby at state mental hospital met me at hotel door wanted to speak with me but cop stepped in between us. At airport the eyeglass bureaucrat said humorous "Is there any last message you want to deliver to the young lady who met you at the door of your hotel?" Also the last I saw of my student guard from breakfast, he was being pushed around a little and asked for identity papers by the police on Konvictskaya Street as I

Czechoslovakia

was being led upstairs in elevator. So I flew off to England on plane, and kept my mouth shut again. I didn't want to make a stink or get anybody I knew connected with me in scandal there, so was discreet from May 7 on when I flew in air to England and also wrote a nice poem *Kral Majales,* I'll send you in a month when printed—big paranoid hymn about being May King sleeping with laughing teenagers—and landed in England and found Bob Dylan (folk singer, you remember, I had his record in Havana?) was there spent days with him watching him besieged by a generation of longhaired English ban the bomb girls and boys in sheepskin coats with knapsacks—and in his Savoy hotel spent a drunken night talking about pot and William Blake with the Beatles, gave a few small readings in London Liverpool Newcastle Cambridge and met my NY girlfriend there, made more film and had a birthday party after reading at Institute Contemporary Arts, took off all my clothes at 39th birthday party drunk singing and dancing naked, the Beatles came at midnight and got scared and ran away laughing over their reputations, then Voznesensky came to town and we met again— we'd seen each other another night in Warsaw—Corso and Ferlinghetti came over from Paris so we hired Albert Hall and filled it with 6,000 hairy youths and bald middle-aged men of letters, Indira Gandhi and Voznesensky sitting at my side holding hands, 17 poets English German Dutch all read, Voznesensky shy to read because *Daily Worker* wrote it up as anticapitalist antiwar demonstration and perhaps too political for his visit, Neruda said he'd come read but didn't, went to some official university scheduled for him alas instead, big funny night all the poets filled with wine, a lot of bad poetry and some good, but everybody happy and England waked poetically a little. A few nights later Ferlinghetti Corso and I read at Architectural Assn. together and Fernandez and Voznesensky and another Georgian poet came, I read from *Kaddish* and Gregory read *Bomb* poem and last Voznesensky got up and read like a

Czechoslovakia

lion from his chest, poem dedicated to all artists of all countries who gave life and blood for poesy, poem imitating sound of Moscow bells in Kremlin towers, he read better than anyone and was happy and came up and kissed me after and stuck his tongue in my mouth like a Russian should in Dostoyevsky, we said goodbye, then I flew to Paris but had no money left I'd taken no money for Albert Hall or other readings so had to walk street all night with Corso first night and finally slept a week upstairs in Librarie Mistral bookstore room with customers sitting on bed reading Mao Tse-tung at 10 AM when I woke, and flew back to NY on still valid Cuban ticket, arrived in NY and as I entered customs was stopped by US guards and taken in to room and searched, they collected the lint from my pockets looking for marijuana. I was scared, I'd stayed with Tom Maschler a few weeks in London and he'd given me his old clothes and I didn't know what he'd ever had in his pockets, but they found nothing tho they stripped me down to my underwear. I saw their letter of orders they negligently left on the desk face upwards. "Allen Ginsberg (reactivated) and Peter Orlovsky (continued)—These persons are reported to be engaged in smuggling narcotics . . ." and meanwhile back in England on May 18 I heard rumors and got phone calls from journalists and found that the Czech Youth Newspaper had big article attacking me as dope fiend homosexual monster who'd abused Prague hospitality so they didn't have enough sense to shut up about their own idiocy. They didn't report any accusations I hadn't already said myself publicly in my own way. I never made a secret of the fact that I smoke pot and fuck any youth that'll stand still for it, orgies etc. that's exactly the reason they elected me May King in the first place—aside from Mantras and Poesy—the journalese rhetoric like an old creaky movie— and they published a drawing and a few selected pieces of dirty writing from my notebook—properly censored so as not to be too offensive— suppressed the fact that I'd been elected May King while they were at

Czechoslovakia

it. Anyway the police there still have my notebook and some poems I didn't copy out—fortunately they can't destroy it or they destroy their own evidence, so it's safe—probably in fact copies of it are being passed around and read by amused litterateurs in the Party it'll find its way down to the students in time even and back to me in 1972 in Outer Mongolia from the hands of a lamaist monk who practices ancient tantric sex yoga or Neruda will find it in his Ambassador hotel room drawer next time he visits Prague.

[...]
Love
Allen

ENGLAND

Allen Ginsberg's expulsion from Czechoslovakia eventually made international news, but there seemed to be a kind of news blackout in the days immediately following his leaving the country. As he predicted, the expulsion was awkward, if not embarrassing, and Czech officials took their time in constructing a reason for their actions, announcing that Ginsberg had been bounced from the country for drug and morals issues that conflicted with Czech laws. Ginsberg remained quiet, as he had in the aftermath of his troubles in Cuba, his reasoning the same: there was no reason to risk the well-being of those he'd been associating with in Czechoslovakia. When the news of his expulsion made the rounds in the newspapers, Louis Ginsberg couldn't resist teasing his son about his troubles. "How come they expelled the King of May?" he asked. "Too much revelry with Pan?"[2]

2. Letter, Louis Ginsberg to Allen Ginsberg, June 15, 1965.

Swinging England, as it turned out, was an ideal place for Ginsberg to recover, an atmosphere that seemed the polar opposite from what he had faced in the Iron Curtain countries. A massive youth movement, spearheaded by the Beatles and the "British Invasion" of the United States, enveloped the country. Help would be the big movie of the summer. The Rolling Stones released "Satisfaction." Bob Dylan toured the country, his concerts and extracurricular antics the subject of the documentary film Dont Look Back. *Young people flooded the stores and boutiques, snapping up bright, colorful clothing that freshened London's streets. Ginsberg enjoyed every minute of it.*

His journals from his time in England begin on a plane, while he was in transit to London from Prague, the poet determined to document his experiences in Czechoslovakia.

"Y E B U OL O N"—a word forbidden to say

May 7—Back to work—on BOA plane leaving Prague airport, Rainy day, & the ship whistling hath begun th' ascent.

And the communist bureaucrats have nothing to offer but fat cheeks[3]
    and eyeglasses and policemen that tell lies
and the capitalists proffer napalm to Viet Nam and money in green
    suitcases to the naked in Dominican Republic
and the communists create heavy industry but the heart
    is also heavy
and the beautiful engineers are all half dead, the secret technicians

3. First draft of "Kral Majales," *CP*, 361, written on plane en route from Prague to London.

England

The reading at London's Royal Albert Hall was a mixed
success, but it gave Ginsberg the opportunity to read an
important new work, "Who Be Kind To," written especially
for the reading. Photograph by John "Hoppy" Hopkins,
"Ginsberg RAH," copyright 1965 Estate of J. V. L. Hopkins.

    conspire for their own glamor
in the Future, in the Future, but now drink vodka
    and lament the Security Forces,
and the capitalists drink gin and whiskey on airplanes but
    let Indian brown millions starve
and when communist and capitalist assholes tangle the Just
    man is arrested or robbed or had his head cut off,
but not like Kabir, and the cigarette cough of the
    Just men above the clouds
in the bright sunshine is a salute tiving in Japan studyio the health of
        the blue
    sky.
For I was arrested thrice in Prague, once
    for singing drunk on Narodini Street,
once of losing my notebooks or sex politics dreams,
    once for having unusual sex opinions
and I was sent from Havana by plane by
    detectives in green uniform,
and I was sent from Prague by plane by
    detectives in Czechoslovakian business suits,
Cardplayers out of Cezanne, the two strange dolls
    that entered Joseph K's room at morn,
also mine, and ate at my table, and
    examined my scribbles,
and followed me night and morn from the
    houses of lovers to the cafes of Centrum—
and I am the King of May, which is the
    power of sexual youth,
and I am the king of may, which is industry

England

in eloquence and action in amour,
and I am the king of may, which is long hair,
    Adam and the Beard of my own body
and I am the king of May, which is Kral Majales
    in the Czechoslovakian tongue,
 and I am the King of May, which is old Human
    poesy, and 100,000 people chose my name,
And I am the King of May, and in a few minutes
    I will arrive in London airport,
And I am the King of May, naturally, for I am
    of Slavic parentage and a Buddhist Jew
who worships the sacred heart of Christ the blue
    body of Krishna the straight back of Ram
the beads of chango the Nigerian singing Shiva
    shiva in a manner which I have invented,
and the King of May is a Middleeuropean honor,
    mine in the XX century
despite space ships and the Time Machine,
    because I heard the Voice of Blake in a Vision,
    of May that sleeps with youth.
And I am the King of May, that I may be ex-
    pelled from my kingdom with
    honor, as of old,
to shew the difference between Caesar's kingdom
    and the Kingdom of the May of Man—
and I am the King of May, the paranoid, for
    the Kingdom of May is too beautiful
    to last more than a month—
and I am the king of May, because I touched

England

my finger to my forehead saluting

a beautiful girl with trembling hands who said

 "one moment Mr. Ginsberg"

Before a fat young policeman stepped between our

 bodies—I was going to England—

and I am the King of May, returning to see

 Bunhill Fields and walk on

 Hempstead heath,

And I am the King of May, on a giant

 jet plane touching albion is airfield

 trembling in fear

as the ship roars to a landing on

 the grey concrete, shakes &

 expels air,

and rolls slowly to a stop under the

 clouds with part of blue heaven

 still visible.

And *tho* I am the king of may, the Marxists

 have beat me up on the street, kept

 me up all night in police station

 followed me through springtime Prague,

 detained me in secret and expelled

 me from out kingdom by jetplane.

Thus I have written this poem on

 Savoy London

The TV on, longhaired Birds wrecking

 their necks in Fauntleroy suits,

outside the Windo Prince Gold

 stands over the mechanic roof—

England

and a great grey clock stands face
 hands over a windowed wall
risen above the aged Galeles of brick
 lightningrod tile in the sky
mull white above spear spire
 iron balcony chimney & watertower
ringing space—and two high pillars
 lifting the hotel roof's
cottage of marble statues seated on an arch
 over a high green room.
In the room myself high and
 one in beard & glasses w/shepherd's
 crook,
one wife blackhaired with gifts of
 brown candy Tanger
one with black camera big baby on his
 lap,
one microphone black bulb, a
 longhaired blonde carrying its
 wrey case—
one boy in grey suede pants, so then he
 sings,
one married businessman with long silver hair,
one boy in striped shirt pink hair and barefoot,
the telephone to overseas, Eisenhower on
 the screen "It's the human race,"
No regrets on the chiaroscuro stage in
Sequins—
Belsen pictures my dear the thin corpses
 and sitting skeletons stunned while

the Russians shelled the faded buildings

   and Stormtroopers marched toward

   Brandenburg Gate—

May 9—Concert in Albert Hall, then to hotel till 3 a.m. w. Beatles. I fell on John Lennon's lap when he said "Move closer," mocking me.

Next nite the 10'th to Albert Hall again—first walk to bus to Embassy & negotiations to reach messages for my notebooks to Prague[4]—then bus to Hotel Savoy & phonecall upstairs & walk to Jonathan Cape Maschler & back by Greek St. to National Gallery—Delis Franscesca [?] & Davinci & Michelangelo & Cezanne then to Hotel & Albert Hall a concert of Dylan Gates of Eden Tambourine Baby Blue[5] & out to hotel & Trattoria restaurant a round table & chicken.

Once again in Worchester Cathedral—the soft white

   light of afternoon on the grey stone.

Long ribs of the roof of the house of silence—and

   high English ladies voices

and basses in the choir under pastel stained glass—

   and the stone effigies of King John asleep—

and 6 years I've been around the world,

   arrived at this spot to worship

the tender voices rejoicing in our anonymous presence,

   How lovely to be back again in England!

4. Ginsberg made repeated attempts to retrieve his stolen/confiscated Czecho-slovakian journals, to no avail.

5. During his stay in London, Ginsberg appeared with Dylan in D. A. Penne-baker's film *Dont Look Back*. Ginsberg is also pictured, clean shaven and wearing a top hat, on the back of Dylan's album *Bringing It All Back Home*.

Guru[6]

It is the moon that disappears
It is the stars that hide not I
It is the city that vanishes, I stay
with my forgotten shoes
my invisible stocking
It is the call of a bell

Written on Primrose Hill looking at the full moon high on Junk 3 a.m.

after

Charring Cross Underground John

For the best	I am 16
sexthrill off	If any man
all take on	wants me make
11 yr. schoolgirl	Date any Monday
knickers down &	————
slowly lick her wet	British Museum
fanny while it	25. Good prick. bum and body
twitches—they all	who likes to fuck
adore it!	Make date, place, time
E Col Cul	after 25 May
Facea Trombetta	any offers *Fred Bloggs*
————	————

6. Notation for "Guru," *CP*, 364.

The Queen	Wanted
for slow death	Man with a polaroid
by torture.	camera

Marianne Faithful	I am
Julie Andrews	Castrated
No Cilla Block	————
for slow death	Fuck me
by Torture—lovely!	England.

Mlada Fronta—C.P.K. News Agency

[...]

I feel like an old poet from greyhaired 1880 years—I sit in front row &
see the Harlequin as he rushes frontstage & leads the row of dancers,
joyfully he jumps & lifts his heels to the universe of red eyes.

Am I an orgiast? God yes! Narcotics! Plenty experiments on con-
sciousness—expansion drugs. Narcotics addict, technically *not*.

*Ginsberg became obsessed with men's room graffiti and devoted many pages to no-
tating the messages, usually pornographic, that he found written on the walls. All were
similar to the one already notated in these journals, though it seemed as if there was
a competition over who might present the most outrageous lines.*

May 25, 1965

Central line Underground—a gentleman with shiny black shoes &
black bulbous derby hat, white celluloid collar, pinstripe blue shirt &
dark blue tie with tiny white circles innumerable [?] a 7 button black
vest, his black coat's second buttonhole jutted striped grey pants & grey
wool socks—reading the Times—thru gold halfeye glasses.

The Lie

is to becloud the Consciousness
I can look him in the eye
   steely gazed, eyesockets fixed
      and rigid
     imitating candor balanced
       eyeball
thinking "I am deceiving him, he thinks I'm
   looking into his eye, but I must be
   careful not to fix my stare
        at his pupil"—
and not go in, as in a warm bath,
softly reading in with tender looks
   that stiffen the cock—
For Consciousness is between me and him,
and if I deceive him, I also cut
   the numbers of feeling between us,
   the thrill of I love you—

or I am naked to your eye,
    I am naked in your soul,
        take me, have me, be mine—
To lie is to cut the senses, to close the
    doors of vision, to guard the ear,
      make touch selfconscious and taste
        an empty tongue—
      to smell my own nose—

Truth to man opens the portals, the six feelers
        outward—like fingertips
    touching forth delicately along the
        ribs of the self,
      Great Many Self we are

Why cut your soul in half and
      feed it to the Karma Crows?—
Why take half soul your portion when
    the truthful infinite opens out
of Muladhara, belly, solarplexus,
    heart, mouth, between the eye
      and sunflowers the top of the head,
        the blossomy Soft Crown
"licked by angels"—petals kissed
    by sweet sixteen or boy or girl
    or newborn babe—
I must uncloud my Consciousness, shit in
    Myself many a fearful lie.

The lie cloud is Fear   the lie cloud is envy,
   The lie cloud is dissatisfaction
     —Sadism to what IS—

Myself and Him with whom I live
   For 80 years no more.

   May 25—read Bricklayer, Green Auto, Now Come poem, Over Kansas, Old Poet Peru, & The End.[7]

O the great song & cry of
   warm heart stirring ache
   thru belly and cock—
the [?] for a second woken
   phantasy asshole thrilled
   and muscles relaxed in the
   morning huge room
      windows open on the
      day's empty stand—
ah draw the curtains and let be
this sexuality, not less than Myself
   desiring eternal life,
   from America come thru to ecstasy in the fingertips,

7. See "The Bricklayer's Lunch Hour" (*CP*, 12), "The Green Automobile" (*CP*, 91), "Fragment 1956" (*CP*, 157), "Over Kansas" (*CP*, 124), "To an Old Poet in Peru" (*CP*, 247), "The End" (*CP*, 267).

England

my god of Jazz revealed in the Word—
But he was originally dismissed, I'm
       scared of being alone with a broom
         up my bum, sweetly coming
         to kneel & to pour my spunk
             on the rust
  Come to essen   my body having [?]
      back to England bringing a poetry reading—
come bring *Fuck You* from America to
      Albion's shore,
Bring mixtures of lust expressed like prayer
  of lark saws magic rising over greenery
or sparrows woken in the black cat's yard—

Come lovely sphinx let forth new
    song [?] wake desire & stir
      knee crags of prophesy—

Invisionable sex   Alone slouching
  round searching for New Bethlehem.
    thru South London's streets—

Wake wake wake wake wake
  gold bodygod & Be!
    Me! Men marching
  longpiped & schotchmen-kilts lifted
    on the holy hill—
I want to meet some long haired

England

golden skotch lad who'll make
me sing under his knees
  "I want your body"
hoarsely dignified a
    Fuck up, mon.

Step forward Liverpool sexual fantatics
    Let my hairy fire spread thru England,
the stain begun in the gentlemen's toilet
explode like spermshit over green
      Tight little isle—

womenfolk fear not, what I begin you get
  doublejoyued multiple in your own cunt
           for Aye!

Friday, 28—Up noon, out looking at art school with Adrian Henri, and ride around Liverpool drinking in dock bars & up on Albion Street, looking at Venetian scaled Roberts Docks—then to Parry's bookstore to reading/w/Horowitz & Pete Brown—and off with Henri to Blue Angel, crowded dark cellar with rock group Melody Makers?—beating up th' ecstasy—then home slept with B—necked & claspt for hours softly naked in bed and finally back turned he put my cock between his legs & I came, sighing—

Saturday, 29—Woke an hour after B, who dressed and went to York —and then out to Adrian's & listened to rock records—read Beatles interview in Playboy—the worried zany conversation—then walked downtown to Walked art gallery & looked over variety new Liverpool exhi-

England

bition paintings—op & other—and the preraphaelites including Dante-Beatrice—and then out Walking to the Gold Clock Pub.

Reporter from Sunday Telegraph phoned from London & read me long AP dispatch re Czechoslovak illusions. Relatively accurate tho vulgar from N.Y.—and said Novotny'd gone on Radio to denounce me on the 19th—or something—I didn't understand all the details by memory. A faded scene. What's happening in Prague?

Brighton Pier, round red wooden
   restaurants, feet running down
    the gangway for the fast boat
down the grey fields of river to the grey
   city in the cloud and mist—
—pikes of harborcrones leaned in the Saturday twilight
Under vast blue open universe mottled
   with planetary steam mass floating
         over the smokestacks,
wharves, lone sailboats at rest (the great green
   river birds atop the twin towers of the 19th century)
leviathan hulks of warehouses ribbed before the city—
the distance, the distance to this old home
   downtowns with Heys and Alleys
   and the Beat Rock Ecstasy in brick basements—the flaxen girls
waiting at the cavern portal for their nightly joy—
and the tide comes in, washed by a boat,
the yellow universe lights up—the warm sun out between
   clouds over the Irish ocean
Shines on Brighton fort and New Brighton Amusement Park Tower,
   clanking with toy cars lifted in the air to its
   grim grey mansard over the Maygreen trees—

England

Too much fish & chips, cockles & mussels
    my stomach sinking, my leg twitching,
music echo on my lap, and a rock tune
    running from my forehead & foot—
Tum Tum Tum Tum/tum tum/tum tum tum tum tum/tum tum
Under the black concrete granite of the Harborside, shaking
    on top of a double-decker bus front seat, miniature cars &
    people on black asphalt out of the window,
the happy hour of Saturday nite, riding downtown past
    Victoria's statue
for an evening of beer and longhaired boys and Nigerian
    music down the Sink.

In the Sink, the stone basement of city[8]
    the vibrations of Vox electronic shudder thru brick & flesh,
    the children beautifully collared and sleeved, with tapered
        silk dungarees,
each pubescent body think and handsome shaking his hips,
each darling daughter alone on the concrete snapping her fingers—
the longhaired guitarist snakes into a silver microphone and
    builds the drum beat to a heavy charge
    and screams on the high note—a circle
    a circle of flesh is formed,
he screams, everybody claps & shudders,
    a circle of flesh dances round
six boys and two girls, shuffling
    left shuffling right hey hey,

8. See "Liverpool Muse," in *Wait Till I'm Dead: Uncollected Poems* (New York: Grove Press, 2016), 50–51.

England

shuffling left, shuffling right, the
Yoruba dance step comes back to Liverpool—

I stop writing and move my hips—the circle is complete.
Albion, Albion your children dance again
Jerusalem's rock established in the basements of Satinic mills.

Sunday—Liverpool
Eating fish maw soup in Chinese restaurant near Lime Street & Station—tonite to hear the Clayton Square band in the rumbling cellar—the Sink.

Lettuce Soup—Toasted crumpets.

Liverpool, June 1, 1965, 8 a.m.
Dream
I have a big huge loft building in New York upstate, an old elevated station maybe—you go up the wooden stairs and it's a long room divided by glass partition & swinging doors with sections—the first room a huge long one, the second smaller and curved around with an exit downstairs there too—good for getting away from police—it's mine, I have a lease on it given me by Huncke and a few friends, some young cats I don't like, junkies I'm afraid—but I want some junk too—I have a long paper of junk in the top drawer of a huge ancient mahogany dressingtable 20 feet length—and the cellophane paper—like that for photo negatives—is itself 2 feet long, stashed in the top drawer—among papers and memorabilia—we all turn on—

There are too many people in the house—damn and the police come too, a couple cops appear at the front door and push Huncke around and a couple at the side back door I'd been thinking so handy for escaping thru—they round up Trocchi's[9] Huncke's friends and take them out, most—they don't go thru my drawer—leave me there—

I think the junkies'd been thru my drawer—I look thru it & the H is all gone, those pigs they shot it *all* up—just came in my room and appropriated it all—I look thru drawer to find old bottle of M.S. (morph sulfate and stropine) and there's a few pills there turned to dry powder but ok, and a few more pills fallen out of cellophane packet, intact— I visualize the pinpricks of the stropine, when I shoot it—in fact I do take it—

I'm out of the house. The big room's Huncke's & friends & the smaller one's mine, I think I ought to close it off—partition between the two—but Huncke'll get the best part?—No I want that—

I'm coming back up my street toward the Elevated line entrance where the giant pad door is—oh! There's the same police hanging around door, talking to a group of Huncke's friends—will they bust me as I come on up?—No, they move from group to phonebox downstairs, but let me thru—

I go in house it's a giant party—but the pad is packed full, it must be *thousands* of people in the house all in pink lights, and all wearing Harlequin costumes, paper noses, black eyemasks, pierrot hats, sitting on the floor in the bedroom in the hall the huge front room—I wander thru, amazed & a little bugged—what has this to do with me, for real?—It was supposed to be a nice homecoming & here's so many completely strange people—I pass the swinging doors to a long downward dipping corridor I'd known before, part of my realm—it's a primary schoolroom—I walk down & see the class in session—Books piled up for their use, a few little

9. Alexander Trocchi (1925–1984), Scottish novelist, editor of *Merlin* literary magazine, and, with Richard Seaver and Terry Southern, editor of *Writers in Revolt: An Anthology* (1962), which featured the work of Beat Generation writers.

England

Ikons of Krishna, brass statues—tiny on the brown desks—why aren't *they* at the party?—I ask, & they all say demurely they don't know, there was schoolwork to do—

I go back to party & try to clear it out—into front door like bartender of English pubs—"Everybody not a member of the immediate family please go home ... Everybody not a member of the immediate family please leave immediately"—the rooms empty out except for scattered groups of friends—that's good, someone'll be left and most folk'll go— I go thru the house calling for the crowd to go home.

Had fallen asleep thinking of consequences of my talk. I'd had drunk with 14 yr. old boy in Chinese [?] place in Liverpool—I'd seen him standing there and said—

Me: Are you sure about it? Are you positive about it?

Boy: Sure of what?

Me (confused silence): Are you sure it's alright to die?

Boy: No

Me: Are you sure it's not alright not to die?

Boy: No

Me: ah death ain't nothing it all goes black

Boy: How do you know

Me: Same thing before you were born, there's nothing to remember.

Boy: But you don't remember when you were one year old, do you?

Me: (thinking) No!—you're absolutely right (thinking) by god I've wondered about that for years and never got the answer. You're a wise man.

The implications for me "simply fantastic," here I'd been going around thinking there was nothing after death simply because I couldn't visualize or remember prebirth.

England

June 4, 1965

And many days passed from Liverpool to London—Back for a party,
John Ashbery[10] read at USIS Embassy theater, quiet and staring down
at texts, then at Cape a gathering of literati for my benefit—Marc Schli-
effer turned up tall in a Russian-Muslim fur cap—next morn June 2 I
woke early & saw Ferhandez Pablo & Marc at breakfast & accompanied
M to the airport with his Muslim US spade coffee sweet beauty clear
nosed wife & children & saw them off at noon.

Thence John Esan & Barbara[11] hired Albert Hall[12] & a mad snowfall
began the second I moved to Miles'[13] flat under the high spikey tower
& that nite at Finches met the poetry gang from [?]—to the East End
all nite till 4 a.m. singing mantras, thence home by cab & woke the next
morn June 3 was interviewed also by N.Y. Times & London Times &
Geo Dowden[14] for PhD—

10. John Ashbery (1927–2017), American poet, 1976 winner of Pulitzer Prize, Na-
tional Book Award, and National Book Critics Circle Award for *Self-Portrait in a
Convex Mirror*.

11. Barbara Rubin, independent filmmaker, sometime girlfriend of Ginsberg's.

12. On June 11, a group of international poets, including Ginsberg, Lawrence Fer-
linghetti, Gregory Corso, and Andrei Voznesensky, read at the Royal Albert Hall in
London, in an event filmed for a documentary. Ginsberg hoped the reading would be
like the breakthrough poetry reading in San Francisco's Six Gallery in 1955, but there
were too many poets reading, and too much of the poetry was substandard, to please
Ginsberg.

13. Barry Miles worked in (and eventually owned) a London bookshop. He housed
Ginsberg for a time during his stay in England and, in later years, recorded Ginsberg
singing Blake songs. Miles wrote the first full-length Ginsberg biography.

14. George Dowden compiled the first Ginsberg bibliography.

England

Ginsberg helped organize an international poetry reading at the Royal
Albert Hall in London. Pictured here, following a press conference
announcing the event, are (left to right) Harry Fainlight, Ginsberg,
Barbara Rubin, Kate Heliczer (back to camera), Michael Horovitz,
Simon Watson-Taylor, and Lawrence Ferlinghetti. Photograph by John
"Hoppy" Hopkins, "B Rubin," copyright 1965 Estate of J. V. L. Hopkins.

June 8, 1965—Voznesensky at London Univ.

"I want to give rhythm of fiery snow in my poem . . . women rushing & jumping into the snow"—

Reads with right fist in the light lifted, when, framed by green blackboard.

"Anas myas"

Rocks back & forth on his heels—

"I heard about Prague . . . but confused . . . what happened?"

"Before I became a poet, yet, I was a student of architecture . . . when I master the [?] there was fire in the architectural college & all my work was burned . . . that's why I became a poet."

Second time hearing architectural fire the rhythms & rhymes become hypnotic-familiar.

". . . is experiment in poem . . . Russian poets write in rhyme . . . and before us there were 2 types of Russian poetry—first type man's rhyme . . . another woman's rhyme—example—for me it seems unnatural, why man w/man & w/w we must get them together"—

"I'm going to read part of my last long poem Beaux Arts . . . I am far from my love . . . and I am remember about your shoes"—

You are sitting waiting for your child
and your face is white

> . . .

and I don't know why women kiss us
> ugly us . . . yes us . . .
thru all earth women are standing alone
> waiting for children

While in London, Ginsberg gave a spirited reading
with Gregory Corso at the Architectural Society.
Photograph by John "Hoppy" Hopkins, "Ginsberg
Reading," copyright 1965 Estate of J. V. L. Hopkins.

and ugly nasty men are running thru them
      in trains—

"I want to give with these long lines
    a music of Moscow bells ... sense that life is
struggle ... and that life for painter and artist is pain"—
    ". . . another line dedicated to the barbarians of the
middle age"

"In pain then is bridge of Art where painter draw pictures ... I noticed drawing of face of Mayakovsky & lines about his love of Lily Brik—I noticed people walked on face of Mayahovsky ..."

There is road near Moscow named Roublishovia—and there is great ancient Ikon painter named Andrei Roubliev—and when I see motorcycles on road it seems they look like angels of Roubliev—the girls with silk dresses like angels wings ... and I don't know what will happen with me when God (he taps his shoulder) takes me out ..."

    June 8, 1965—4–6 a.m.—H.

        Who Be Kind To[15]
Be kind to yourself, it is only one and perishable
of many on the planet, thou art that
one that wishes a soft finger tracing the line of feeling from

15. First draft of "Who Be Kind To," *CP*, 367.

England

nipple to pubes—
one that wishes a tongue to kiss your armpit, a lip to touch your
    cheek inside your whiteness thigh—
Be kind to yourself Harry, because unkindness comes when the
    body explodes
napalm cancer and the deathbed in Vietnam
is a strange place to dream of palm trees leaning over and
    angry American faces
grinning with sleepwalk terror over your last eye—
Be kind to yourself, because the bliss of your own kindness will
    flood the police tomorrow,
because the cow weeps in the field and the mouse weeps in the
    cat hole—
Because the rain comes over Guatemala and washes all the god
    statues away in the next thousand years—
Be kind to this place, which is your present habitation, with
    derrick and radar tower and flower in the ancient brook—
Be kind to your neighbor who weeps solid tears on the television
    sofa—
He has no other home, and bears witness to nothing but the
    hard voice of telephones—
click, buzz, switch channel and the inspired melodrama disappears
and he's left alone for the night, he disappears in bed—
be kind to your disappearing mother and father gazing out the
    terrace window
as milk truck and hearse turn the corner and say no goodbye—
Be kind to the politician weeping in the galleries of Whitehall,
    Kremlin, White House, Louvre and Phoenix Terrace
aged, large nosed, angry, nervously disliking the bald voice

England

box connected to
electrodes underground converging thru wires vaster than a
    kitten's eye can see
on the mushroom shaped fear-lobe under the ear of sleeping
    Dr. Einstein
Crawling with worms, crawling with worms, crawling with worms the
    Hour has come—
Sick, dissatisfied, unloved, the bulky foreheads of Captain
    Premier President Sir Comrade Fear!
Be kind to the fearful one in front of you who's remembers the
    lamentations of the bible
and the prophesies of the Crucifixion, Adam Son of all the porters and
    char women of Bell gravia—
Be kind to yourself who weep under the morrow moon and hide
    your bliss hairs under raincoat and suede levis—
For this is the joy to be born, the kindness received thru
    strange eyeglasses on a bus thru Kensington,
the finger touch of the Londoner on your throat,
    that borrows light for your cigarette,
the smile of the morning at Newcastle Central station, when
    longhair Tom blond husband greets the bearded Stranger
    of Telephones—
the boom born that bounces in the joyful bowels as the Liverpool
    Minstrels of Cavernsink
raise up their joyful voices and guitar in electric Afric
    hurrah for Jerusalem—
the saints come marching in, & twist & shout, and gates of Eden
    are named in Albion again
Hope sings a black Psalm from Nigeria, and a white psalm echoes

England

in Detroit and reechoes in Nottingham to Prague—
and a Chinese psalm will be heard, if we all live our lives for
  the next six decades—
Be kind to the Chinese Psalm in the red transistor in your breast-
  pocket
Be kind to the Monk[16] in the 5 Spot who plays lone chord-bangs
  on his vast piano,
lost in space on a stool and hearing himself in the nightclub
  universe—
Be kind to the heroes that have lost their names in the newspapers
and hear only their own supplication for love, the peaceful kiss
  of sex in the giant auditoriums of planets,
hear only myriad nameless voices crying for kindness in the
  orchestra balcony, crying for hope of their own joy,
screaming in anguish that bliss come true and birds sing another
  hundred years to their white-haired babes
and poets be fools of their own desire—O happy Anacreon
  angelic Shelley
guide these new-rippled generations on space ships to
  next Universe—
the prayer is man and girl, the only god—Lords of the Kingdoms
  feeling, Christs own living ribs—
Bicycle chain & machine gun, fear sneer & smell cold logic of
  the Dream Bomb
Come on Saigon, Johannesburg, Dominica City, Pnom-Penh,
  Pentagon Paris and Lhasa—

16. Jazz pianist, bandleader, and composer Thelonious Monk (1917–1982), whom Ginsberg met at the Five Spot Café, a jazz club in New York City.

England

Paredon! Who goes to the wall?

and create the giant worm that eats the universe and dies?

Be kind to the universe of self that trembles and shudders and

    Thrills in XX Century

Wakening to its own noise alone in the universe,

the newborn babe with no father but its self—

and opens its eyes to see the myriad of its eyes—

and opens its belly to the butterflies of tenderness—

and opens its [?] to feel the myriad flowers—

    blessedness open as I am to thee—

A dream! A dream! I don't want to be alone!

    I want to know that I am loved!

I want to crowd my lips and ears and eyes and belly

naked over our myriad bodies! I want the orgy of our own flesh,

    orgy of all eyes happy, orgy of the soul kissing and

    blessing its mortal-grown body,

orgy of tenderness beneath the neck, orgy of kindness to thigh

    and vagina—

the soft vibration of desire given with meat hand and cock,

desire taken into mouth and ass, desire returned returned

    to the last sigh & the happy laugh of innocent babies!—

Tonite let's all make love in London as if it were 2001 the years

    of thrilling god—

and be kind to the poor soul that cries in a crack of the pavement

    because he has no body—

our prayers to the ghosts and demons, the lackloves in the U.N. &

    frightened Congresses, who make sadistic noises on the

    radio—

England

statue destroyers & tank captains, unhappy murderers in Mekong
& Congo—

The age of the snake—

For a new kind of man has come to his bliss to ending the
cold war/that he has borne since the days of the
snake against his own kind flesh.

All familiar like an old father's voice everywhere lying head a pillow
at dawn, chirp birds, a newscaster in another apartment, jetplane above
whoooking, mail dropped in slot—
I'd dozed off into junk visions—a large file of mufti clad soldiers turning the corner walking upstreet toward a London downtown subway—
"I feel as if I am the unique one here" says one voice in the crowd—
I think, that's curious, a thought
"I am the only or a special here today"—says the insistent voice—
I think nonsense, but I look up & see it's a corpse dressed in black funeral clothes formal stretched out on a litter, being borne off—a flash of understanding, ah the claimant had a true claim. I'd misunderstood myself.

Dream in Evening—in closed dark party meeting a big colored man
whom I adored—grabbed his cock, he grabbed mine & was kissing me,
I woke—

England

June 13, 1965

Studying the Signs

Piccadilly fine white Lights[17]
a wet glaze on asphalt floor
the Guinness time house clock in the sly mist
Look up in the earthy black deep
yellow lamps of Cathay blinking
and red Swiss watch neon under regent arch
Sun and Alliance Insurance Group granite
—and a piece of sweet chocolate in the checks—
"Everybody gets torn down" as a high
black taxi passes with yellow light door
around the curv'd [?] Iron railing
lit with red blazon Sigma Underground—
ah where the cars glide slowly around Eros
Shooting down on one standing in Empire's hub
To look up past the shining silver breast on Man's
Sleepy face under half spread-iron wings—
Swan & Edgar's battlement walls the moving circus
with princely high barred windows' darkened
office shadow stairways bank interior behind
cast green balconies emblemed with single birds
afloat like white teacups—Boot's Blue Strip
alit above the bottled door scaled down
by the white weight machine's mirrored

17. Early draft of "Studying the Signs," *CP,* 371.

clockface centering plateglass Revlon
slimming biscuit plaque and alchemide
red pharmacy bottle perched on street
display—a *severed head* "relished
uproariously" above the Masque'd Criterion
Theater Marques, with Thespes & Ceres
white plaster Graces lifting their arms
in the shelled niches above fire gongs
on the white pillared façade whose Masard
gables lean down blue black sky
thin flagpole—Like the prow of Queen
Mary boat the great checkered signs had
figure *players* package, blue capped
Navvy encircled in his life-belt a sweet
bearded profile against the 19th century Sea—
and a huge red *delicious* Coca Cola signature
covering half a building back to Gold [?] Cathay
cars stop 3 abreast for the light, race forward,
youths in black turtleneck cross the fence to Boots
straightway, the night gang in sweaters & ties
sip coffee at the Snoo-Matic corner opendoor—
where couples in white pants and blue wool chests
bump their blond shoulders passing by a boy
leaning in cartoon cinema door lifts hand
and puffs white smoke and waits agaze—
and a wakened pigeon that fluttered under streetlamp
now promptly walks and pecks the empty grey pave
as deep blue planet-light changes the low sky dawn.

2 or 3 months ago when I was skippering around the Dilly Morning, tatty head (—Spouse) What ho! Wench!

At Bunhill Fields, June 1965

Irish wishes go—
the sweet golden clime, at Blake's grave,
   Where "nearby lie the remains"
in Bunhill ironfence green tree
   cemetery of white stones
      in the grass—
and birds whistling duskly in the trees
with grey clouds of late day passing
      toward the Thames,
is this place, where I am still in life
in my body—to see the moment I am
   born with sneakers on the paved
   walk of the graveyard
& I see the daylight uplit in the Living
   universe this itself is the sweet
      golden clime,
Clime of this planet, this air, these clouds,
   this birdsong, this setting sun,
      and this self with eyeglasses and
      girls with cameras returned awake—

(Drowse Murmurs)[18]
They drew together for the trick of vocal flattery that exists when you wake up at dawn in the middle of the night with happy sphinx like lids

18. Early prose notes for "Drowse Murmurs," *CP*, 365.

England

mysterious to the eyeball heavy anchored together the mysterious signature, this is the end of the world, whether the atom bomb hit it or I fall down into death all alone nobody help help

It's me myself am I caught in throes of Ugh! They got me whom you lately loved, who wanted to be loved on soft cloth beds, who stuck his cock in the wrong way like a lost animal, what wd Zoology say in Abstract Square in Park Bench Sat watching the spectacle of this time Me it's my body carrying me around it's my body not me that's going to die, it's my ship sinking forever, O Captain the fearful trip is done! I'm all alone, I have no more to offer myself, this is human, and the cat that licks its ass, also hath short term to be a furry specter as I do I awaken by my own thought last leap up from the pillow as the cat leaps up on the desk chair to resolve its foot lick, I lick my own mind, I observe the pipe crawling up the brick wall, I see the pictures on the room sides emblem hung with nails Funny abstract oils mysterious glyphs, girls naked, letters & newspapers the world map colored over for emphasis somebody born—my thought's almost lost, I absorb the big earth lamp hung from the ceiling for ready light, I hear the chirp of birds younger than I and faster doomed, the jet plane whistle hiss roar above the roofs stronger-winged than any thin jawed bird—the precise robot for flying in the air's stronger than me even tho metal fatigue may come before I'm 90—I scratch my hairy skull & lean on elbow as an alarm clock of Sat morn rings next door and wakes a sleeper body to face his day. How amazing to be here, now this time in newspaper history, where earth planet they say revolves around one sun and sun on outer arm of Nebula slowly revolves pinwheel around center so vast slow big this speckles invisible molecule I am sits up in solid motionless early dawn high thinking in every direction, photograph serial nebula photograph death blank photograph this wakened brick minute bird song pipe flush elbow lean in soft pillow to scribe the green sign Paradis.

England

June 22, 1965   Paris

Tired Paris
Pharmacie des Arts blinks
Next the couple's busy this decade
that sharp woman looks round, a man.
I too tired
Sit coffee select scribbling
gleam of long haired heroes
the war was Algeria now Ben Bella coups

White hair from 1914
Still reads Sartre & Bossuet on sidewalks
Still meets crosslegged friends,
palefaced, cigarette hanging out,
Hare lipped, Arab, American crew

Drest for business or police work,
White skirts, journals, Livre des Monstres
The best bookstores, one fat Irish drunk,
The café will not close till 3 a.m.,
Everyone fatigued.
And Rimbaud's Face on display
25 different ways on Right Bank Gallery—
That white boyish breast & pink nipples
and chestnut-haired armpit still For Sale,
and a new kind of Arab beard cropped
Black round reactionary chin eyeglasses.

England

These awnings, of many years' rains,
Neon lettering Le Mabbullion, Le Bar Americaine,
gabble croque-monsieurs, yawns, the promise
of Xmas on Earth, Baudelaire so familiar
his tombstone's next door, Balzac & Rodin
old tired café bores, Roditi & Giacometti
drinking coffee with an eyelid on new boys & girls,
fresh bodies for the Skull Factory. And at night
when the streets are closed, bright lights gleaming
in a few mahogany café mirrors, 7 years ago.

25 June '67 *[sic]*

Returned, the tall moonfaced Bankok boy, black
   shining hair brushed over his eye
    with a Siamese cat, jewel-collared
     set on his cashmere sweater—

and a German blonde whose sex I know not, with
   hair perfect girl, black leather strap
    hung long to her knee, and several Pomeranian
     youths atwaddle in the rear—

A mod came by in checkered suit and open
   oscar wildeish collar, striding serene
    as a lone Beatle—
Everybody's got hair, even the bald make style—

And one blonde French rocker, perfect faced
   For the marble antiquities room, white sweater arms
   Wrapped round his neck

Ah Texas the brilliant Spaniard, I should have lept
    up from my rattan chair at the Floore
    & followed him down the greenleaved pavement—

There was an Arab sheik, short legged in
    Burnoose & flowing wool—
the slow stride of corderoy, sailcloth, denim,
    suede, poplin, taryline, charcoal
    hip bones buttocks and thin ankles—
Turtlenecks, open collars on blue shirts, it's all
    men I see, adams apples in thin folk with
    striped ties from WWII—
one young feminine Morean face leans over his raisin juice—
the flicker of a smile, the darling handshake & lisp of sisters,
    eyebrows rising & falling like comic antennas—
Artaud sat here and croaked his gut, shaking hands
    with young Englishmen in monogramed blazers—
I sit here alone with my larynx cracked, silent at last after
    gabbling 20000 miles from Alameda thru La Rampa
    Nova Mesto Gorky Novy Swiat & Trafalgar—
Where's Don Cherry's[19] face?—in the Fishy Cat—where's
    Genet's snubnose & Michaux's wrinkles and
    Louis Ferdinand's rheum?—
"... going to Leslies, & the Fiacre"—an unlikely group of
    powerful queens—"all of the cirque-oui"
and Africans with blueblack foreheads, hands

19 Don Cherry (1936–1995), jazz trumpeter often associated with Ornette Coleman, was a friend of Ginsberg. Cherry contributed to the 1991 call-and-response reworking of Ginsberg's 1971 poem "Hum Bom!" (*CP*, 1004).

England

hanging out of their suitsleeves below their knees—
so relaxed walking by you'd never know they
were nervous about this revelation—
the moment returns to a noisy street in Warsaw,
   I also return to my eyes—
and a tall blonde Swede whom I slept with 2 days ago
   is just sitting down, enchanted—
"You know, I love Vietnamese ..." and my boy
doth smile next the Orient owlface charmer—

   26 June 1965
Dawn, the bright white disk raying
   down from Notre Dame's Square tower,
Louis Armstrong gravelvoiced on the
   Croissant café jukebox,
No place to sleep all night in my sneakers,
   from Cupole to Pergola by taxi,
the key didn't fit in the door,
   slow round the old cathedral & walked long
   green trailers of vine [?] on the river,
Sleepers by the Seine, young lovers lying on
   bridge kissing, a hardon thru blue jeans as the
   blonde sucked his mouth from above—
and passed also the astronomy wall where
   Libre Algerie signs were chalked 6 years ago—
Entered an old familiar café & stood by the cash register
   Where I used to buy Matines [?]
passed by veils of green branches hung with chestnut spike
   nobs—thru them the delicate tower & angelos of Notre
   Dame's belly—

An all nite café, a French gangster explaining knife gestures
    & revolver flourishes to tough delicate brown Algerians—
and I'm tired, and the sun warms the page, and the pen's blue
    as my heart
and was alone, & unrecognized in my garish black hair
    circling the streets looking redsweatered boulevardiers
    in the eye,
& casting my eye down for shame—Who am I? I asked in a big
    café mirror.
Sat on a bench and watched the gang from the Boheme break up,
    each couple separate,
the negroes paired off walking up St. Germain looking back,

a blond boy like Neal with Greek chest in white sweater sleeves
    uprolled on white muscles—
off with a boyish negress in shorthaired slax—
and thought of Kerouac drunk at little café in the Isle St. Louis—
    talking with Lady Sorbonne 'bout the Mass—
and two dutch boys counting in the golden morn

29 June 1965

Blue ocean, blue sky, an apron of Atlantic clouds—
Plato could have never dreamt of this.
The long jet wing rises & falls slowly.

An orange booklet of Louis Sabe Sonnets on the plastic table.
Eyes closed, I'm sleeping flying to America after half a year.
Old man, veined hands folded over the bulges in his checkered
    lap—tie & belt—
and I'm almost 40 yrs. myself—going back home.

England

Atlantic City, boardwalks, somewhere up ahead along the peninsuloa
    of mist—fine place to bathe.
    Not in here.
                            Ugh.

"O Smile, O foreheads, locks, arms, hands and fingers!
O plaintine late, voila bow and voice!"

Jan. 18 left America, June 29 returned to N.Y.C.
    "Time to go back I've been gone a half year."

OM! N.Y.—Faceless buildings—stopped & searched at Customs. Angst
        & now slight pain in
left breast—
    Emptied out pockets of old used clothes given by Machler—
        suspicious granules of tobacco
& what?—probably nothing, they let me go—
    On the table a letter of Feb. 18 or Mar. 23—Allen Ginsberg
        (reactivated) Peter Orlovsky
(continued)
    "These persons are reported to be engaged in smuggling narcotics."

SELECT BIBLIOGRAPHY BY AND ABOUT ALLEN GINSBERG

Ginsberg, Allen. *The Best Minds of My Generation: A Literary History of the Beats*. Edited by Bill Morgan. New York: Grove Press, 2017.

——. *The Book of Martyrdom and Artifice: First Journals and Poems, 1937–1952*. Edited by Bill Morgan and Juanita Lieberman-Plimpton. New York: Da Capo Press, 2006.

——. *Collected Poems, 1947–1997*. New York: HarperCollins, 2006.

——. *The Essential Ginsberg*. Edited by Michael Schumacher. New York: HarperCollins, 2015.

——. *Journals: Early Fifties, Early Sixties*. Edited by Gordon Ball. New York: Grove, 1977.

——. *Journals: Mid-Fifties*. Edited by Gordon Ball. New York: HarperCollins, 1994.

——. *The Letters of Allen Ginsberg*. Edited by Bill Morgan. New York: Da Capo Press, 2008.

——. *Wait Till I'm Dead: Uncollected Poems*. Edited by Bill Morgan. New York: Grove Press, 2016.

Ginsberg, Allen, and Louis Ginsberg. *Family Business: Selected Letters between a Father and Son*. Edited by Michael Schumacher. New York: Hyperion, 2001.

Ginsberg, Allen, and Peter Orlovsky. *Straight Hearts' Delight: Love Poems and Selected Letters*. Edited by Winston Leland. San Francisco: Gay Sunshine Press, 1980.

Morgan, Bill. *I Celebrate Myself: The Somewhat Private Life of Allen Ginsberg*. New York: Viking, 2006.

Schumacher, Michael. *Dharma Lion: A Biography of Allen Ginsberg*. New York: St. Martin's Press, 1992. Reprint, Minneapolis: University of Minnesota Press, 2016.

Schumacher, Michael, ed. *First Thought: Conversations with Allen Ginsberg*. Minneapolis: University of Minnesota Press, 2017.

Bibliography

ALLEN GINSBERG

(1926–1997) was an American poet, philosopher, and writer. He was a member of the Beat Generation during the 1950s and a leader of the counterculture that followed. His poetry collection *The Fall of America* received the National Book Award for Poetry in 1974.

MICHAEL SCHUMACHER

has written extensively about Allen Ginsberg and the Beat Generation. His books include *Dharma Lion: A Biography of Allen Ginsberg* and *First Thought: Conversations with Allen Ginsberg*, both published by the University of Minnesota Press. He is the editor of *The Essential Ginsberg* and *Family Business: Selected Letters between a Father and Son* (correspondence between Louis and Allen Ginsberg). He lives in Wisconsin.